Mastering Unreal Engine 4.X

Take your game development skills to the next level
with one of the best engines on the market

Muhammad A.Moniem

BIRMINGHAM - MUMBAI

Mastering Unreal Engine 4.X

First published: June 2016

Production reference: 1240616

Published by Packt Publishing Ltd.
Livery Place
35 Livery Street
Birmingham B3 2PB, UK.

ISBN 978-1-78588-356-9

www.packtpub.com

Credits

Author
Muhammad A.Moniem

Reviewer
Moritz Wundke

Commissioning Editor
Amarabha Banerjee

Acquisition Editor
Larissa Pinto

Content Development Editor
Divij Kotian

Technical Editor
Mrunal M. Chavan
Anushree Arun Tendulkar

Copy Editor
Safis Editing

Project Coordinator
Ritika Manoj

Proofreader
Safis Editing

Indexer
Hemangini Bari

Production Coordinator
Aparna Bhagat

Cover Work
Aparna Bhagat

About the Author

Muhammad A.Moniem started in the industry at a very early age. He taught himself everything related to the game development process even before he joined college. After becoming a software engineer, he started to teach himself the art of game design and game art techniques. As a self-taught person, he was able to find his way into the industry very easily, which led him to be hired for big, medium, and small companies, titles, and teams.

Throughout his career, he has been able to contribute as a full-time or part-time employee or freelancer on games for a wide range of platforms, including Windows, Mac, iOS, Android, PS4, Xbox One, and OUYA. He has also worked with technologies such as VR, AR, and Kinect. Muhammad started using Unreal Engine 3 in 2007, moved to Unreal Engine 4 when it became available to the public in 2014, and has used UDK for some indie games.

Eventually, he was able to establish his own one-person game company/team as a part-time independent developer. A lot of his indie games have received recognition or have been finalists at international indie game events, such as IGF, Indie Showcase, IGC, and Tokyo Game Show. You can get in touch via twitter @_mamoniem

He has also worked on *Learning Unreal® Engine iOS Game Development, Packt Publishing*, which is available at `https://www.packtpub.com/game-development/learning-unreal-engine-ios-game-development`, and *Unreal Engine Lighting and Rendering Essentials*, which is available at `https://www.packtpub.com/game-development/unreal-engine-lighting-and-rendering-essentials`.

Acknowledgments

I would like to thank all those people who helped me get this book to your hands. A special mention for all the team members at Epic Games for their hard work on Unreal Engine and for the great decision of making the engine for everyone with the source code for free.

I would like to thank all the people at *Packt Publishing* who worked on this book. They helped me a lot and were patient when I missed the schedule because of my personal obligations. Thanks for helping me and teaching me once again about how to write a book.

I want to express my pleasure of having a lovely wife and wonderful kids in my life. You are my gift. You are a very supportive family, thanks Loly for giving me the best environment to write one more book, and thanks for believing in all my personal projects since you came to my life. You always working too hard for this family! Thanks Joe, Mary, and Oni for being noisy, sweet, and lovely kids all the way. You are a delight to my eyes!!

Yunus, thanks for being the new hope, this book for you…Only for you buddy!

Father and mother, thanks for raising me the way you did and teaching me how to self-learn, it helped me a lot to learn and pass the knowledge to others.

Last but not least, all my friends and the good people I met around the world, you definitely helped me somehow, at least with your trust and belief. Even if you were an online friend, I'm sure I still owe you something…Thank you everyone.

Dear God, thanks for being Muhammad, I like being this person. And thanks for everything I've achieved, please keep those wonderful people around me ☺

Alhamdulillah…It's the last line to write…!

About the Reviewer

Moritz Wundke, also known as Moss, started programming at the age of 12 and he always knew that he would write games for a living. After finishing his Bachelor in computer science at the University at the Balearic Islands in 2007 he started working with the Unreal Engine 3 at Tragnarion Studios. He left the studio in 2014 and joined the Spanish social game developer PlaySpace working on over then titles and shipping their games to more than 23 million players. In his career he has been able to work with nearly all major platforms, such as the NDS, Xbox 360, PS3, PS4, Android, iOS, Windows and Mac. Apart from his day job, Moritz is an official community moderator of the Unreal Engine community, Engine Contributor and freelance Unreal Engine consultant. He has worked for companies such as Deep Silver on Dead Island 2 and Red Goddess: Inner World for Yanim Studios.

I would like to thank my wife Cecilia for being so patient while I worked late nights and not throwing away my rig and even myself with it.

www.PacktPub.com

eBooks, discount offers, and more

Did you know that Packt offers eBook versions of every book published, with PDF and ePub files available? You can upgrade to the eBook version at `www.PacktPub.com` and as a print book customer, you are entitled to a discount on the eBook copy. Get in touch with us at `customercare@packtpub.com` for more details.

At `www.PacktPub.com`, you can also read a collection of free technical articles, sign up for a range of free newsletters and receive exclusive discounts and offers on Packt books and eBooks.

`https://www2.packtpub.com/books/subscription/packtlib`

Do you need instant solutions to your IT questions? PacktLib is Packt's online digital book library. Here, you can search, access, and read Packt's entire library of books.

Why subscribe?

- Fully searchable across every book published by Packt
- Copy and paste, print, and bookmark content
- On demand and accessible via a web browser

Table of Contents

Preface

This book is an in-depth guide through the process of creating a high quality game from scratch, starting from importing and implementing assets and ending up with packaging the game for release and making patches, with all the steps in-between. The main aim of this book is to make a game that looks awesome, and cover advanced stuff using C++ extensively to build the logic for the game.

What this book covers

Chapter 1, *Preparing for a Big Project*, shows how to create a new project, set it up, edit its settings and making it ready to rock. Also, the advanced assets pipeline will be discussed so that readers can bring in their models into Unreal Engine.

Chapter 2, *Setting Up Your Warrior*, explains how to make the game's hero! We will be building a character controller mapped to the keyboard and mouse using C++. You will learn how to create the logic for the character, switch weapons, attack, and move with C++. The class will be converted to blueprints. You will learn how to add in animations and physics to make it move using C++.

Chapter 3, *Designing Your Playground*, shows how to build the game world! We will be using the editor tools and brushes to build a level, apply lighting and materials to it, and make it ready for the first round of testing the game's logic.

Chapter 4, *The Road to Thinkable AI*, shows how to build the game's creatures AI, which are going to detect the player and attack them based on distance, sight, and/or the noise made by the player. All scripting will be done in C++. Animations will be taken care of by the editor and some other cool options.

Chapter 5, *Adding Collectables*, spices things up with some collectables! We will learn about some of the triggering and overlapping events, more about adding new classes, and adding some physics to the collectable items.

Chapter 6, The Magic of Particles, shows how to add in some particles to complete the coolness! We use cascade to build particles for the enemies, weapons, and collectables, and learn to tie these to the game logic.

Chapter 7, Enhancing the Visual Quality, shows how to make the game better looking by focusing on the most important rendering features of the engine, to make things pretty. You will learn to bake light maps.

Chapter 8, Cinematics and In-Game Cutscenes, covers the tools required to build an in-game cut-scene for a better gameplay experience and story direction.

Chapter 9, Implementing the Game UI, shows how to add a solid UI to the game is what will get the players going "Hell Yeah!" Make use of Unreal Motion Graphics (UMG) to tinker with different screen sizes and build a superb looking UI for your game.

Chapter 10, Save the Game Progress, shows how to write a "save and load" function in order to save the progress in order to be able to resume the game later.

Chapter 11, Controlling Gameplay via Data Tables, shows how to use data tables to drive the gameplay values for the enemies and so on (it is widely used in tons of game genres, such as Tower Defense, RPG, Roguelike, RTS and so on)

Chapter 12, Ear Candy, shows how to add audio experience to the gameplay. You will learn how to cue the audio and use the clips in the scenes.

Chapter 13, Profiling the Game Performance, masters the various editor debugging and profiling tools to define the performance issues.

Chapter 14, Packaging the Game, you will learn how to make an executable of the game for release. We also add a splash screen to show you're the boss, cook the game, and then use the project launcher to release it.

What you need for this book

In order to be able to follow along with this book, you need to have a good foundation of C++, as the book mostly focuses on building an Unreal game using C++. You also need to have Unreal Engine installed and Visual Studio, and both be available for free.

If you are on a Mac or Linux, you'll definitely need another IDE to use with Unreal Engine, as Visual Studio is not supported on those platforms, but you'll still be able to go with the book smoothly.

Good game design and level design skills are great and will help, but they are not essential!

Who this book is for

This book is for game developers who have basic knowledge of Unreal Engine and also have basic C++ scripting knowledge. This is ideal for those who want to take the leap from a casual game developer to a full-fledged professional game developer with Unreal Engine 4.

Conventions

In this book, you will find a number of text styles that distinguish between different kinds of information. Here are some examples of these styles and an explanation of their meaning.

Code words in text, database table names, folder names, filenames, file extensions, pathnames, dummy URLs, user input, and Twitter handles are shown as follows: "The game we are going to create during the course of this book is called Bellz."

A block of code is set as follows:

```
UCLASS(config = Game)
class AGladiator : public ACharacter
{
  GENERATED_BODY()
```

New terms and **important words** are shown in bold. Words that you see on the screen, for example, in menus or dialog boxes, appear in the text like this: "Otherwise inside the launcher, just hit the **Launch** button of the editor version you want."

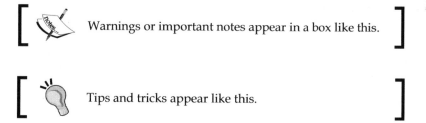

> Warnings or important notes appear in a box like this.

> Tips and tricks appear like this.

Reader feedback

Feedback from our readers is always welcome. Let us know what you think about this book—what you liked or disliked. Reader feedback is important for us as it helps us develop titles that you will really get the most out of.

To send us general feedback, simply e-mail feedback@packtpub.com, and mention the book's title in the subject of your message.

If there is a topic that you have expertise in and you are interested in either writing or contributing to a book, see our author guide at www.packtpub.com/authors.

Customer support

Now that you are the proud owner of a Packt book, we have a number of things to help you to get the most from your purchase.

Downloading the example code

You can download the example code files for this book from your account at http://www.packtpub.com. If you purchased this book elsewhere, you can visit http://www.packtpub.com/support and register to have the files e-mailed directly to you.

You can download the code files by following these steps:

1. Log in or register to our website using your e-mail address and password.
2. Hover the mouse pointer on the **SUPPORT** tab at the top.
3. Click on **Code Downloads & Errata**.
4. Enter the name of the book in the **Search** box.
5. Select the book for which you're looking to download the code files.
6. Choose from the drop-down menu where you purchased this book from.
7. Click on **Code Download**.

You can also download the code files by clicking on the **Code Files** button on the book's webpage at the Packt Publishing website. This page can be accessed by entering the book's name in the **Search** box. Please note that you need to be logged in to your Packt account.

Once the file is downloaded, please make sure that you unzip or extract the folder using the latest version of:

- WinRAR / 7-Zip for Windows
- Zipeg / iZip / UnRarX for Mac
- 7-Zip / PeaZip for Linux

The code bundle for the book is also hosted on GitHub at `https://github.com/PacktPublishing/Mastering-Unreal-Engine-4X`. We also have other code bundles from our rich catalog of books and videos available at `https://github.com/PacktPublishing/`. Check them out!

Downloading the color images of this book

We also provide you with a PDF file that has color images of the screenshots/diagrams used in this book. The color images will help you better understand the changes in the output. You can download this file from `http://www.packtpub.com/sites/default/files/downloads/MasteringUnrealEngine4X_ColorImages.pdf`.

Errata

Although we have taken every care to ensure the accuracy of our content, mistakes do happen. If you find a mistake in one of our books—maybe a mistake in the text or the code—we would be grateful if you could report this to us. By doing so, you can save other readers from frustration and help us improve subsequent versions of this book. If you find any errata, please report them by visiting `http://www.packtpub.com/submit-errata`, selecting your book, clicking on the **Errata Submission Form** link, and entering the details of your errata. Once your errata are verified, your submission will be accepted and the errata will be uploaded to our website or added to any list of existing errata under the Errata section of that title.

To view the previously submitted errata, go to `https://www.packtpub.com/books/content/support` and enter the name of the book in the search field. The required information will appear under the **Errata** section.

Piracy

Piracy of copyrighted material on the Internet is an ongoing problem across all media. At Packt, we take the protection of our copyright and licenses very seriously. If you come across any illegal copies of our works in any form on the Internet, please provide us with the location address or website name immediately so that we can pursue a remedy.

Please contact us at copyright@packtpub.com with a link to the suspected pirated material.

We appreciate your help in protecting our authors and our ability to bring you valuable content.

Questions

If you have a problem with any aspect of this book, you can contact us at questions@packtpub.com, and we will do our best to address the problem.

1
Preparing for a Big Project

When you are about to create a C++ game using Unreal Engine, it means that you are going to create a big project. The two specific reasons for such a choice are: you are a core programmer and not familiar with the blueprints concept, or you want the game to run faster. Either way, you are about to get the right start here.

It's been said several times that C++-based games are quite a bit faster (10 times faster) than games made with blueprints. Although that was hearsay on the Unreal forums, the fact is that it is partly true. All games made with Unreal are equal in performance to those relying on the same technology and engine code base. However, when things get complex, it gets a little slower, and that speed difference is not as noticeable; it is something measured in milliseconds.

Starting a C++ project with Unreal is quite different, as it is not something that can be done inside the editor anymore. You'll need all the help of the IDE and, based on your platform, the setup will be different. My setup currently while writing this book is Windows 10, Unreal 4.10 and Visual Studio 2015. Apart from Google Documents, that's all that I need to create my data tables, and that's all that is needed!

By the end of this chapter, you will be able to:

- Start a new Unreal Engine C++ project from scratch
- Set the project and editor settings to match your needs
- Map any input device to match your game design
- Import and export assets in and out of the Unreal Editor
- Migrate assets between the different Unreal projects
- Retarget animations between the different skeletons
- Add the required modules and header files to the project code

Overview of the game

The game we are going to create during the course of this book is called `Bellz`; it's definitely a word without a meaning. Its name came from the Hell Bells, as we are planning to put some unique bells around the maps!

The game is built with C++. While it is a C++ project, about 5% consists of necessary blueprints and other different graphs!

Bellz is a third-person RPG, where you have a mission loaded from Excel tables, weapons to use with different attributes, and evil enemies to escape from or to hunt. It looks simple, and the fact is, it is, but it holds all the needed elements to create a visually appealing AAA game. So that we stay on the same page, this game will take you step by step through the processes of:

1. Starting a C++ project based on a blank template.
2. Creating a player controller.
3. Building enemies, behavior trees, and blackboards.
4. Creating animation graphs and retargeting different animations.
5. Loading game-required data from the design data tables.
6. Adding camera animations and cut scenes to the game.
7. Adding audio effects and visual effects to the game.
8. Creating and building appealing maps.
9. Optimizing the game as much as possible.
10. Debugging the game performance.
11. Packaging the game to players.

The following is a screenshot of the final game:

Creating a C++ project

With the goals set, let's get started by launching the Unreal launcher. If you already have an Unreal Editor instance running, that is not a problem; just choose to make a new project from within the **File** menu and that will launch the proper screen of the launcher. Otherwise inside the launcher, just hit the **Launch** button of the editor version you want. After a few seconds of loading, the editor project selection window will appear. Do the following:

1.   Switch to the **New Project** tab.

2.   Under **New Project**, switch to the **C++** subtab.

3.   Choose a **Basic Code** project type.

4.   Set the target to **Desktop/Console** as that's our target!

5.   Set the quality to **Maximum Quality**.

6.   Remove the starter content, it will not be useful at all.

7.   Give your project a name, but make sure to remember that name, as a lot of the code will be using it. Mine is called `Bellz`. I would say go ahead and name your project with the same name so you can easily follow along with the tutorial without any confusion or naming conflicts.

8.   Finally hit **Create Project**!

If that was your first time creating a code project (which I guess is the case for the book's target audience), the project will take quite a time, it is not going to appear within a second like the other blueprint-based projects.

A C++-based project needs to copy some header files, build a Visual Studio solution/project (or Xcode if you are running on Mac), add the necessary code to the project, build files, inputs, the engine, and so on, and then finally run the Visual Studio command-line tool to compile and launch the project editor.

Now that you have a basic project, shall we go ahead and learn more about the C++ game project structure?

Yes!

But why?

Well, an Unreal project could increase to a crazy size at some point, especially if you are going to source-control your project using Git or SVN. You have to be wary about the space, as some free hosting services put a limit on the file type and file size you are using within your repository.

By opening the `game project` folder you will have these files and folders; some new files and folders might appear in the future as long as we keep adding stuff to the project. This is what I had by the end of the project:

Name	Type
Binaries	File folder
Build	File folder
Config	File folder
Content	File folder
Intermediate	File folder
Saved	File folder
Source	File folder
Bellz	PNG File
Bellz	SQL Server Compact Edition Database File
Bellz	Microsoft Visual Studio Solution
Bellz	Unreal Engine Project File

While the folder is full of subfolders and files, it makes much more sense to break it all down. If you understand how the project directory works, it will be easy to understand how the game director works, and how you can optimize the size of the project.

- `Binaries`: This folder holds `.dll` files and executables that will be autogenerated during the compilation time.

- `Build`: A folder for all the necessary files to build the editor or the game itself.

- `Config`: A whole folder for the configuration files, basically a bunch of text files that hold a lot of the settings you set for the project and the game from within the project setting and the editor settings. You can do changes here, but it is not that easy to locate exactly what you want. However, it's a good place to search for the causes of problems.

- `Content`: The `Content` folder hosts all the assets, blueprints, maps, Marketplace assets and any other item you use to build your game. Any folder you create inside your editor to hold some assets will end up inside the `Content` folder. Code files will not be included inside the content, in case your game is based on C++ not blueprints.

- `Intermediate`: The majority of the files underneath this folder are temporary files, all of them being generated while building the game or the engine, which means deleting this folder's content will not affect you, as all the content will be regenerated as soon as you build.

- `Saved`: The `Saved` folder contains lots of different saved files, some are backups that are saved every once in a while, some are autosaved copies of the assets, and other files are the save data of the game itself (saved using the save API).

- `Source`: This folder contains all the game code. Any C++ classes you are going to add in the future for the project will end up in this folder.

- `PNGImage`: The icon file for the project, which has the same name as the project; it is not necessary for it to represent the final build, but will be mainly used to visualize the project at the Unreal Launcher library section. Keep in mind that this image must be a square of 192 by 192 pixels. You can change it either by directly replacing it, or through the project settings.

- `SQLFile`: This is an `.sdf` format file named with the project name; you don't have to worry that much about it, as Visual Studio will be generating a new one every time you open the solution.

- `Visual Studio solution`: The Visual Studio solution for the game code has the same name as the project. You can open it directly, or you can launch it from within the Unreal Editor itself through the **File** menu. Keep in mind that the project options section of the **File** menu is very dynamic. If you have a C++-based project (such as the one we are creating) the menu will always give you two main options, the first to refresh the Visual Studio project and the second to open the Visual Studio project.

But if you made a blueprint-based project, and at some point you wanted to convert it to a code file, you will find that the project options of the **File** menu display only one option for the Visual Studio, which is **Generate Visual Studio Project**.

- `Unreal Engine Project`: An Unreal Engine project file that has the same name as the project and has the extension `*.uproject`. You can easily open the project using it, either by double-clicking on it or by browsing for it from the Unreal Launcher.

The project settings

Now we have a project set and running. However, that's not enough for us to start adding code, assets, and logic for the game. A game project has tons and tons of settings and options, which will have been set to default values when you create a new project, and every time you make a new game or project, you have to set those settings to specific options that fit your needs and your goals.

Accessing the project settings is very easy as you only have to click on the **Project Settings** button at the end of the **Edit** menu button.

First things first, I like to always set the overall information about my project at an early stage, so I don't have to worry about it later. From the **Description** section of the project settings, you can set the company name, and its homepage; also you can assign the logo for the project to be displayed on the launcher and description of the project and its name.

The most important part for this C++-based project is to set the copyright notice. By defining a piece of text here, it will be automatically added to all your newly created C++ files. So you have a copyright added to your code… Just in case!

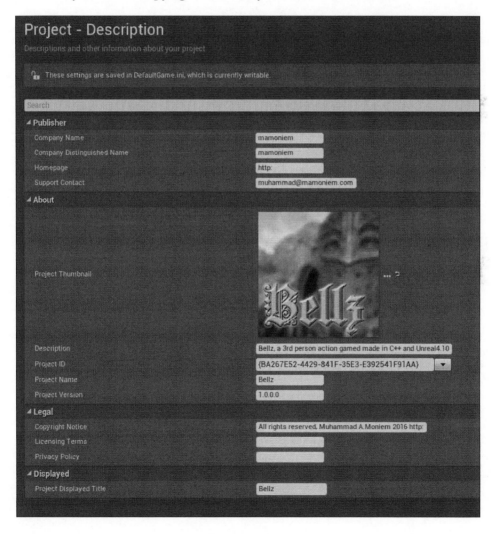

Another important option to set is the map to be used as the default map for the game and for the editor. I agree that we don't have maps set yet but once you have a map, you need to set it inside the **Maps & Modes** section; so you make sure that every time you run the editor, you don't have to reload the map you want.

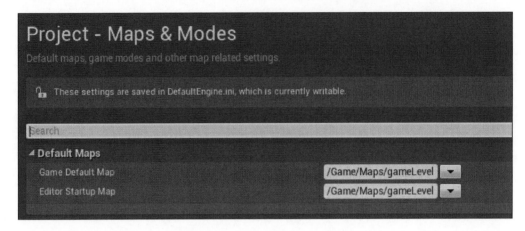

Finally, I would like to set the targeted platforms. I already know that my game will be running on PCs and consoles, so there is no need to label my game as an Android or iOS game for example. Therefore, you can just uncheck the untargeted platforms from the **Supported Platforms** section.

The editor settings

To access the editor settings, from the **Edit** menu, just choose **Editor Preferences**. If you are using a Mac, you might find it in a different place, usually it is called **Preferences** or **Editor Preferences** and it is listed under the **Unreal Editor** menu.

There is not much that needs to be changed within the editor settings, as it is mostly about personal, preferred settings while working with the editor. I don't mind sharing the few changes I made for the editor of `Bellz`, but feel free to ignore them and apply your preferred settings, or don't apply any editor settings at all if you prefer to keep it that way.

Under the **Loading & Saving** section of the **General** settings, I managed to disable the autosave option for any asset type; that way I make sure that the editor saves only on my demand, and I'll not get too many unnecessary files, keeping my project size as small as possible. Also, disabling the source control (if you are not using it, or you are using another source control system) is a good way to go with a smaller project!

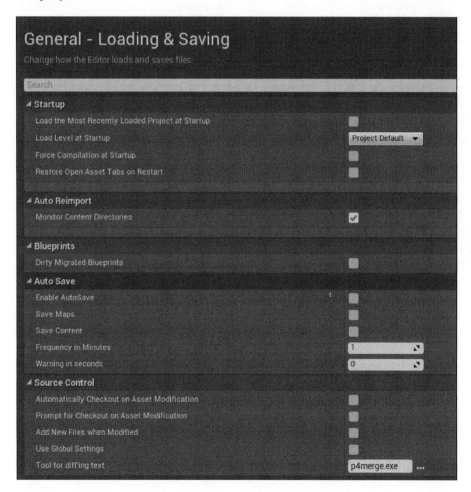

From the **Play** section of the **Level Editor** settings, make sure you enable **Game Gets Mouse Control**; this way I make sure that the game has the advantage of using the mouse over the editor.

And that's it. There are lots of changes I used to make to the editor, but there were mostly related to changing the colors to fit my experience and keeping the overall visual look of the objects the same between all the applications I was using. For example, changing the color of selected objects to match the selected objects in Maya viewport, so I keep things consistent. But those two options are the important ones that have an impact on my experience while working.

Mapping the inputs

While the input setting relies on the project setting, I always like to discuss it as an individual topic. If you have come from an engine structuring background, you probably know that the inputs are an independent topic just like rendering, networking, and so on.

Any game built within Unreal Engine (or any game in general) must have the input class, which defines the whole input for the game. Fortunately, Unreal Engine has made this step easier, and has given you the chance not to worry about input handling. It does this for you at a lower level of the engine core, and gives you a nice and easy-to-use interface, where you can map some predefined input keys, buttons, and axes, and name them. You can then refer to these buttons by code using their respective names.

Unreal Engine supports a lot of input devices, which has made the input mapping list huge, and it is better to learn more about the supported devices in order to make this huge list easy to manipulate. The inputs that are supported are:

- **Gamepad**: This contains the mapping for all the buttons and axes used by any gamepad type

- **Keyboard**: This contains the mapping for all the keyboard keys

- **Mouse**: This contains the mapping for all the mouse buttons and axes

- **Motion controllers**: They contains the mapping for any motion device, such as Razer for example

- **Gesture**: This contains the mapping for some gestures integration, which could be used with any touch device (mobile, touchpad, and so on)

- **Steam**: This contains the mapping for the special buttons of the Steam controller; all other Steam controller buttons are accessible through the gamepad inputs

- **Xbox One**: This contains the mapping for the special buttons of the Xbox One controller; all other Xbox One controller buttons are accessible through gamepad inputs

- **Android**: This contains the mapping for the special buttons of Android devices (Back, Volume, Menu, and so on)

And that's how the list of inputs looks by default while every section is folded; unfolding those sections will give you an endless list of keys and buttons that you can map for your game and for different platforms and devices.

In order to use these inputs for your game, you have to select some keys and give them names; this is called the process of **Binding Keys**. But before diving into this process, you will have to understand the different types of binding within Unreal Engine.

Unreal Engine supports two main binding types; they are divided by the sensitivity of the input key/button. This means that the input button/key could fire a couple of events when it is pressed and/or released, or it will keep firing events as long as it is pressed. The two main types of bindings are:

- **Action mapping**: Action mapping should represent a button or key press, and then within the code you can call some logic based on pressing that key

- **Axis mapping**: Axis mapping should represent a value change of the pressure on the button, which usually works with the trigger buttons of a controller or the thumb sticks of the controller as well

Here are few more points to remember before we start the mapping process:

- The game will be using the keyboard and mouse as PC inputs and will be using the controller/gamepad as the console input (you can still use the controller with PCs, though).

- I highly recommend that you use the same names I used to map my keys; if you change any, you have to be aware that you have to change them within the code as well.

- To add a new action mapping or axis mapping, you just need to hit the = sign next to the action and/or axis title. But if you want to add more buttons to the same action or axis, then you need to hit the + sign next to the action map itself.

Now you are ready to go. By opening the project settings from within the **Edit** menu, and then navigating to the **Input** options under the **Engine** section, you have access to the inputs mapping. You can now start mapping your key inputs.

- **Action mappings**: This contains the following options:
    - **Jump**: Will be using either Spacebar or the controller lower face button to perform the jump on press

- ° **Attack**: Will be using the LMB or the controller right trigger to perform attack.
- ° **ChangeWeapon**: Will be shuffling between weapons on pressing the **Tab** button or the **Gamepad Right Shoulder** (the one above the trigger).

The end result of this action key mapping should eventually look something like this:

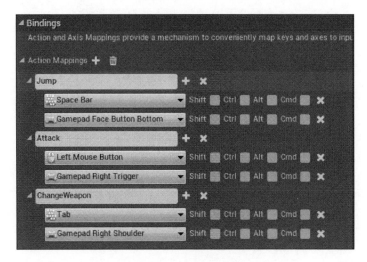

- • **Axis mappings**: This contains the following menu:
    - ° **MoveForward**: Will be using the keyboard's **W** or **S** or **Up/Down** arrow, or the controller Y axis of the left thumb stick, to move the player forward and backward. The value of 1 means forward and the value of 0-1 means backward.
    - ° **MoveRight**: Will be using the keyboard's **A/D** or the controller X axis of the left thumb stick to move the player right and left. The value of 1 means right and the value of 0-1 means left.
    - ° **TurnRate**: Will be using the keyboard arrows or the X axis of the right thumb stick of the controller to rotate the camera sideways.
    - ° **Turn**: Will rotate the camera sideways using the mouse.
    - ° **LookUpRate**: Will be using the Y axis of the right thumb stick of the controller to rotate the camera up and down.
    - ° **LookUp**: Will lookup using the mouse Y axis.

The end result of this axis key mapping should eventually be something like this:

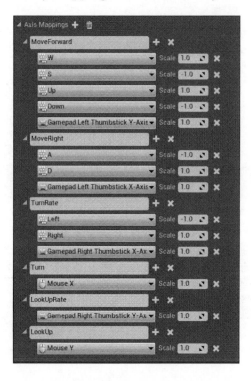

Now you have successfully mapped the game inputs. Keep in mind that you might need to map more keys in the future, but those are the keys I needed for `Bellz`. If you need more you can keep adding and mapping keys based on your game design. Personally I found those inputs are enough for our current example.

If you still remember the project directory we mentioned earlier in this chapter, there was a `config` folder for the project. If you access this `config` folder, and you open the `DefaultInput.ini` file using any text editor, you will find the input mapping that you've already done at the end of the `DefaultInput.ini` file. This means those inputs are modifiable at any time because the shipped game will have a similar file eventually!

Migrating assets

In some cases, you might have an asset within an Unreal project that you want to use within another project. And because Unreal content is converted into `.uasset` files, it is not that easy to just copy assets from the `Content` folder of a project into another `Content` folder of another project.

For this game, we are about to create the basic animations of the default Unreal Engine mannequin character, to be used by my character. Therefore, by opening any of the Unreal projects and by selecting the required animation files, you can just right-click on them and choose **Migrate** and then choose the new project you want to copy assets to.

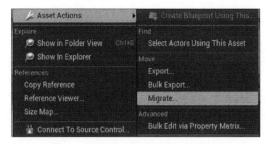

That way, all the assets with the required dependencies will be copied to the new project. However, achieving it by just doing a window-level copying will not guarantee you move all the required files. In my case, when I was copy animations the editor found that I needed to copy the character mesh, skeleton, and the materials as well. Those have been selected automatically for me and set alongside the targeted animation files.

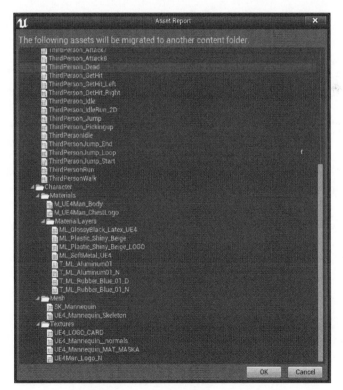

Finally, a typical OS window will pop up to ask you to choose the destination folder/project you want to migrate the assets and all its dependencies to.

Using MarketPlace assets

Now as a single-person project (me or you, we are both working as individuals now), you can't make the entire game all by yourself. In other words, time, and the goal of this book, do not allow us to do that. Thus, that's the reason behind relying on some free assets, or you might like to get some of it outsourced. It is all up to you.

For Bellz, I used a mix of assets provided by Epic games; they are free to use and you can get them from the launcher. The assets are labeled with Infinity Blade (yeah, those assets are a free giveaway from Epic and the developer of the game), and they are really top-quality assets.

While those assets look perfect, not that many animations come with the packages so I used some of the free animations provided by Epic and asked a friend to make some other animations for me to use.

A good exercise here is to follow the migrate process we discussed earlier in this chapter in order to migrate some of the custom animations I've made in the book's project, and move them into your project.

In order to get the packages installed, you have to download them first from the **Marketplace** section of your launcher, then you will find a button next to those packages that displays **Add To Project**. I've added warriors, enemies, weapons, and the grass environment to my project. Feel free to add them as well (I highly recommend them) or get your own assets.

There are three types of environment presented for free; you are free to pick the one you want. I just liked the grassy one. After making your decision about which to use of the free packages, all that you have to do is to hit the **Add To Project** button. Keep in mind, some of the Marketplace packages don't have the **Add To Project** button, and they have only a **Create Project** button; with those packages you'll need to create a whole new project in order to be able to use them or migrate some of their assets to your current project.

This will take you to a whole new section of the launcher, and you probably have never been there before. It displays all the valuable projects that could match this package. It is all about the engine version and the package version which usually have to match, and Epic might change this condition in the near future. Anyway, I made my choice as **Bellz**.

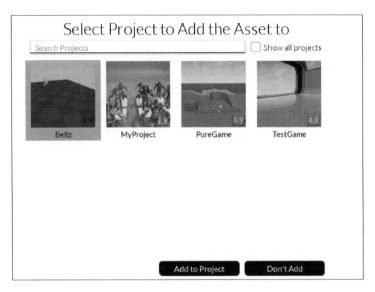

Now it will take some time to load and add the directories and the assets to your project. Go ahead and redo the process for the other packages you want to add to the project (the warriors, enemies, and weapons).

Keep in mind that, if you are using Windows, you don't have to relaunch the project. In a Windows version of the editor, once you add a package to the project through the launcher, you can locate them right away from within the editor. But if you are running Unreal on a Mac, you have to relaunch the editor in order to find the assets inside the project.

Feel free to take your time to check the characters, enemies, weapons, and the environments and all the animations provided by them. Also spend some time migrating any animations you want from the project sample that came with the book, and decide which assets you are going to use with your instance of `Bellz`, and delete any other unneeded assets, such as all other characters, enemies, and weapons. Those files are large, and will heavily increase your project size, so, it's a good idea to keep the project as clean as possible as we go.

Retargeting animations

When I was choosing my characters, I picked the bear as my main game enemy. The choice came as a result of several factors. First, I liked the two attack animations that the bear has, it is very strong and has great key poses. Second and most importantly, the bear has no idle, walk, or run animations, and it's a good opportunity to check some of the Unreal tricks of duplicating animations from a skeleton to another different skeleton. This is called **animation retargeting**.

By default, when you import an animation for the first time, you will be asked to either use an already made skeleton asset from within the project, or to import the asset skeleton and build a skeleton asset out of it. For several animations of the same character, you will keep reusing the skeleton asset, but once you import a different character it'll force Unreal to create its own skeleton structure asset.

Now, as you might have noticed, each enemy of the **Infinity Blade** assets has its own skeleton assets, and our main focus here is to somehow get an idle animation alongside the running and/or walking animation for the bear. As you noticed, the bear has only two animations!

ExoGame_Bears_   ExoGame_Bears_   ExoGame_Bears_
Attack_Melee   Attack_Melee_B   Attack_Melee_C

Now if you check what the closest animal is in body structure and skeleton hierarchy to the bear (and included in the assets), you will find the wolf asset. This asset has all that we need and more, it is very similar to the bear, and it has walking and idle animations, alongside other attached animations. The goal now is to retarget and close the walk and idle animations of the wolf and use them with the bear. After we finish that, we will retarget the walk animation once more, and change its speed factor in order to make it look like a running animation (a run is just a fast walk, huh?!), and that will save us the time of creating animations or assets from scratch. It will even save us more time if we want to send the bear asset back to Maya or 3dsMax to add some more animations for it.

The retargeting process is very simple; you can consider it as the following steps:

1. Create an intermediate skeleton structure (called **Set up Rig**).
2. Define the **Source** character skeleton (the wolf), based on the intermediate skeleton.
3. Define the **Target** character skeleton (the bear), based on the intermediate skeleton.
4. Retarget the required animation from the source into the target.

While we have a plan, let's get started in retargeting the animation. By opening the wolf skeleton asset, you will be inside the Persona editor. At the top there is a button called **Retarget Manager**. Hit it!

That will open the retargeting window for you; it is very simple, you need to create the skeleton by hitting **Add New Retarget Source** and then start assigning the wolf bones to the correct slots of the intermediate skeleton. You don't have to fill them all, you just need the animated bones to be assigned. Keep in mind, at any time, if you need to assign more bones that are not shown on the intermediate skeleton, you can press the **Show Advanced** button in order to display more bone options to assign. Nevertheless, from my experience with this wolf skeleton asset, those basic bones are enough.

After assigning the bones you should end up with something like the following:

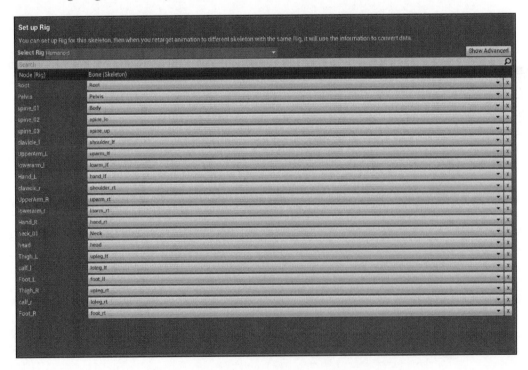

Now, let's do the same thing with the bare bones. Open its Persona, and start assigning the bones to an intermediate skeleton. There are two things you might notice here: the wolf has one more bone within the legs, and it fits its real bone structure. In addition, the wolf has a tail, while the bear skeleton has no tail. That will not affect us too much, but make sure not to assign something wrongly. Feel free to ignore those extra bones from the wolf.

After assigning the bones, you should end up with something like the following:

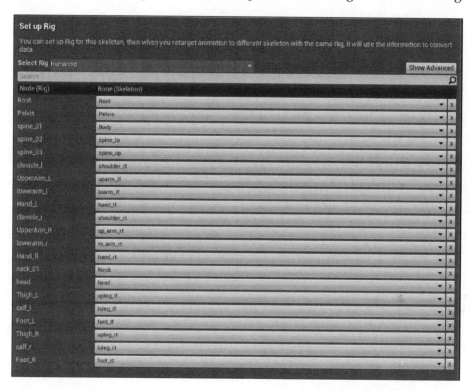

Now it is time to do the final step, which is retargeting (cloning) the animations themselves from the source to the target. By accessing the animation assets of the wolf (under the `animations` folder within the `wolf` folder), you can select any of the animations (let's start with the idle animation); right-click and, from **Retarget Anim Assets**, choose **Duplicate Anim Assets and Retarget**. That's enough to take you to the final step of retargeting.

The **Select Skeleton** window will show up. This window will already have the retargeting source skeleton selected and display its character. It requires you to select the target (which is the bear), by selecting the bear skeleton (the one we have already assigned to the intermediate skeleton) and hitting **Select**; that will copy the animation right away for you, and set it to the animation for the bear.

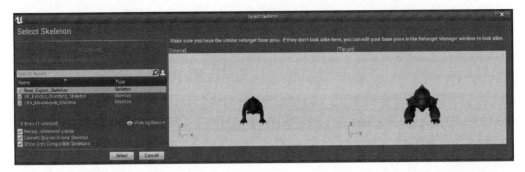

Now it's time to rename the animation to something which makes more sense. The new animation will still have the name of the wolf, but it has a thumbnail of a bear character, and it is only playable over the bear skeleton; thus you probably need to rename it bear.

Do retarget all the animations you want, but don't forget to rename them and move them to the `bear` folder, just to keep things organized.

After you are done duplicating/retargeting all the animations you want, I would recommend you duplicate the walking animation again for the bear, but this time name it run. After you have done the duplication, double-click on the animation asset. That will run Persona again, but this time it will be activating the **Animation** tab, not the **Skeleton** tab like before.

From the left side, there is a panel called **Anim Asset Details**. Make sure to set **the Rate Scale** under the **Animation** tab to **2.0**, which will change the speed of this animation asset. By having it run fast, it really looks like a real run. Now we have managed to get lots of animations working and running for the bear, without the need to do a single animation frame!

Summary

You went through the process of starting a big game from the ground. You learned how to select a base C++ code project, which is not based on any other premade code, and totally understood the project structure, which folders are important, and which folders you can simply ignore.

You also learned about how and where to find the project settings and the editor preferences, and you got an idea about what type of settings you can find there, and how to adjust some of them to fit your needs.

All games have inputs, and now you know where you need to map those inputs for your game. You are not only aware of how to set up game inputs, but also you know all the input types and the limits of supported input devices with Unreal Engine.

All games have assets, and now you have learned how to be tricky while working: how to integrate packages from the Marketplace, or move assets between different projects without any trouble by just migrating them, not only copying them.

Animations are essential, but sometimes we have to retarget animations in order to fix some problems we have or to fasten the process. You now know all the needed steps and skills to be able to retarget any animation into any skeleton.

Now with all of that fresh in your mind, I highly recommend you dive into the next chapter right away. Let's start writing code and building our player controller from the ground up.

2
Setting Up Your Warrior

Once we have the project set up and running, it is time to start making the game itself and put something together that we can call a playable game.

The most important part of any game is the player controller. Regardless of the game genre and type, the player has to control the game somehow. It may be in the form of controlling the environment or controlling a character through the environment, or even something else.

Because the game we are building here is a third-person type of game, our players will have to control a character (I'm calling him `The Gladiator`). This character will be based on the Unreal character class, as it gives us many benefits and saves us lots of time because the character class is basically a `Pawn` class and pawns are actors that are controlled either by the player or AI. The character class we are building is going to be fully controlled by mouse and keyboard or the gamepad controller.

Keep in mind that we are building our own character class from scratch and not basing our character on the Unreal one, so this process will take a long time. Almost 90% of Unreal game characters are based on the unreal character class, and that's the reason behind having some base classes shipped with the engine.

The character controller we are going to create will be able to walk, jump, control the camera, play animations, switch weapons, affect enemies, get affected by enemies, show some statistics in the UI, read weapon data from the data tables and, most importantly, die when it is the time to die!

By the end of this chapter, you will be able to:

- Build the character class in C++
- Write movement logic
- Map key inputs into the player controller logic
- Build the character animation blueprint
- Add an animated mesh, and display animations from the character class
- Add sockets to the skeletons
- Build animation blend spaces and use them
- Assign and use any character as the default game character

The code project

We have already created the project and launched Visual Studio. Once you open your project's Visual Studio you'll find it is not empty. There are some classes and files that have been generated for you automatically to start you off and give you a minimal base for a game that you can use and run.

The Visual Studio solution will contain two major projects:

- UE4: This is listed under the Engine folder of the solution, and it is a project that contains the important header files, tools, plugins, and so on, of the Unreal Engine, so you don't have to worry about it most of the time.
- Bellz: This is the game project and listed under the Games folder of the solution, which holds the name of your game. Also you'll find this project has some base code files, Builder scripts, and the GameMode class. Those are there to make sure you've something that can run.

Feel free to keep browsing files, read the auto-generated comments, and learn more about them. Eventually, at certain points, we will have to go through almost all of those auto-generated files and make some changes to some of the files to fit our needs.

At the end of the day, the auto-generation process gives us the minimum necessary, and we will need to change and adjust that content to fit the game type we are processing.

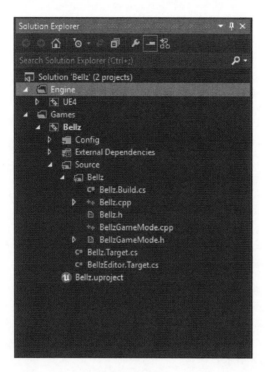

Creating the C++ class

When it comes to creating or adding a C++ class into your game, there are lots of ways you can do it. From the **File** menu you can choose **New C++ Class**. However, the most common method is by just clicking on the big **Add New** button in your content browser and selecting **New C++ Class**.

Using either way will add the new class into your `Source` folder (revise the project directory structure in *Chapter 1, Preparing for a Big Project*) of your project.

By default, all C++ game projects will have a slightly different project structure, but most importantly, you will clearly see a section called **C++ Classes** in the outliner of the content browser and a folder with the game name underneath it. This is where any new code files should be by default. If you check this folder now from within the editor, you will find only one class whose name as game name + `GameMode`. This is an autogenerated class generated while creating the project. It is the first and only class included with your project for now.

Once you hit that magical button, you will be taken to the **Add C++ Class** wizard. The first screen of the wizard will ask you to choose a parent class. Any class you are going to create, most of the time should have a parent class, and I have to say that there are tons of full games that have been made without the need to create a class that is not inherited from a parent class of the unreal class list.

The parent class screen offers you the most important and the most common class types, but you also have the choice to pick a parent class from this list by marking the small checkbox at the upper-right that says **Show All Classes**. You will get access to the full class list for the engine.

Let's just select the **Character** class type at the moment and that will show you the selected class source as a `Character.h` file. If you are good, then let's proceed with the wizard by pressing **Next**.

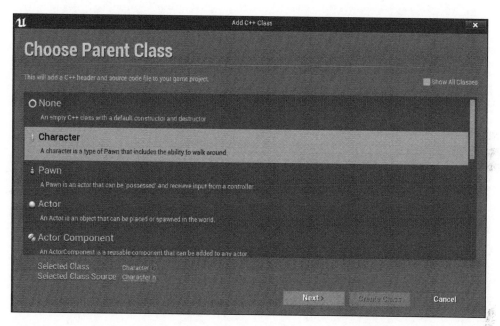

The second screen of the class wizard is the last screen of that short wizard. With this screen you can give a name to the newly created class and define a path for it. I called my class `Gladiator`; feel free to use a name of your choice, but then make sure to correct your code while reading the code for the example project.

The path of the class can be changed and you can set it in a different folder, but most of the time, and this is the most common behavior, you leave it as is and keep all the files inside a folder named with the project name within the source folder of the project.

The main reason behind the process of having a game name folder inside the `sources` folder is that, in some cases, you will need to add extra code to the game that is not Unreal-related, possibly some code files (headers of source files) for an external library, a plugin, or maybe a server implementation for a multiplayer game, so the `sources` folder should be organized for that reason.

Another way people used to structure their code directory is by marking some classes as `public` while marking others as `private`. As you can see in the second screen of the wizard next to the class name, you can define if the new class is going to be public or private; if you make this choice, Unreal will create a new folder of that type in order to have the class inside.

If everything is OK, and you are good with the class name and the path, hit **Create Class**, and that will launch Visual Studio (or Xcode if you are on OS X) with the game solution loaded and the new class source file and header file opened for you.

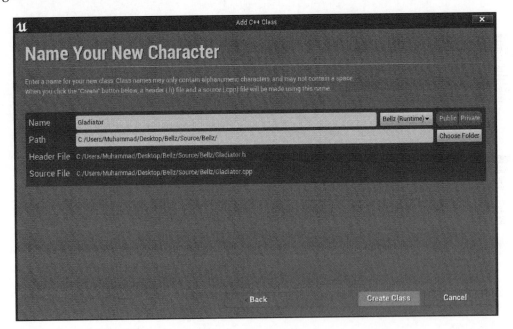

Keep in mind that all the code for this project was written at the same time. The game was built before starting the process of writing this book so you might find some pieces of code that do not make any sense at the moment because it was written for use later on.

In a real game project you'll be building your game step by step and the `character` class, for example, will not be done first; you'll keep adding to it and improving it all the time. Because this is an educational book, and everything should be described in its own chapter, you will find almost all the pieces related to a covered topic within its own chapter.

Editing and adding code

After opening Visual Studio, you will have the base code for the header file and the `sources` file of the `character` class we just created. This base code is not essential; you can edit it or remove the majority of it, but for our game's purposes we will keep it.

The header file will usually look like this by default:

```
1    // Fill out your copyright notice in the Description page of Project Settings.
2
3    #pragma once
4
5    #include "GameFramework/Character.h"
6    #include "Gladiator.generated.h"
7
8    UCLASS()
9    class BELIZ_API AGladiator : public ACharacter
10   {
11       GENERATED_BODY()
12
13   public:
14       // Sets default values for this character's properties
15       AGladiator();
16
17       // Called when the game starts or when spawned
18       virtual void BeginPlay() override;
19
20       // Called every frame
21       virtual void Tick( float DeltaSeconds ) override;
22
23       // Called to bind functionality to input
24       virtual void SetupPlayerInputComponent(class UInputComponent* InputComponent) override;
25
26
27
28   };
29
```

As you can see, header files start with including the character header file from the Unreal Engine game framework, and then include the generated header of the newly created class we just made.

An Unreal Engine class should have the macro UCLASS above it, otherwise you will probably get a compiler error.

The class, by default, will include several public functions that are, in order:

- Constructor: This is necessary to hold any code that is used to build the class (or any blueprint based on that class) during edit time
- BeginPlay: The override of the virtual void BeginPlay class, which is going to be called once the game starts
- Tick: This is also an override of a virtual void from the base class, and that method will be called every frame as long as the object exists
- SetupPlayerInputComponent: Another override of a virtual function from the base class, and this one is called to set up and map the key inputs (the ones we made in *Chapter 1, Preparing for a Big Project*) to the class

In addition, the source file for the Gladiator class should have all the implementations of those functions defined within the header file.

```cpp
// Fill out your copyright notice in the Description page of Project Settings.

#include "Bellz.h"
#include "Gladiator.h"


// Sets default values
AGladiator::AGladiator()
{
    // Set this character to call Tick() every frame.  You can turn this off to improve performance if you don't need it.
    PrimaryActorTick.bCanEverTick = true;

}

// Called when the game starts or when spawned
void AGladiator::BeginPlay()
{
    Super::BeginPlay();

}

// Called every frame
void AGladiator::Tick( float DeltaTime )
{
    Super::Tick( DeltaTime );

}

// Called to bind functionality to input
void AGladiator::SetupPlayerInputComponent(class UInputComponent* InputComponent)
{
    Super::SetupPlayerInputComponent(InputComponent);

}
```

The base code of the source file is almost empty; it is just declarations for the methods. But one thing to notice here is that the `object` constructor contains a Boolean value named `PrimaryActorTick.bCanEverTick`; setting it to `true` will make sure this object and all its instances use the `tick` function (called every frame). So if your class is not going to call a tick, or you want an easy way to disable a tick for a class and its objects, just mark this value as `false`.

The Gladiator header (.h) file

Now let's jump back to the header file again, and let's start adding some more functions and variables to it so we can start building gameplay logic for the character and make something that fits our target.

Considering that a class based on `FTableRowBase` and called `AGameDataTables` will be used later to read the gameplay data from Excel tables; here is the header file code I ended up with.

To make it easier to understand the code, I would like to breakdown all the variable components and methods into a set of chunks; that way it will be very easy to understand them.

Everything starts with the includes, just like any form of C++ coding you are used to making, including the header files that are going to be used or referenced and must be done at the top of the code.

```
#pragma once
#include "GameDataTables.h"
#include "GameFramework/Character.h"
#include "Gladiator.generated.h"
```

Defining the class itself is essentially a step directly after the `include` statements.

```
UCLASS(config = Game)
class AGladiator : public ACharacter
{
   GENERATED_BODY()
```

`BeginPlay`: This is the virtual void of the override `BeginPlay` from the `Character` class base and this one will be called once the game is started.

```
virtual void BeginPlay() override;
```

`CameraBoom`: This is a `USpringArmComponent` that will be added to the character blueprint that is based on that class. This component will be used to control the camera.

```
//Camera boom positioning the camera behind the character
UPROPERTY(VisibleAnywhere, BlueprintReadOnly, Category = Camera, meta
= (AllowPrivateAccess = "true"))
class USpringArmComponent* CameraBoom;
```

`FollowCamera`: This is the camera itself that will be viewing the game and following the player. This one will also be added to the blueprints.

```
//Follow camera
UPROPERTY(VisibleAnywhere, BlueprintReadOnly, Category = Camera, meta
= (AllowPrivateAccess = "true"))
class UCameraComponent* FollowCamera;
```

`EffectSprite`: This is a `Paper2D` sprite component (Paper 2D is the main 2D framework for Unreal Engine 4.x). There are lots of ways we can use this to achieve an on-screen draw texture, but this one is the easiest and most flexible. I managed to add a sprite component that is very close to the camera, and then we can use it to draw whatever effect we need.

```
//The sprite used to draw effect, better and more contrallable than
using the HUD or Textures
UPROPERTY(VisibleAnywhere, BlueprintReadOnly, Category = Effects, meta
= (AllowPrivateAccess = "true"))
class UPaperSpriteComponent* EffectSprite;
```

`AGladiator`: This is the constructor, and as mentioned earlier, it is used to build the object in edit mode.

```
public:
AGladiator();
```

`BaseTurnRate`: This is a `float` variable in degrees to control the camera turn rate.

```
//Base turn rate, in deg/sec. Other scaling may affect final turn
rate.
UPROPERTY(VisibleAnywhere, BlueprintReadOnly, Category = Camera)
float BaseTurnRate;
```

`BaseLookUpRate`: Another `float` variable to control the camera, but this time it's for lookups. This one is also in degrees.

```
//Base look up/down rate, in deg/sec. Other scaling may affect final
rate.
UPROPERTY(VisibleAnywhere, BlueprintReadOnly, Category = Camera)
float BaseLookUpRate;
```

`JumpingVelocity`: This is a `float` variable to determine the jump velocity.

```
//Base Jump velocity
UPROPERTY(VisibleAnywhere, BlueprintReadOnly, Category = "Player
Attributes")
float jumppingVelocity;
```

`IsStillAlive`: This is a Boolean variable to tell us what the current state of the layer is. It is a very important variable, as most of player behavior and inputs will be based on it.

```
//Is the player dead or not
UPROPERTY(EditAnywhere, BlueprintReadOnly, Category = "Player
Attributes")
bool IsStillAlive;
```

`IsAttacking`: Another Boolean variable to report if the player is attacking now or not. It is important for animations.

```
//is the player attacking right now?
UPROPERTY(EditAnywhere, BlueprintReadOnly, Category = "Player
Attributes")
bool IsAttacking;
```

`WeaponIndex`: This is an integer to determine the current active weapon index. The player could have several weapons; to be able to load the weapon's data, it is a good idea to give each weapon its own index.

```
//the index of the current active weapon.
UPROPERTY(EditAnywhere, BlueprintReadOnly, Category = "Player
Attributes")
int32 WeaponIndex;
```

IsControlable: Sometimes the player is not dead, but you also need to take the control out of his hands, maybe because the character is carrying out an attack, or maybe because the player paused the game. So this is a `bool` variable meant to tell us if the player is in control now or not.

```
//To be able to disable the player during cutscenes, menus, death....
etc
UPROPERTY(EditAnywhere, BlueprintReadOnly, Category = "Player
Attributes")
bool IsControlable;
```

TablesInstance: A `datatable` variable to hold the active instance of the game tables. It is just here to load some data.

```
UPROPERTY(EditAnywhere, BlueprintReadOnly, Category = "Game
DataTables")
AGameDataTables* TablesInstance;
```

GetIsStillAlive: A getter method to return the value of the `IsStillAlive` Boolean variable.

```
//Return if the player dead or alive
UFUNCTION(BlueprintCallable, Category = "Player Attributes")
bool GetIsStillAlive() const { return IsStillAlive; }
```

OnSetPlayerController: A method that takes a parameter of `true` or `false`, and uses it to set the status of the player controller. So it is here we take the control from the player, or give it to him at a certain moment.

```
//Enable or disable inputs
UFUNCTION(BlueprintCallable, Category = "Player Attributes")
void OnSetPlayerController(bool status);
```

OnChangeHealthByAmount: A method that takes a `float` value, and reduces the total player health using it. It is usually used when the player gets damaged.

```
//the attack effect on health
UFUNCTION(BlueprintCallable, Category = "Player Attributes")
void OnChangeHealthByAmount(float usedAmount);
```

OnGetHealthAmount: This is a `getter` function that returns the `TotalHealth` value of the player as a `float` value.

```
UFUNCTION(BlueprintCallable, Category = "Player Attributes")
float OnGetHealthAmount() const {return TotalHealth;}
```

OnPostAttack: A method that holds some procedurals after the player has done an attack.

```
UFUNCTION(BlueprintCallable, Category = "Player Actions")
void OnPostAttack();
```

GetCameraBoom: A getter method to return the CameraBoom component variable.

```
//Returns CameraBoom subobject
FORCEINLINE class USpringArmComponent* GetCameraBoom()
  const { return CameraBoom; }
```

GetFollowCamera: Another getter method to return the FollowCamera component variable.

```
//Returns FollowCamera subobject
FORCEINLINE class UCameraComponent* GetFollowCamera()
  const { return FollowCamera; }
```

MoveForward: A method that holds the code responsible for player movement to the forward and backward. Notice that it is a BlueprintCallable in order to be able to use it from the Gladiator class blueprint instances.

```
protected:
UFUNCTION(BlueprintCallable, Category = "Player Actions")
void MoveForward(float Value);
```

MoveRight: A method that holds the code responsible for player movement to the left and right.

```
UFUNCTION(BlueprintCallable, Category = "Player Actions")
void MoveRight(float Value);
```

Jump: A method that is responsible for applying the jump action to the character based on the base character class.

```
UFUNCTION(BlueprintCallable, Category = "Player Actions")
void Jump();
```

StopJumping: A method that is responsible for stopping the jump, and resuming the idle/run animation.

```
UFUNCTION(BlueprintCallable, Category = "Player Actions")
void StopJumping();
```

OnAttack: A method that is responsible for attacking.

```
UFUNCTION(BlueprintCallable, Category = "Player Actions")
void OnAttack();
```

OnChangeWeapon: A method that is responsible for switching between weapons.

```
UFUNCTION(BlueprintCallable, Category = "Player Actions")
void OnChangeWeapon();
```

TurnAtRate: A method that is responsible for applying turns to the following camera.

```
//Called via input to turn at a given rate.
void TurnAtRate(float Rate);
```

LookUpAtRate: A method that is responsible for applying the camera look-up rate to the follow camera.

```
//Called via input to turn look up/down at a given rate.
void LookUpAtRate(float Rate);
```

TotalHealth: A float variable that holds the player's total health (the current health), as at any moment the player's health gets reduced, that will be the final value. Some people like the approach of creating two variables:

- TotalHealth: This is the base and default health
- CurrentHealth: This represents the current health status

Feel free to use any approach you want, but I like to make one health variable for such a small game.

```
//The health of the enemy
UPROPERTY(EditAnywhere, BlueprintReadWrite, Category =
  "Player Attributes")
float TotalHealth;
```

AttackRange: A float variable that holds the current weapon attacking range.

```
//The range for the enemy attack
UPROPERTY(EditAnywhere, BlueprintReadWrite, Category =
  "Player Attributes")
float AttackRange;
```

`SetupPlayerInputComponent`: Another override of a virtual function from the base class, and this one is called to set up and map the key inputs (the ones we made in *Chapter 1, Preparing for a Big Project*) to the class.

```
protected:
//APawn interface
virtual void SetupPlayerInputComponent(class UInputComponent*
InputComponent) override;
  //End of APawn interface
};
```

As you can see, there are some stylings that have been applied to the code. It looks weird, strange, and unique at first glance, but once you get used to writing Unreal code you'll get very familiar with these things.

The styling I used involved some access specifiers and macros, which include:

- `Public`: Any variables or methods listed underneath this access specifier will be public
- `Private`: Any variable or method listed underneath this access specifier will be private
- `UPROPERTY`: This is used before a variable and is a macro to define attributes for the variable, such as how and where it should or could be changed or seen, and its category to make sure it is listed in the correct place
- `UFUNCTION`: This is used only before a function and is a macro to define attributes for a function, such as how and where it should or could be called, and its category to make sure it is listed in the correct place

The Gladiator source (.cpp) file

Because source files always contain more than 20x more code than the header files, I would like to follow a different approach here in explaining the code. I will break down the source file into blocks, one by one.

The includes

As we mentioned earlier, any C++ file or even header file must start with the `include` statements. You don't have to include everything; some of the `include` statements will be there by default but others might be needed while you are building up the code.

Even if your game example is different and you wanted to have different functionalities, you might need to include more headers.

```
#include "Bellz.h"
#include "Gladiator.h"
#include "GameDataTables.h"
#include "PaperSpriteComponent.h"
#include "GameDataTables.h"
```

As you can see, now the included header files have been increased to include those we have formed from the auto-generated source file.

Because the game will be reading data from Excel sheets, I managed to import the `GameDataTables` header file, so we will be able to deal and work with the data table classes. For the same reason, I managed to import the `GameDataTables` header file, so we'll be able to get the data through the object instance of the data itself.

Because we've made a `Sprite2D` component within the header file, I needed to be able to control this sprite at any given moment and also needed to be able to control anything related to this sprite component at the constructor while building our character. To be able to do all of that, I need to be able to access that component, which can be done through the `PaperSpriteComponent` header file.

Keep in mind that, if you are not able to load this header file, it might be because Paper2D is not in your `include` path, so you need to add several additional `include` paths in the project settings of your game project.

```
C:\Program Files (x86)\Epic Games\4.10\Engine\Plugins\2D\Paper2D\Source\Paper2D\Classes
C:\Program Files (x86)\Epic Games\4.10\Engine\Plugins\2D\Paper2D\Source\Paper2D\Public
C:\Program Files (x86)\Epic Games\4.10\Engine\Plugins\2D\Paper2D\Intermediate\Build\Win64\UE4Editor\Inc\Paper2D
C:\Program Files (x86)\Epic Games\4.10\Engine\Plugins\2D\Paper2D\Source\Paper2D
```

The constructor

You might be familiar with the term constructor. It has exactly the same function within Unreal games. It will be execute the set of commands you enter once the object instance has been created.

```
AGladiator::AGladiator()
{
  //Set size for collision capsule
  GetCapsuleComponent()->InitCapsuleSize(42.f, 96.0f);
```

```
    TotalHealth = 100.f;
    AttackRange = 25.f;

    jumppingVelocity = 600.f;

    //set our turn rates for input
    BaseTurnRate = 45.f;
    BaseLookUpRate = 45.f;


    //Don't rotate when the controller rotates. Let that just affect the
camera.
    bUseControllerRotationPitch = false;
    bUseControllerRotationYaw = false;
    bUseControllerRotationRoll = false;


    //Configure character movement
    GetCharacterMovement()->bOrientRotationToMovement = true; //
Character moves in the direction of input...
    GetCharacterMovement()->RotationRate = FRotator(0.0f, 540.0f, 0.0f);
// ...at this rotation rate
    GetCharacterMovement()->JumpZVelocity = jumppingVelocity;
    GetCharacterMovement()->AirControl = 0.2f;


    //Create a camera boom (pulls in towards the player if there is a
collision)
    CameraBoom = CreateDefaultSubobject<USpringArmComponent>(TEXT("Came
raBoom"));
    CameraBoom->AttachTo(RootComponent);
    CameraBoom->TargetArmLength = 300.0f; // The camera follows at this
distance behind the character
    CameraBoom->bUsePawnControlRotation = true; // Rotate the arm based
on the controller


    //Create a follow camera
    FollowCamera = CreateDefaultSubobject<UCameraComponent>(TEXT("Follo
wCamera"));
    FollowCamera->AttachTo(CameraBoom, USpringArmComponent::SocketName);
// Attach the camera to the end of the boom and let the boom adjust to
match the controller orientation
    FollowCamera->bUsePawnControlRotation = false; // Camera does not
rotate relative to arm
```

```
    EffectSprite = CreateDefaultSubobject<UPaperSpriteComponent>(TEXT("
ClawEffect"));
    EffectSprite->AttachTo(CameraBoom);

    //Note: The skeletal mesh and anim blueprint references on the Mesh
component (inherited from Character)
    //are set in the derived blueprint asset named MyCharacter (to avoid
direct content references in C++)

    IsStillAlive = true;
    IsAttacking = false;
    WeaponIndex = 1;

    //by default the inputs should be enabled, in case there is
something ned to be tested
    OnSetPlayerController(true);
}
```

Inside the constructor, we have to put all the logic that will be applied directly in the following three cases:

- If you switch back directly to the editor after writing the code, you should see that the changes that have been made inside the constructor have already taken place

- Once you create a blueprint based on the class, all the code within the constructor will be executed after creating the blueprint instance in the editor

- Once you spawn a blueprint based on the class at runtime (while the game is running), all the constructor logic will already have been applied (unless you changed it inside the editor)

Because of the nature of the constructor, I managed to put any default value, add any default component, or add any default objects, inside it. As you can see from the constructor logic, I have done the following, in order:

- Applied a size (width and height) to the `capsule` component of the `character` class.

- Added a default value of `100` to the total health variable holder, and added a default value of `25` to the attack range variable.

- Applied a jump velocity to the character (this value is inherited from the base character class). Feel free to experiment with values, I found `400` to `600` works well for me.

- Applied default values for the `BaseTurnRate` and the `BaseLookupRate` values, so I now have some values to control the camera when necessary to control it. The higher the values, the faster the camera moves; the lower the values, the slower the camera moves.

- Then I worked on applying values to some of the default members of the character base class. Those values include:

  ° Setting `boolOrientRotationToMovement` to true; that way I make sure the character mesh will be rotated in the direction of the movement

  ° Settting `RotationRate` variable to make the default rotation rate for the character

  ° Applying the default velocity value we stored earlier to the `JumpZVelocity` variable

  ° Adding some `AirControl` value to make sure the character behaves well

- Then I started to work with the spring arm component called `CameraBoom` that we declared within the header file. I started by creating the component itself, to add it to a category of its own name. Then I attached it to the root of the object, added a `TargetArmLength` value of `300` to it, and finally I set the Boolean named `bUsePawnControlRotation` to `true` to make sure that the spring arm will be rotated based on the controller.

- While I'm creating the new components and applying some parameters to them, it is time to create the camera and attach it to the player controller. After creating the camera component as `FollowCamera` and assigning it to a category, I attached it to the spring arm component (as a child) and finally disabled its `bUsePawnControlRotation` component to make sure that the camera doesn't rotate relatively to the spring arm component.

- Now I have created a paper sprite component (`Paper2D`) and assigned it to the `EffectSprite` component; that way I make sure it will always be rotated with the mouse/gamepad, which applies the camera rotations based on the `CameraBoom` component attached to the player.

- Then I set some of the variables I have to their default values, including the Boolean `IsStillAlive` to mark the player as alive at the beginning, and then I set the value of the `IsAttacking` variable to `false`, because it makes sense that, once the game starts there is definitely no attack! Finally, I set the `WeaponIndex` component to the first weapon I want to be used.

- Finally, we call the method, OnSetPlayerController and pass a true value to it to make sure that once the game starts, the player, by default, has control over the camera. This could be changed later based on the level, the scenario, and so on.

BeginPlay

BeginPlay is a little different to OnConstruct, which is the constructor executed once the object has been created, which means it is executed either once the instance has been made at runtime, or inside the editor while building the game. Beginplay is only executed at the start of the game, or once the object is instantiated at runtime, as long as it has never been executed inside the editor.

```
void AGladiator::BeginPlay()
{
   //Ask the datamanager to get all the tables datat at once and store
them
   //AGameDataTables dataHolder;
   for (TActorIterator<AGameDataTables> ActorItr(GetWorld()); ActorItr;
++ActorItr)
   {
     if (ActorItr)
     {
       //print theinstance name to screen
       //GEngine->AddOnScreenDebugMessage(-1, 10.f, FColor::Green,
ActorItr->GetName());

       //Call the fetch to the tables, now we get all the datat stored.
Why? simply because keep readin everytime from the table itself is
going to cost over your memory
       //but the most safe method, is just to read all the data at
once, and then keep getting whatever needed values from the storage
we've .
       TablesInstance = *ActorItr;
       TablesInstance->OnFetchAllTables();

     }
   }
}
```

Because `BeginPlay()` is the first thing to take place for the class instance once the game runs, I didn't have much to do for now except getting the current data table instance from the level so I can store it and use the data from it. Some of the data is useful for the player, such as the weapons data, and that made it important to keep an instance of it inside the player controller.

Using the `TActorIterator` type was my choice, as it is the best way yet within Unreal to look for objects of an X type within the level. I used it to look for the type `AGameDataTables`, which is a class type we are going to create later, and once I found it, I called its member function `OnFetchAllTables` which will get all the table data and store it.

Feel free to comment this part, and not even use it until you reach the data table chapter. It might make more sense there but again, it makes the game go back and forth between classes. However, each chapter here has to be as independent as possible.

SetupPlayerInputComponent

This is one more default method that Unreal adds by default you can totally ignore calling it at all, but as long as we have inputs required it is the best place to bind them.

```
void AGladiator::SetupPlayerInputComponent(class UInputComponent*
InputComponent)
{
  //Set up gameplay key bindings
  check(InputComponent);
  InputComponent->BindAction("Jump", IE_Pressed, this,
&ACharacter::Jump);
  InputComponent->BindAction("Jump", IE_Released, this,
&ACharacter::StopJumping);

  InputComponent->BindAction("Attack", IE_Released, this,
&AGladiator::OnAttack);
  InputComponent->BindAction("ChangeWeapon", IE_Released, this,
&AGladiator::OnChangeWeapon);

  InputComponent->BindAxis("MoveForward", this,
&AGladiator::MoveForward);
  InputComponent->BindAxis("MoveRight", this, &AGladiator::MoveRight);
```

```
    //We have 2 versions of the rotation bindings to handle different
kinds of devices differently
    //"turn" handles devices that provide an absolute delta, such as a
mouse.
    //"turnrate" is for devices that we choose to treat as a rate of
change, such as an analog joystick
    InputComponent->BindAxis("Turn", this,
&APawn::AddControllerYawInput);
    InputComponent->BindAxis("TurnRate", this, &AGladiator::TurnAtRate);
    InputComponent->BindAxis("LookUp", this, &APawn::AddControllerPitch
Input);
    InputComponent->BindAxis("LookUpRate", this,
&AGladiator::LookUpAtRate);
}
```

`SetupPlayerInputController` is one of the most important functions from the base character class. This is the function responsible for assigning the keys from the input settings (the ones we set in *Chapter 1, Preparing for a Big Project*, inside the project settings), to functions within this class (or maybe other classes if you wish).

As you may remember, we added two types of key input in *Chapter 1, Preparing for a Big Project* , which were:

- `Actions`
- `Axis`

Now, it is time to bind the inputs and in order to do this we use a function based on the key input type, and that means that, as we have two key input types, we also have two types of binding functions:

- `BindAction`
- `BindAxis`

Both interfaces look the same; you have to pass the key name that we have defined inside the input settings and pass the function that should be called in that input event. It is not only everything that you can pass, but also a specific type of the input event. For example, you can fire the function on when the input key is released or pressed.

Jump

This is a very short, but useful function. Lots of people used to map the `jump` function with the key in the `SetupPlayerInputComponent` directly, but I always like to have an independent function for jump processing.

```cpp
void AGladiator::Jump()
{
  if (IsControlable && !IsAttacking)
  {
    bPressedJump = true;
    JumpKeyHoldTime = 0.0f;
  }
}
```

As you can see, I made sure first that the player is in control and is not in attacking mode. If both conditions are met, then I can go ahead and change some parameters, which will apply the jump directly from the character base class.

StopJumping

When a jump takes place, lots of things will depend on it. Some logic will be executed but, most importantly, animations will be played based on that action. That is the reason behind adding another function to be called when a jump is done, because other animations will need them.

```cpp
void AGladiator::StopJumping()
{
  if (IsControlable)
  {
    bPressedJump = false;
    JumpKeyHoldTime = 0.0f;
  }
}
```

The `StopJumping` function is not very complex, and in fact it only does the exact opposite of the `jump` function.

OnAttack

While there isn't too much to do when the player hits the **Attack** button, changing the status of the attack itself is enough to drive the animations inside the animation blueprint.

```
void AGladiator::OnAttack()
{
  if (IsControlable)
  {

    IsAttacking = true;
  }
}
```

The OnAttack function is simple here, as it is only going to set the Boolean value of the attack to true. This value is going to be used from the animation blueprint in order to display the attack animation.

The attack effect itself is measured by the overlapping spheres of the weapons and that's the reason behind not having too much logic within the attacking function.

OnPostAttack

Here is another reverse of a function; a function that is only doing the opposite of the previous function.

```
void AGladiator::OnPostAttack()
{

  IsAttacking = false;
}
```

A good implementation to be used here is to make them both one function with a Boolean parameter to be passed. Then, based on the case, we pass a true or false value. But I prefer to make both separate functions, just in case I need to add something special for either of the two functions.

OnChangeWeapon

Sometimes in such a game, the player needs to switch between weapons; this might make more sense with a very large game with tons of different weapons, but I wanted to add it here in a minimal fashion as it is sometimes essential to have it.

```
void AGladiator::OnChangeWeapon()
{
  if (IsControlable)
  {

    if (WeaponIndex < TablesInstance->AllWeaponsData.Num())
    {
      WeaponIndex++;
    }
    else
    {
      WeaponIndex = 1;
    }
  }
}
```

The main idea here is that, whenever the player switches between weapons, all that we do is change the weapon index, and based on that index we can:

- Load a different weapon mesh
- Load different weapon data from the data tables (information that includes the weapon's name, icon, damage, and so on)

So as you can see, every time the player hits the **Change Weapon** key, this function gets called. The function is very simple. It checks the current weapon index variable and, as long as it is less than the amount of the weapons found on the game data table, it adds 1 to the current weapon index variable. If it is not, then it sets the weapon index variable to 1 to start from the first weapon in the table again.

TurnAtRate

This is one of the functions mapped to a certain input. Its main job it to rotate the camera up and down, but the good part of it is that it is mapped to ready-made code from the Unreal Engine `Character` class.

```
void AGladiator::TurnAtRate(float Rate)
{
  if (IsControlable)
  {
    //calculate delta for this frame from the rate information
    AddControllerYawInput(Rate * BaseTurnRate * GetWorld()-
>GetDeltaSeconds());
  }
}
```

The base character class has a method called `AddControllerYawInput`. It is meant to apply a yaw rotation to the controller. Here we make sure this method is going to be called when the proper input calls the `TurnAtRate` method and applies it to the value of the `BaseTurnRate` float we have created in the header file.

LookUpAtRate

As we mapped some keys to move the camera up and down, it makes sense to add a similar functionality to move the camera from side to side:

```
void AGladiator::LookUpAtRate(float Rate)
{
  if (IsControlable)
  {
    //calculate delta for this frame from the rate information
    AddControllerPitchInput(Rate * BaseLookUpRate * GetWorld()-
>GetDeltaSeconds());
  }
}
```

We are going to do with the pitch as we did with the yaw. The base character class has a method called `AddControllerPitchInput` to apply a yaw rotation to the controller. Here we make sure that, every time this method is called, when the proper input calls the `TurnAtRate` method and applies it to the value of the `BaseLookUpRate` float we have created in the header file.

OnSetPlayerController

This simple function is very effective as it is going to control almost all player inputs. This function's main job is to change the value of the Boolean called `IsControlable`. The value of this Boolean is checked before any player input to verify whether the player has access to the input or not; based on that, the game will process the player input and translate it to functions.

```
void AGladiator::OnSetPlayerController(bool status)
{
  IsControlable = status;
}
```

For example, this function is called by the end of the constructor with the value of `true` to make sure that, once the object instance is created, the player has control over it. At the same time, when the player tries to do any input, such as attack, you'll find that the `attack` method called `AGladiator::OnAttack()` does nothing before it checks for the Boolean `IsControlable` to see if it is `true` or `false`.

OnChangeHealthByAmount

Now let's do something interesting. It is not only interesting because we are going to do a math function that will decrease and increase the player health, but also because it will be calling a function from the blueprint, yes, C++ code calling blueprint logic!

```
void AGladiator::OnChangeHealthByAmount(float usedAmount)
{
  TotalHealth -= usedAmount;
  FOutputDeviceNull ar;
  this->CallFunctionByNameWithArguments(TEXT("ApplyGetDamageEffect"),
ar, NULL, true);
}
```

The player health by default is `100`, stored in the variable named `TotalHealth`; this value is not going to stay as is during the gameplay.

The player has to take some damage from the enemy's attacks and eventually lose some health. Or maybe you want to add some new features to the game such as health pickups; then you need a quick way to be able to change the current health value, which will be eventually displayed through the UI.

That's the main job of this function: it takes a specified amount of health, and subtracts it from the main health.

As you can see, there is a call for an internal function being made using the method `CallFunctionByNameWithArguments`; this means that the C++ code is going to call the blueprint function.

Let's be clear, anything that can be done using C++, can be done using blueprints, but sometimes accessing components and applying some settings is easier via blueprints. The idea here was to present a way that you can call a blueprint function from within the C++ code.

The function being called here, which is called `ApplyGetDamageEffect`, is meant to display an overall screen effect that shows that the player has taken some damage at that moment. We will build its logic in the blueprint later in this chapter, but let's be clear about what exactly this function is going to do in order:

1. Get the level post-processing volume that is dedicated to displaying the hit effect and save a reference to it so it becomes easier and faster the next time we call the function, as we will already have a reference for the volume and then will display this volume effect.
2. Get the `sprite` component we created in the header file, enable it, and play some fade animations for it. So yeah, making fade effects based on a `float` value is a lot easier through blueprints and timeline nodes.
3. Finally we create some camera shakes to simulate the damage to the player.

Once we're done with the C++ code and have created our blueprint based on that class, we will be working on beautifying it and adding some blueprint logic. That's where we will implement the logic for the `ApplyGetDamageEffect` method.

MoveForward

Now we come to a very important part of the controller system, where we will be writing the code to move the player forward and back, using the keys we have mapped earlier at the top of the class.

```
void AGladiator::MoveForward(float Value)
{
  if ((Controller != NULL) && (Value != 0.0f) && IsControlable &&
!IsAttacking)
  {
```

```
    //find out which way is forward
    const FRotator Rotation = Controller->GetControlRotation();
    const FRotator YawRotation(0, Rotation.Yaw, 0);

    //get forward vector
    const FVector Direction = FRotationMatrix(YawRotation).
GetUnitAxis(EAxis::X);
    AddMovementInput(Direction, Value);
  }
}
```

The AGladiator::MoveForward function is called when the move forward input key is triggered. This function has to first check whether the controller exists, and the value of the movement is not 0, as well as whether the player has control now or not. Finally, it checks to see whether the player is not in attacking mode. If all the conditions are met, then the function will get the rotation of the controller and the yaw rotation of the controller, and that's very important information in order to decide which forward direction will be used to move.

After getting the direction and storing it as a vector as the Direction variable, it is a good time to apply the movement using the base class method, AddMovementInput, to apply the movement with the value that came from the input key, and the direction we just calculated.

Understand that the value passed might be positive or negative, and that will define the direction: forward or backward.

MoveRight

As we've created a function to move the player along the front-back axis, we have to create another one for the side to side movement.

```
void AGladiator::MoveRight(float Value)
{
  if ((Controller != NULL) && (Value != 0.0f) && IsControlable &&
!IsAttacking)
  {
    //find out which way is right
    const FRotator Rotation = Controller->GetControlRotation();
    const FRotator YawRotation(0, Rotation.Yaw, 0);
```

```
    //get right vector
    const FVector Direction = FRotationMatrix(YawRotation).
GetUnitAxis(EAxis::Y);
    //add movement in that direction
    AddMovementInput(Direction, Value);
  }
}
```

The `AGladiator:: MoveRight` function is called when the `move right` input key is triggered. This function has to check first whether the controller exists and the value of the movement is not 0, as well as whether the player has control now or not. Finally, it checks to see whether the player is not in attacking mode. If all the conditions are met, then the function will get the rotation of the controller and the yaw rotation of the controller; this is very important, in order to decide which direction is the right way to move.

As with the `move forward` function, after getting the direction and storing it as a vector as the `Direction` variable, it is a good time to apply the movement using the base class method called `AddMovementInput` with the value that came from the input key, and the direction we just calculated.

Understand that the value passed might be positive or negative, and that will define the direction: right or left.

Compiling the code

Now with everything done for the controller, you're ready to jump back to the editor to make use of it. In order to have the code we made executed by the editor, you need to compile it first. Otherwise, the game will keep behaving as if this code has never been added.

There are different ways you can use to do that, both accessed from a different place. So you can:

- From within the Visual Studio itself, right-click on the game project from the **Solution Explorer** window and hit **Build**, and that will do the build for you. If there are any errors, you'll see them in the output panel; otherwise, you will get a success message.

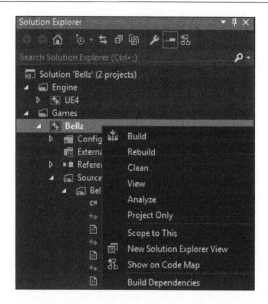

- From within the Unreal Editor itself, you can simply hit the **Compile** button from the top bar. If there are code errors, Unreal will show you a failed message with a failed sound effect.

But anyways, regardless of the method you used, if compilation takes quite some time you can still make it faster as you can copy `BuildConfiguration.XML` from the unreal Engine installation directory (for example): `C:\Program Files (x86)\Epic Games\4.10\Engine\Programs\UnrealBuildTool`.

Paste it in your Unreal Engine documents folder (for example): `C:\Users\<user>\Documents\Unreal Engine\UnrealBuildTool\`.

The last step is changing a small value from this XML file, which is `ProcessorCountMultiplier`, to 2 or 4 is set to 1 by default.

```
<ProcessorCountMultiplier>1</ProcessorCountMultiplier>
```

Animation assets

Even after we have made all the code we need, it is still not enough to get the character running in the game; and doing exactly what the code is saying. The code is just a way to do things, but in order to see it needs some way of being visualized.

In *Chapter 1, Preparing for a Big Project*, we managed to import some of the free assets to the game, one of those assets was the warriors in the free packages from Unreal Marketplace. If you haven't added it to the project, then follow the steps we have used in *Chapter 1, Preparing for a Big Project*, and add those characters to the game.

Adding sockets to the skeleton

Double-click on the character you want to use in order to open it in the animation editor, Persona, and there you need to switch to the **Skeleton** tab in the upper-left corner. From there, you have access to the entire skeleton.

Because I know that my player will be using his right hand to hold weapons, I wanted to visualize this so it becomes very easy for me to understand how, exactly, the animation looks.

Select the **hand_r** joint from the bones list and by right-clicking you can choose **Add Socket**; this will add a socket that can hold items. I named my socket sword, name the one you made as you wish!

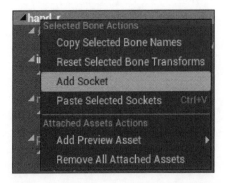

Now you right-click again, but this time on the socket itself (the socket we have just created), and choose to **Add Preview Asset**.

That will open a small menu for you to choose an asset to use as a preview. Pick one choice but keep in mind that the asset you choose will only be a preview, only appears inside the character editor, and will not be spawned in-game, or even in any other editors; it is just a preview asset to test your animations.

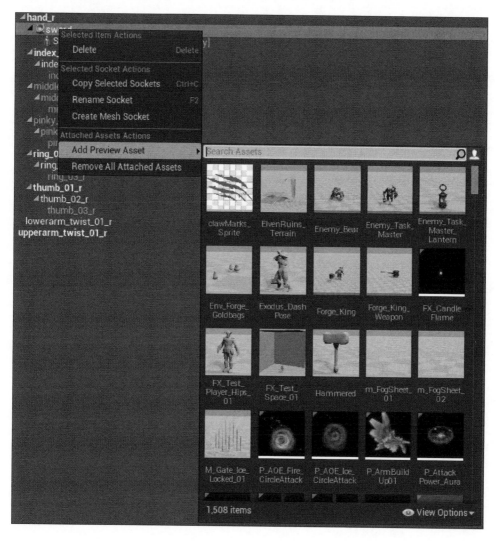

Keep moving the socket, and position and rotate it until you get a good result. It has to be very accurate, as this position will be used later to hold weapons.

Creating the blend space

Now it is time to create the animation blueprint. In order to be able to create the fully working animation blueprint we still need to create one more thing: an animation blend.

The animation blend is meant to implement a blend between several animations, and the goal we want to achieve here is to blend between the idle, walk, and run animations.

Using animation blend is one of the most fun, yet simple, tasks you can do with Unreal Editor. By simply creating an animation blend 1D asset from the content browser, you are half-way there.

Right-click inside the content browser and choose **Blend Space 1D** from the **Animation** section; this will pop up a window for you to choose the targeted character skeleton. Choose it, and name the animation blends as you wish.

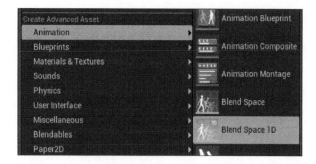

Open the animation blend space. The way it works is that a vertical line in the middle represents the blend over time.

On the right-hand side you can see all the animations listed for the character; by simply dragging and dropping animations into the space, you are assigning them. I simply put the walk animation at the bottom and the running animation at the top, then the walk animation in the middle, but shifted it a little to the bottom to make sure the blend between the idle and walk is quick, but the blend between the running and walk takes more time and inputs.

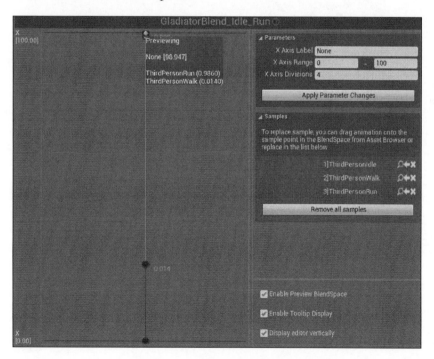

If everything is OK and you like the result then hit **Save and Close this Editor** window, as we are going to create the animation blueprint.

The animation blueprint

As the name implies, the animation blueprint is a way to handle the relationship between animations in the form of diagrams, charts or whatever you call it.

Creating an animation blueprint asset is as easy as creating the blend space. From the same animation section of the contextual right-click menu of the content browser, you can choose **Animation Blueprint**.

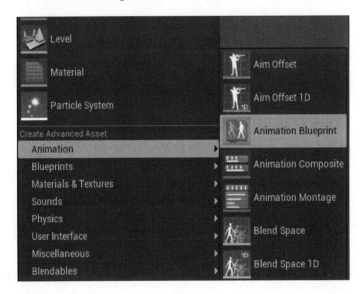

The animation blueprint is a special type of blueprint; however as long it has the word **blueprint** in it, this means that it has to share some characteristics of the normal blueprint. This means that the animation blueprint not only contains a bunch of animation nodes, graphs, and state machines, it also has variables, functions, events, and almost anything you can find within a typical blueprint, such as an actor blueprint for example.

Because the best use of the animation blueprint is to utilize almost each section of it, which means a huge part of the animation handling process will be involving code or logic creations, in order to do that I managed to add some variables that will be used to build the logic.

Those variables are:

- inAir: This is a Boolean variable that gets the in air value from the character class.

- movementSpeed: This is a float variable that is going to control the movement speed; based on that, we will be handling the animation blend space we made earlier in the previous step.

- isAttacking: This is a Boolean variable that stores the original value we get from the gladiator class.

- isStllAlive: This is a Boolean variable that stores the original value we get from the gladiator class.

- attackAnimationIndex: Because I'm planning to have more than just an attacking animation, I wanted to have an integer index; based on that index I'll be loading a certain animation. We are going to add logic to randomly give an index.

Once everything is alright, we can start building some logic within the animation blueprint. This logic will be mainly focusing on updating some statues and storing values inside the previously created set of variables.

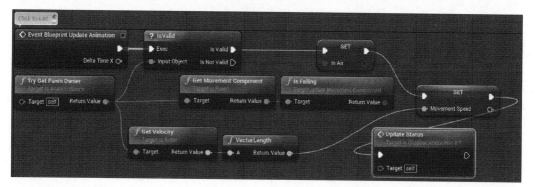

The logic is simple! As you can see, all that it is doing is getting the character controllers that are using this animation blueprint instance, and then getting the *is falling* status and applying it to the local variable inAir, and then doing the same thing with the velocity but applying it to the local variable movementSpeed. Finally it calls a custom event called UpdateStauts. All this happens with every single frame.

The **Update Status** event is not doing anything special, in fact, it is doing almost the same thing, but this time it is not accessing the character controller; instead, it accesses the gladiator class of the character that is using this animation blueprint instance.

Then it gets the isAttacking and the isStillAlive values from there and assigns them to the local variables. Finally, it makes a random number between two values; the maximum value matches the number of the attacking animations I want to shuffle between.

So, why do we get all those values and store them in local variables?

The answer is simple. In order to apply a certain animation at a certain moment, we have to define some conditions for it, and this is how the state machines work: once a condition takes place, the animation blends from one state to another based on that condition.

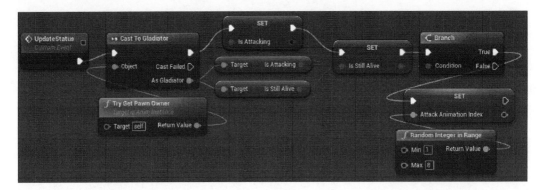

The last, but not least, piece of logic is to tell the code that the attack animation is done, by calling the OnPostAttack method we made earlier inside the Gladiator class using the animation notifications. However, this step needs preparation first!

So let's open any of the attacking animations either by choosing the animations section from the upper-right corner of the animation blueprint, or by double-clicking the animation itself from the content browser.

By dragging the timeline, you can jump to any frame of the animation. I wouldn't suggest going to the end of the animation, as lots of animations contain a few extra frames at the end, but I would say go to the moment where the character actually finishes the attack, and you can right-click on that, on the timeline, and choose **Add Notify**; this will allow you to enter a name for a notification.

A notification is simply a call for a function at a given moment; this means that you can call functions at certain moments in animations, which is great. You can do lots of awesome things using this feature; for example you can spawn some particles or play a sound effect every time the character's foot hits the ground!

Anyway, I managed to name my notification OnAttackEnd. Remember the name you use, and apply it for all the attack animations you have. Remember, once you create a notification, you can reuse it for all the other animations under the same animation blueprint, which means that, if you have another attack animation for the same character, you can directly add the same notification and you don't have to a create new one.

Once you are done adding the notifications you want for any attack animations, or any other animations you have, you can go back again to the logic section of the animation blueprint and there you can find the newly added method listed within the event of the right-click menu.

Add that event and, simply use it to call the `OnPostAttack` method from the gladiator class of the character controller that is using this animation blueprint instance.

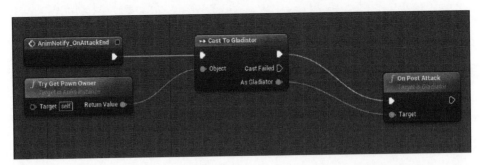

Now, the last step in completing the animation blueprint is to add the animation state machines themselves. From the main graph of the animations, you can add a main animation state machine and name it anything you want. This one will be the main one, usually we call it Default. Connect it to the final animation pose.

That means, whatever happens inside this Default state machine will be used as the final pose for the character animation blueprint at the current frame.

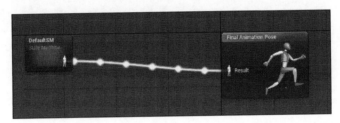

When you double-click on the Default state machine it will take you inside it, which is empty. All that you have to do is add states, name them, and give them conditions.

You can create states from the right-click menu and you can connect them by just dragging and dropping lines out of them, just like blueprint nodes.

I managed to added several statuses, such as:

- **IdleToRun**: This displays the animation of the blendspace we made, to blend between idle, walk, and run
- **Jump Start**: This plays the start of the jump animation, and it is not loopable

- **Jump Loop**: This is a loop for the middle part of the jump animation, and it has to run and loop as long as the character is in the air

- **Jump End**: Once the character gets on the ground, the end of the jump animation should play once

- **Die**: If the player is dead, we play the death animation

- **Attack**: You can add as many attack states as you wish to fit the amount of attack animations you have, but make sure that the amount matches the maximum value of the `attackIndex`

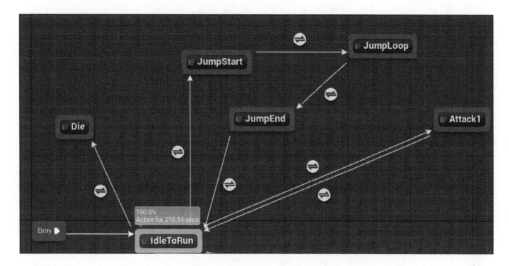

It might look complex, but state machines are one of the most fun and easy topics in animation programming as it takes the load from the code side, and makes it more visual and easy to digest.

Once you drag a line out of a state to another state, you will have a little circle with a double directional arrow; this is called the condition. If you double-click it, it will take you to a graph where you can put some logic: this logic will be the condition that will trigger the transition between the two states.

If we take the transition between Idle and Die, it will simply be the value of the Boolean called isStillAlive; double-click the condition circle between both states to see it.

Build any logic you want. It does not have to be one condition, you can add as many as you wish. Moreover, you don't have to double-click to open the graph every time you want to check the condition; you can simply hover with the mouse over the condition circle, and it will display a conclusion of the logic for you, if there is any logic inside it.

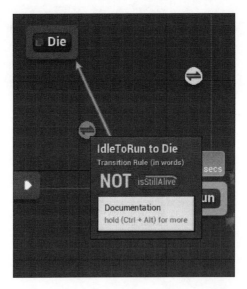

However, regarding the state itself, if you double-click it you will find that you can attach an animation or another state machine and you can keep branching state machines as much as you wish. I'm sure you wouldn't do this, as there are tons of ways to achieve any result, simply.

By opening any of the states, let's say the Die one, you may find it has only a Play animation node; you can simply put it on the right-click menu.

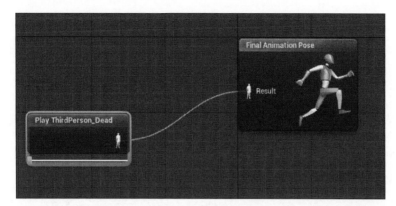

The most important part here is the settings section that is activated when you select the play animation node, as it gives you two main (and important options, among others):

- **Sequence**: From this drop-down menu you can select which animation should be played.

- **Loop Animation**: This defines the type of animation. Because sometimes you can blend between animations when it is done, if the animation is looped it will never be done and that means no blend is going to happen. So it is very important that, once you add a play animation node, you decide carefully if it is going to loop or not.

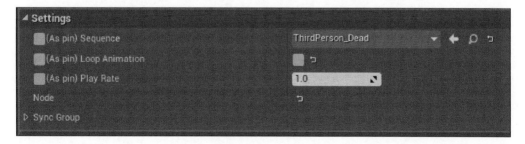

Building the blueprint

Now with everything done on the animation blueprint side, it is a very simple step to get it all together. First, hit **Save** on the animation blueprint and close it; we don't need it again.

You can now right-click inside the content browser, and choose to create a blueprint. This will open the classes list to choose a base class for this blueprint. The ones on the top are the most popular ones, but we want to create one based on our Gladiator C++ class we made at the beginning of this chapter. So, you can look at the bottom section and type the class name in the search box and you will find it. Use it and create the blueprint. Give it a name and remember this name, as we are going to use it in the final step of this chapter in order to use it as the default pawn.

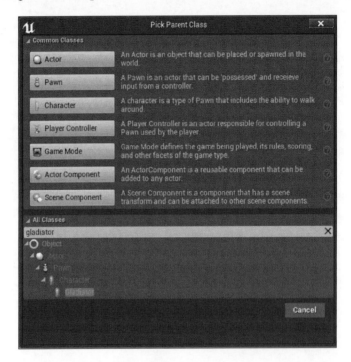

Once you have the blueprint, double-click on it in order to open it, and don't panic because it doesn't look like what you expect, or does not look like a normal blueprint based on an actor.

What you are seeing is called the default view and it is displayed usually for blueprints based on C++ classes. You can see a note telling you that, so you can hit the **Open Full Blueprint Editor** button in this note in order to open the normal blueprint.

Don't be worried, the default view is still accessible but in a different way. While in the full blueprint editor, if you want the default of any of the components, you can just hit the **Defaults** button on the top bar and it will load the default for you in the right-hand panel.

Now you can see, and locate all the components we have created at the constructor of the Gladiator class, such as:

- **CameraBoom**: Sprint Arm Component
- **FollowCamera**: Camera Component
- **EffectSprite**: Paper2D Sprite Component

You'll not only find these three components, even though those are the three components we've created through the C++ code, there will also be other components that are, always there, by default, within any blueprint based on a character class.

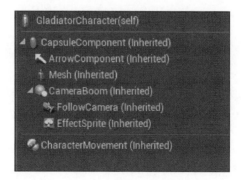

Now the last step in creating the player blueprint, is to assign some default values. As there are tons of default values for each of the components, you can go around them and tweak them to fit your needs. The most essential ones to give you a working character now are the assets.

Select the **Mesh** component from the components list, and open its default values by clicking on the defaults button on the top bar.

In the animations section you need to ask it to **Use Animation Blueprint**, and assign the animation blueprint we created earlier in this chapter.

Then select the **Skeletal Mesh** character you want to use from the free assets you have imported in to the project.

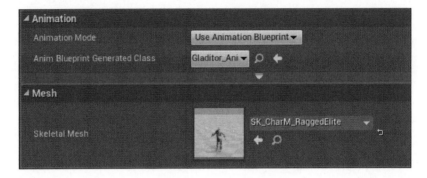

Now, you finally have a fully working character…But wait a second, there is still one more thing to make it perfect.

As you can see, the character mesh is not well aligned inside the capsule (the collision), so you probably need to select the mesh again and keep adjusting its rotation to face the correct direction of the capsule and adjust its vertical axis positioning, as it is flying on air now. A few tweaks, but it will make things a lot clearer.

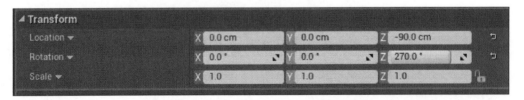

Adding the blueprint to the GameMode

Once everything is in place, all that we need now is to make sure that the GameMode class for the game (or for this level) is going to load our Gladiator blueprint by default once the game starts.

Open the Visual Studio project again, go to the `BellzGameMode` source file, and add this piece of code inside its constructor, in order to set the `DefaultPawnClass` by defining which blueprint is to be used by specifying its name and path within the project.

```
static ConstructorHelpers::FClassFinder<APawn>
PlayerPawnBPClass(TEXT("/Game/Blueprints/GladiatorCharacter"));
  if (PlayerPawnBPClass.Class != NULL)
  {
    DefaultPawnClass = PlayerPawnBPClass.Class;
  }
```

And now, if you start an empty level with the basic elements, or even one of the free asset levels, you'll have the Gladiator fully interactive inside the level.

Summary

You went through the process of creating your first HUGE steps. You not only saw how to build a C++ class inside Unreal, but also learned how to apply the C++ knowledge you have to Unreal's version of C++.

You also learned some hints about the Unreal Engine C++ styling code, what Macros are, when to use them, and how to use access specifiers within Unreal.

You not only built your first `gameplay` element, and the cornerstone of the game, but you also learned about the different components of the Unreal environment, such as `Paper2D sprites`, `Camera`, `SpringArm`, and so on. You got yourself into a lot of Unrealliology!

Creating the C++ class is only half-way to using it. A class without an actor or blueprint in the scene is nothing. You have to learn how to build blueprints and actors based on your class, you have to learn how to communicate between C++ and its blueprint instance, and you have to learn how to modify your blueprints based on C++; you made real progress in mastering this.

While you already know how to define inputs in project settings, this is useless without integrating those inputs inside the game; you have now learned in the course of this chapter how to map inputs by code, and convert them to real logic.

You learned about taking a character mesh and animations, then how to use them together; how to build a fully playable character; how make an animation blueprint; and how to set its rules. You also gained lots of knowledge about blending animations, making blend spaces, adding sockets for skeletons, and much more.

Now, while you have all this in mind, I would suggest you start a project from scratch and try to make almost the whole thing from scratch several times. That way you will be sure you are able to make it alone without turning back to the book. The first time it will appear difficult, so refer to the book again; later, however, you'll be a master it!

Now let's take a rest, and forget about code for a second. The next chapter is all about levels and map design.

3
Designing Your Playground

While we have a player made with a character controller, it is time to build what should look like a level, where we can spawn our character and start running around.

Building a level should sound like a fun task, but in fact it isn't. It is more of an artistic task, where you have to imagine, create, and build a level from nothing. You will be constructing your worlds, maps, and levels. Unreal tools make it easy, but still you need what should be called an artistic vision to build great worlds.

By the end of this chapter, you'll learn about the following topics:

- The requirements of the level and the aspects of level designing that we care about in this game
- How to place assets into the map
- How to use different brush types to place different type of assets
- How to add lights and baking lightmaps of the level
- How to create water surfaces to make the level more visually appealing
- How to set a player start point
- How to add and display the navigation mesh for the level to make it ready for the AI

With our targets defined, go ahead and spend some time thinking about the map you want to create, how you want it to look, and how long you want the player to spend while playing it. Once you finish this little brain-storming session with yourself, come back to this page again!

The art of level design

While this is not a level design book, I've to say that designing a level and design in general is not about tools, techniques, and technology. In fact, it has nothing to do at all with techniques or engines. It is an artistic and creative thing.

But there are always major points that you have to keep in mind while designing a level; these points depend on the game itself, its genre, its story, and lots of other factors. But for Bellz, I've found the following points come in handy to the game:

- The level has to tell a story: I need the player to tell the story of the level through it. I don't want to show the player a movie describing what happened here before he came to the level, and I don't want to display text to tell what happened at this place. But I want my level itself, and the positioning and selection of assets, to tell the story of the place on its own.

- The level needs to look eye-catching: Having a fantastic game is not only a result of using good and polished assets, but also of the way the assets are placed and used. I need my level to use top high-end quality. I need to put a sky dome, moving skies, sun light, and water that moves. I need to add anything that makes it look amazingly real.

- The level has to be efficient: This means that I need to use the fewest possible resources as possible. We are talking here about a top-quality game; we can't add things forever. We have to be worried about the performance, the size, and the quality. The level has to be modular and bidirectional. It has to be modular when it uses fewer assets, but in a different way; the same assets should create different things. It has to be bidirectional when I do force the player to move all over the place several times.

Those are the factors I care about for this game, but the art of level design has lots and lots of tricks and todos. If you are interested recommend you start with the following article at Wikipedia, where you can learn more skills about the level design process and get an overall idea: https://en.wikipedia.org/wiki/Level_design.

I would suggest you spend some more time, if you are interested, and read these episodic articles on Gamasutra.com all about level design, at: http://www.gamasutra.com/blogs/DanTaylor/20130929/196791/Ten_Principles_of_Good_Level_Design_Part_1.php.

As we have already imported the needed assets from the launcher in *Chapter 1, Preparing for a Big Project*, you can now start placing the assets to build the map you have imagined.

Placing assets into the world

Now is the time to actually start visualizing the world and make it real through the process of asset placement. This is an artistic step, where you have to use your imagination in order to place the assets. The process of placement itself is just a matter of dragging and dropping items from the content browser into the map, just as expected!

As we have mentioned earlier, level design has to be modular, which means that we use as few pieces as possible in order to construct the final level, but we combine these together in different ways in order to give differently composed items.

If you have imported the assets package from the Unreal launcher, as we discussed during *Chapter 1, Preparing for a Big Project*, you'll end up having this set of modular assets ready to be used in the map designing process.

When I say "composing the modular assets together to build different pieces", I mean that we can take the column asset, for example, and just place it in the world to look like this:

On the other hand, I can add another decorative asset to it in order to give it more effect, such as adding damaged ground bricks, to give the feeling and story that something happened near that, as follows:

Alternatively, I could even combine both together and add one more asset to give a good visual of the bridge, as follows:

As you can see, with all three cases the asset has a different role, and it does not even look the way it should as an individual asset.

Now, you know what you have to do. It is all about combining assets and positioning them. Go into the content browser and start dragging and dropping the items into the map. You may need to drop the same asset several times; you can simply copy and paste it with *Ctrl + C*, and so on, as you would do with a piece of text.

I would suggest that you first make an outline on paper, when you have a chance to keep changing, erasing, and updating the design, which will make things faster for you in the editor, and perhaps will save you some time while removing and adding loops.

The point is that design is a more artistic area that depends on personal choice, where you can just imagine what you can do with the set of assets in hand, and you can keep trying. Keep what you like; if you dislike something, simply remove it. It is a process of dragging and dropping items into the map; apart from these, you can just position, rotate, and scale assets to give the feel you want.

Using brushes to enhance level design

Your world is not yet ready for players or enemies, as all those meshes you've used mostly have no collisions. This means that the player will fall from the ground and can go through walls.

When you import assets, you have the choice to build colliders for them — colliders that almost fit the shape of an asset. But this is costly when you do it for tons of assets. From a level design perspective, designers prefer to put the assets and then collisions as a layer of geometrical shapes while laying out the level.

Unreal Engine has a variety of range of meshes and shapes that could be used for different purposes. One of the most interesting shape types is brushes, called **BSP**. These shapes are not only placeable, but are also modifiable at the vertex and face level, which means that you can use several cubes to build a complex shape. The currently supported brush shapes are the following ones, which can be accessed from the **BSP** section of the **Modes** panel.

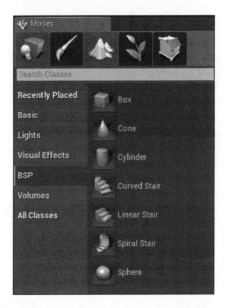

Now, the goal is simple! While those brush shapes could be invisible, we will be throwing lots of them around the map, and making them invisible and not renderable. At the same time, we will be enabling collision for them. This way, the brushes we use will be behaving as invisible walls.

Using this method will guarantee that, regardless of the amount of collision surfaces we have in the level or in the game in general, they will be basic shapes at the end of the day: no hulls, no convex shapes, no mesh colliders that are costly in large numbers.

In order to convert any brush shape you create into a blocking surface, you have to run through the following two important steps:

1. After creating the shape itself, you will need to convert its actor to a blocking surface by setting the value **Convert Actor** of the **Actor** settings from the **Details** panel to **Blocking Volume**.

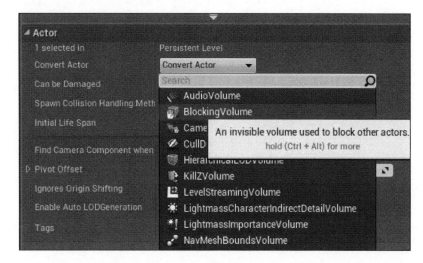

2. Converting to a blocking volume will add few more settings to the brush in the **Details** panel. All you have to do now is set **Collision Presets** to something that fits your need. I found **Invisible Wall** or **Block All Dynamics**; both choices will get the job done.

Adding lights to the level

Now we have a map that is well made and well designed; it has all we need to serve our story, and it also has collisions and layouts to give the player a good and realistic experience.

Talking about realistic experience, our level still isn't lit, which means that it is not going to be visually appealing or even realistic (if the game has to be realistic). This means that we need to add some sort of lighting to the map in order to make it clear and vivid!

The process of lighting a map is an artistic process in its core, where you have to decide where to put the lights, the color for each light, and even the type of light, and the angle for its rotation. All these factors affect the final result and that will in turn affect the player's experience. But while it seems so artistic, it is also a very technical topic, as you have to be aware of light types, shapes, and performance in order to guarantee a smooth experience.

In case you have no experience with lighting within Unreal Engine, I highly recommend you to read one of my previous Unreal books, *Unreal Engine Lighting and Rendering Essentials* (`https://www.packtpub.com/game-development/unreal-engine-lighting-and-rendering-essentials`). It is all about mastering lighting and rendering within Unreal.

For such a level, or in general for most of my games, I do count on lightmaps, which we will discuss next, in order to get the best quality and the best performance. But also, building the lightmaps itself requires us to add some lights throughout the earlier level.

Now, you probably have a map that looks different from the one I have, so the number of light sources or even the light settings might be different. But in my case, I needed to put the following:

- **Directional Light**: **Directional Light** is essential for any outdoor scene and, perhaps, for some indoor scenes, as it is simulates sunlight (infinite rays in one direction), which means that it is probably essential for the map you've created too. The most interesting part of **Directional Light** is that rotating it will give you a different timing of the sun and it has the ability to create light shafts! You can find the **Directional Light** source inside the **Lights** section of the **Modes** panel. Adding it to the map is a matter of drag and drop. Then, you can change the color and light settings that will make your level look the way you want it to.

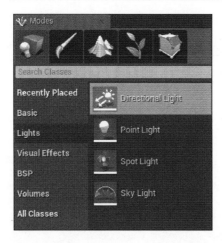

- **Point Light**: **Point Light** is less important than **Directional Light**, and you might make an entire game without the need to use one! **Point Light**, as its name implies, emits light from a point in all the directions in a spherical shape; the emitted light is not infinite, unlike **Directional Light**, which means the light rays decay after a specific distance that you can define. I put a few point lights in my map to enhance the visual; it well good for fire and such light sources that light specific distances. Point lights are accessible from the **Lights** section of the **Modes** panel, and are placed by dragging and dropping them into the level.

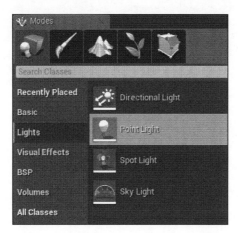

Put in some point lights if your map requires them; they don't have that much effect on performance, but they do have a huge effect on the visual, especially if they have a variation of different colors rather than the main sky/directional light color.

- **Lightmass Importance Volume**: **Lightmass Importance Volume** is one of the volume types that you can find inside the **Modes** panel under the **Volumes** section.

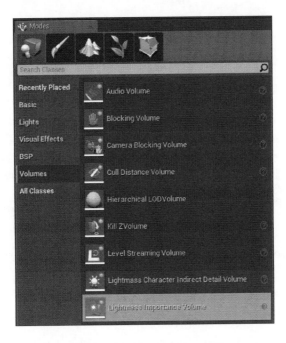

Also, you can create one from scratch in a shape that fits your needs. If you have just created a brush, as we mentioned earlier, you can convert it into a **Lightmass Importance Volume** rather than into **Blocking Volume**.

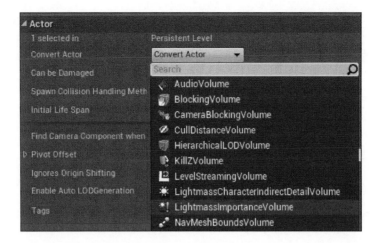

Lightmass Importance Volume is very essential as long as you are using lightmaps and as long as you have a huge level. Sometimes, there are a lot of meshes and details out of the player's reach, for example, far away mountains, and you are sure that the player will not be reaching it. In cases like these, you need to somehow exclude those items from the process of building the lightmaps.

Building lightmaps is a matter of throwing photons around the level while having lots of faraway meshes. This means throwing more and more photons and, at the same time, taking even more time while building the lightmap itself this is even worse at the end, when you get huge lightmap files!

So, if your levels have some parts that are not required to be lit, I would recommend you put in a **Lightmass Importance Volume** and scale it to fit the playable and reachable area of the level. In my case, the following is how it looks when it just includes the playable section of the map.

Now with all that in the level, I bet you have a very vivid and visually appealing level, with everything lit and looking as nice as it should. But, as we are making a game that needs to run almost 60 frames per second, we have to worry about the performance, not only on the development machine, but also on the weakest computer a player might have. This means that we have to start baking and saving some lightmaps, which we will do next.

Building lightmaps for a level

Lightmap is a term used for a lighting concept, where all the light data is saved in maps and the lights themselves are disabled at runtime. This means that there will not be a real-time lighting for those baked objects. This is widely used in games in order to reserve GPU calculations for something else.

The process of building a lightmap (lightmass) itself is not complex; it is just a case of hitting the **Build** button. But what takes some time is the tweaking done before the button is pressed.

The rule of lightmaps is that only static objects can be baked into lightmaps, which means any movable item at the level will not be written to lightmaps, and that includes, but is not limited to, characters and enemies. This means that you have to make sure that the Mobility setting inside the **Details** panel for all the items that are not meant to move in your scene is set to **Static**.

That takes us half-way to lightmaps. The other important setting is the resolution of the lightmap of an object. As we mentioned, lightmaps are like images with light values, which means that they have a resolution. The lower the resolution, the less detail and quality you will get, but with faster building time and VRAM resources usage. The higher the resolution, the better quality and detail you will get, but with more building time and a higher risk of texture streaming crashes with some players. Therefore, you have to balance its value and define what matters and will be seen closely by the players and what is out of reach.

Each object has a **Lighting** section in the **Details** panel, where you can set some values for light-related settings and tweak them.

Once everything is OK and you are good with the chosen values for your static meshes, just hit the **Build** button from the top bar and this will build everything (including the navigations, if any). For faster results, you can hold this button to choose one of the suboptions, which is basically **Build Lighting Only**.

Now, the level looks even prettier and its performance and rending cycles are faster. It is time now to add one more detail to the level, which is water. As the water will look live and moving, it will not need to be included into the lightmaps, so let's add it now.

Creating water surfaces

When it comes to creating an entire game from scratch, you have to be productive and smart about consuming time and resources. Sometimes, you have to rely on things that are already made with Unreal. For example, we could build this game based on a **Third Person Game** template. This might have saved us the time we spent creating the player controller, but we managed to create it from scratch in order to build it in a way that fits our needs.

But there are other things that were made by the Epic team for us in order to make life easier and faster, just like the popular Ocean shader that was made and shared during Unreal's live streams.

We could spend lots of time trying to create this shader from scratch, but eventually we will end up with something not very close to it. This shader can be found with many Unreal free examples in the **Learning** section of the launcher, and it is free to use for all types of projects; it is really used in a wide range of games.

Fortunately, this shader is one of the **Infinity Blade** assets we have imported into our game in *Chapter 1, Preparing for o Big Project*. This means we already have the shader material within the project. You can easily find it by typing its name M_Plains_ Ocean at the content browser search tab.

Once you find it, I would highly recommend spending some time understanding it, just in case you want to add more details or even changes in order to adapt the visuals of your map.

Now, let's come back to creating the water surface. Creating a water surface is a matter of creating surfaces that hold the Ocean shader, which means that you can create a plan mesh or cube, and apply this shader to it. Or you can even create a custom mesh in Maya or 3dsMax and export it to Unreal. It doesn't matter what type of mesh, but eventually, you have to create a mesh with a sizable number of vertices and just drag and drop the Ocean shader on it.

In my case, I used a plain mesh, scaled it to fit the level boundaries and even a little more, and then applied the Ocean shader to it.

Player Start

Your level is still not playable yet or, to put it another way, in another meaning, hitting **Play** might not make any difference. This means that we need to add something to allow us to spawn the player and start using the controller we have created in *Chapter 2, Setting Up Your Warrior*. In order to be able to spawn a player at any given position, we need to either drag and drop the player Gladiator Actor blueprint into the start point or use the **Player Start** actor and position it at the start point.

The **Player Start** actor can be found in the **Basic** section of the **Modes** panel, and as with anything else found within the **Modes** panel, you can use it by simply dragging it into the level. The **Player Start** actor has no settings to be changed other than its position, which will be the position for spawning the player. But still, it has all the default setting you can find within any other actor type, such as a tag or rendering state, which will not affect its function.

Now, drag and drop the **Player Start** actor at the position where you want the player to start the level.

While **Player Start** seems like a very basic and simple actor, but it is really one of the most complex things within Unreal, as it gets its complexity from its rules. To be able to work perfectly, you have to know what rules the Player Start actor has. The **Player Start** set of rules that I found after a few experiments with Unreal is:

- You can have no **Player Start** in your level, but once the game starts that will make your player fall from the sky at the latest known camera position during edit mode.

- Having a player controller (the one defined in **Game Mode** as the default **Pawn Class**) inside the level is enough to make its position as the player start. This means that the engine will ignore the player's start position, and will start from where you dropped your player controller during the edit mode.

- You can have more than one player start actor inside the level, but once you hit start, the engine will use the most recent one as the actual player start.

- You can't place the player start in a wrong position, for example, half-way inside the ground. Unreal will report that as a bad position by tagging its gizmo with **Bad Size** icon, but will not fix it for you most of the time. Sometimes, the engine will fix the character spawn position at runtime, while it doesn't at other times. So, you have to be sure that your player start is not titled the **BAD size**!

The navigation mesh

We have a complete level that looks perfect. The player is autospawned at runtime and we can run through it. But still there are a few more things that are needed for the level that aren't level design-wise, but it are needed for the game logic itself. One of those missing parts is the navigation mesh.

If you don't know what the navigation mesh is, it is the path finding implementation that is used within Unreal Engine in order to find a point via another point. Alternatively, in another meaning, it is used to let an enemy find what he is seeking for. With that said, it means even if we have enemies, they will not be able to navigate through the world until there is a valid navigation mesh.

Adding a navigation mesh in Unreal Engine is a very simple task. It lets you focus more on creating and pitching your enemies and their behaviors while navigating with one step.

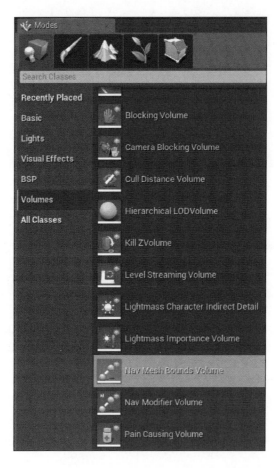

By dragging and dropping **Nav Mesh Bounds Volume** from the **Volumes** section of the **Modes** panel, you have already placed a navigation volume that is responsible for creating the navigation mesh.

By default, this volume will look like a cube volume. You can scale it to fit all the level or you can create several ones; it is up to you. However, the rule is that the walkable area at your level must be covered with the navigation volume, regardless of the several volumes or only one volume. I managed to use only one volume to cover all the walkable areas, and increased its scale to fit my level.

Now, if you want to see your navigation mesh itself, just press *P* on your keyboard and you'll see all the walkable areas colored in green. It will automatically update any time you move stuff and assets around your level.

Summary

Now, you have something you can show to your friends as a game. While it is not a complete game, you have a great character controller that was made from the ground up and an awesome level, where the player can navigate and your friends can test what you have achieved so far. But still, what do you have to show for it?

Well, you have learned some tips about level design, which probably gave you the chance to make a better design than what you had in mind, and you learned how to place assets to construct a level. You also learned how to put the player within the level to start navigating through it. We also learned all the rules, tips, and tricks of the **Player Start** actors, and how to use them in different ways.

If we talk about how polished your level is looking, well, simply and easily you have added water surface that made the level look gorgeous.

Adding the navigation mesh was a tricky step that will make our process faster later. You learned how to add navigation volumes, how to display the navigation mesh, and the rules to follow while adding navigation volumes.

Adding light to the level will allow you to control its mode and day time. You learned how to add light to your level, and how to implement settings for it in order to bake the light to make the game performance better at runtime. With all you have learned, I'm sure you ended up with a nice playground for your character.

While we now have the character and the playground, let's go ahead directly and create some enemies in the next chapter.

4
The Road to Thinkable AI

Usually, when we speak about creating a game, we all just think about enemies, evils, and the bad guys. Of course, games are beyond that. But enemies are what usually make a game what it is; enemies and AI are a huge part of the fun. Enemies are what usually give you a goal to finish a level, to use a weapon, or even to take a mission.

Apart from this, on the other side of the game, involving us, the developers, we all are more interested more in AI as the most important part of the game development process. It is not only the graphic quality and performance that make a game more special than the previous one, but also topics such as AI and how smart and lively your AI is.

When it comes to creating AI for your game, Unreal Engine comes with amazing content. Have you ever liked games such as *Mass Effect*, *God of War*, and The *Batman Arkham* series? All these games have been made with Unreal Engine (Unreal Engine 3 most of the time), and all of them have a remarkable AI and boss fights that we cannot forget even after 100 years!

The thing with Unreal Engine is not the games that have been made with it, but the number of tools and subtools that are supported by the engine, which allow you to tune and detail your enemies and AI behaviors. They are useful for even the smallest tasks.

That's the topic of this chapter: understanding the tools, asset types, and how to code in C++ all within the Unreal Engine ecosystem in order to add AI to our game.

By the end of this chapter, you'll be able to:

- Build an enemy class and write down all the required gameplay code
- Build logic to detect the player based on the navigation mesh we built earlier using **Nav Mesh Bounds Volume**

- Use a wide range of AI-related assets, such as **Tasks**, **Services**, **Blackboards**, and **Behavior Trees**
- Use the behavior tree editor to build the needed behaviors for AI
- Add various triggers playing different roles
- Enhance the code that the animation notifies in order to call a function at a precise moment
- Practice creating animation blueprints and retargeting

Let's get started!

The overall idea

When it comes to building enemies, or AI in general, you have to understand the whole game, its concept, and the game design, probably through the **Game Design Document (GDD)**. Knowing these aspects earlier will make the job easier for you and your team, and for the plan that you'll come up with in order to construct a whole AI system.

In general, there is one thing that has always been almost the industry standard: basing everything in inheritance classes. This really makes sense, as all enemies, regardless of their types or behaviors, have to share something at the end of the day. It's where you have to create a base AI class and inherit all the enemies from it. Or it might be more detailed; if the enemies themselves are from different classes, let's say animals, humans, and mechanicals, then you need a class for each, inherited from the base class, and then the enemies themselves will be inherited from this first inheritance. Something like this:

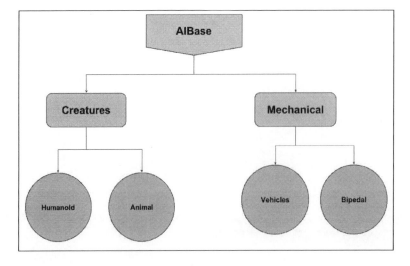

It doesn't have to be exactly the same, but this is one way to do such an example: you can, for example, directly split the left-hand side into **Humanoid** and **Animal**, without inheriting them from **Creatures**, which is inherited from the base. It is just down to you, your game, and your design.

While Bellz has a very small design goal (it shouldn't be a massive game, just a one-level game) and the assets and animations that I was able to get was for one enemy, I managed to create the whole AI within one class; I named it `Enemy`. But in the event you are planning to create several enemy types and classes, I would recommend you use the basic C++ inheritance; it works just the same here with Unreal.

The other part I want to mention is that having an AI system within Unreal is not just a matter of coding several C++ files full of logic. Other things need to be done in a different way; for example, in order to control the animations we would need an animation blueprint, just like the character controller we made in *Chapter 2, Setting Up Your Warrior*, the `Gladiator` class. Or in order to give the enemies the appearance of a mind, we need to build a behavior tree that is full of decisions to take and make. But to get a behavior tree, we need to create tasks and services, which are basically behaviors themselves. And that's how we are going to build our enemy sample: piece by piece, as all of those things are required.

The AI assets

As we discussed earlier in this chapter, the process of creating AI within Unreal Engine requires a recipe of several assets. Each of these assets is there for a different reason, and it does its own unique job. These assets are:

- **Behavior Tree**
- **BTTask**
- **BTService**
- **Blackboard**

Let's look at these assets individually.

Behavior Tree

The **Behavior Tree** asset could be considered as a different type of blueprint, but it does not hold too much logic or coding; it holds several connections between different tasks, better described as behaviors.

A behavior tree could be very complex or simple; it depends on your AI system and the goals you have for it.

The best part about behavior trees is that they have their own editor with a unique visual aspect and not many types of nodes to use. Although the node types are few, they are enough to bring your AI to life.

Creating a behavior tree could be done by right-clicking inside the content browser and then finding it underneath the **Artificial Intelligence** section.

In my case, I've created one and called it EnemyBT.

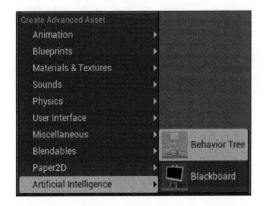

While the behavior tree has several types of nodes or commands that you can use, there are always two main things you'll be using; they are not considered as assets, but you can think about them as functionalities for the **Behavior Tree** asset. They are as follows:

- **Composites**: The composite node's main job is to select which task (branch of the tree) should be executed. All composites have numbers inside circles and these numbers represent the order the behavior tree will be following.

- **Decorators**: A decorator is just like **Service** or **Task**; it is something that you can add to a composite in order to empower its functionality. For example, you can use a decorator of the **Blackboard** type, in order to get a value from the **Blackboard** asset, to be used a specific tree branch.

BTTask

As the name implies, this type of blueprint represents a task that the AI will be doing. And while it is a blueprint, you'll be able to put the logic inside it as you do with a normal blueprint.

Also, you can write the logic in C++ for it, and then call it through the blueprint. Regardless of the way you will be using it, a node within the behavior tree will represent the whole thing itself.

Personally, I prefer globally to code these tasks with a blueprint as long as they don't have too much logic; other times, I like to get a mix of both, blueprints and C++ code.

In order to create a task, you need to go through the default process of creating a normal blueprint. Then, you need to base it on a class named `BTTask_ BlueprintBase`.

As my AI sample will need only one task, I have created one asset of that type and named it `EnemyAttackTask`.

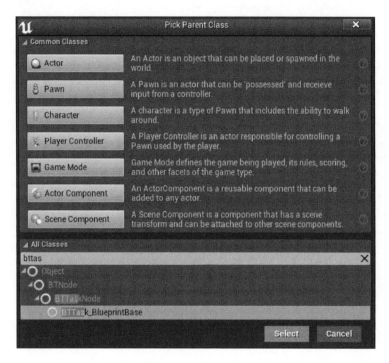

BTService

The service works just like a task, but the difference is that it is going to be called all the time. Even the way it is called from within the behavior tree is still the same.

You can add the **BTService** asset as you are adding a new blueprint, just like the task. But this time, you will be basing it on the class named **BTService_BlueprintBase**.

I have created only one service, as my example AI will need only one, and I called it `EnemySearchService`.

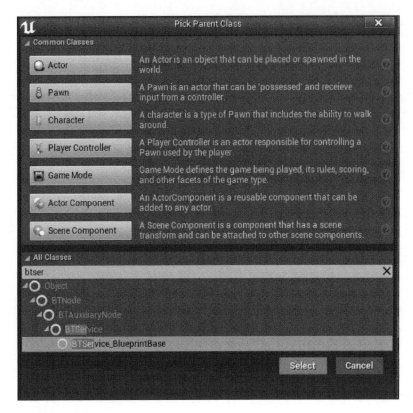

Blackboard

Blackboard is very simple, but an important asset type. You can consider it as a data container, because that is simply its job. When you open the **Blackboard** asset, all that you need to do is add variables in the form of data. Later, you can use this data inside the tasks of the behavior trees.

Creating it is very simple, as you can find it inside the right-click menu of the content browser under the **Artificial Intelligence** section.

I've created one for my AI and named it EnemyBlackboard.

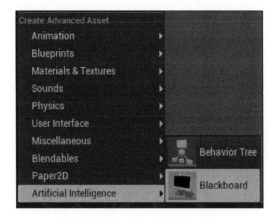

Now, we have prepared our AI system. Nothing has happened yet. In fact, we don't have enemies yet, but we have set up the base structure of the system. Now, what we need is to write some logic, but most importantly we need to prepare some animations that will allow us to code the enemy easily.

The animation blueprint

Any character or skeletal entity within your game, as long as it will be moving and executing animations, must have an animation blueprint to handle and manage the animation based on the set of the rules you define.

We have already discussed the process of retargeting the animations and preparing the assets in *Chapter 1, Preparing for the Big Project*. And we have discussed the process of creating and setting the rules for the animation blueprints in *Chapter 2, Setting Up Your Warrior*. Also, we have discussed blend animation and how to blend different animations in *Chapter 2, Setting Up Your Warrior*. I would suggest that you go ahead and build the animation blueprint and the animation setup for your character.

I will show off the setup I made for my bears. Feel free to clone it or improvise as much as you wish based on your game design and the type of enemies you have and with the knowledge you have gained from *Chapter 1, Preparing for the Big Project* and *Chapter 2, Setting Up Your Warrior*. I guess it is time for you to do the process for the enemies based on what you can remember.

Like anything else with game logic, variables are the kings; functions and methods do everything (almost everything). But without variables, methods and functions are useless. So, let's add some essential variables in order to be able to proceed with the process.

1. The most important part is the variables. I have created a set of variables to control the animations and use them as conditions to control the animation states. The unique one is the integer called **attackIndex**. This is basically a randomized value between 1 and 3 in order to get a random index. Based on this number, I'll display a random attack animation.

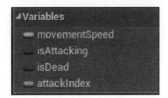

2. The animation graph contains only one state machine, the main one. I named it Default and it is the only one there.

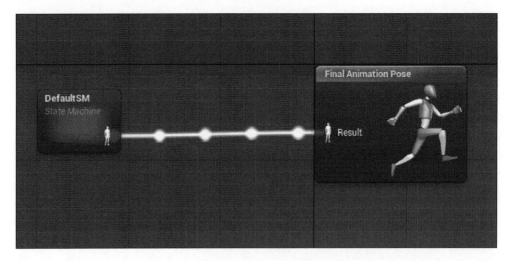

3. Within the state machine, I have created several states. I blend between them based on several conditions. These conditions are the variables I've created earlier. And the values of these variable, as you will see later, are taken from the C++ code.

4. The way a connection and condition have been added is simple. By just dragging and dropping an arrow from a state machine to another, the connection will happen and a conditional little gizmo sphere will appear. By opening it, you'll be able to add any logic, similar to the blueprints logic, in order to act like a condition for that transition between statuses. As you can see, I have made three attack statuses, displaying them based on the **attackIndex** random value. It is a good thing to keep some variations!

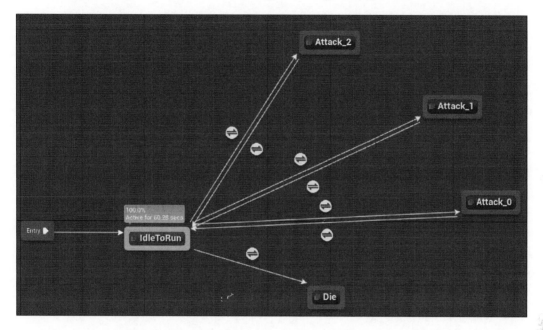

5. Then, I would like to split the animation blueprint logic into two parts. The first part gives the velocity of the enemy, which will then be applied it to the movementSpeed variable. This variable will be used to build a blend node between idle, walk, and run!

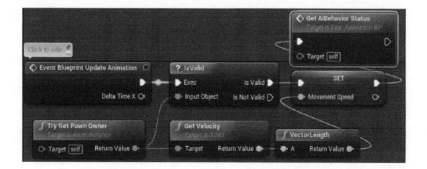

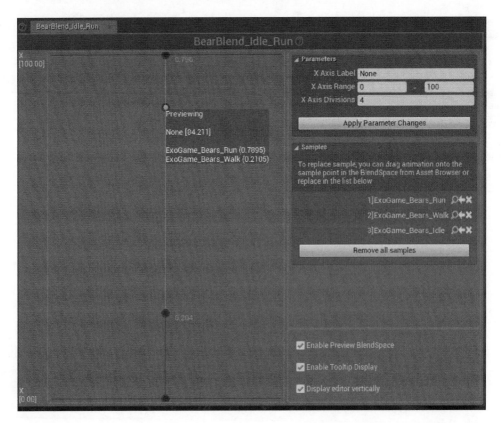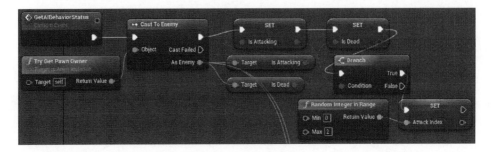

6. The second part is a custom event that I've created. It is called **GetAIBehaviorStatus**. All that we need to do is fetch the value of the `isAttacking` and `isDead` variables from the C++ code that we made earlier. And finally, it will set a random value for the attack index. So, each time the enemy attacks, it will display a different attack animation.

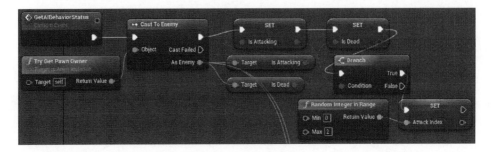

7. The last thing within the animation blueprints system I made is a blend space, just like the one we made in *Chapter 2, Setting Up Your Warrior*, in order to blend between idle, walk, and run.

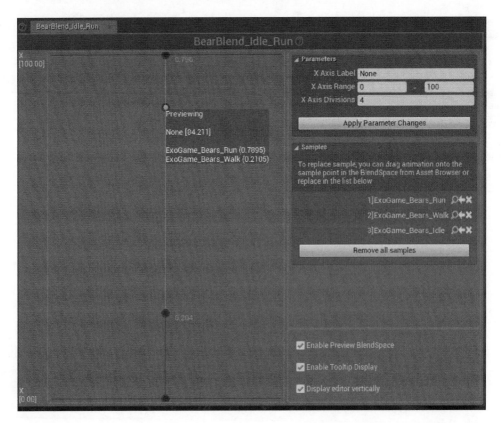

Now, with all the animations in place and having created several assets for the AI (the **Task**, **Service**, **Blackboard**, and **BT**), it is time to write down the functionalities and make the BT itself. Let's go ahead with the C++ part, as the process of building the behavior tree will require a piece of the code.

Building the C++ logic

You are probably guessing that we are going to create an enemy class that will hold the logic for our enemy. As I mentioned earlier, I'll not be inheriting several AI classes from each other, as I will have only one enemy. But, in fact, we are going to create two new classes for the project based on the base class of each. The new classes will be as follows:

- Enemy: This class will be based on the ACharacter class, which means that it will have a lot of properties, such as our gladiator, as Gladiator as well is inherited from Character.

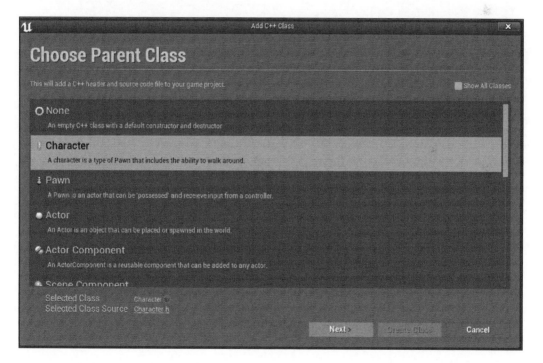

- EnemyAIController: This one will be based on AAIController. While the ACharacter-based class takes its movement through inputs, the AAIController-based class takes its movement through the environment, the navigation mesh, for example.

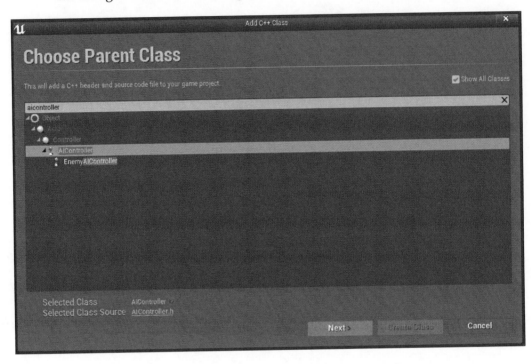

Now, after adding both the classes and before we start doing anything within Visual Studio, you will find yourself able to differentiate between them via their icons. This is how both look in my project.

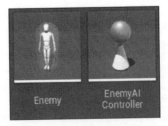

We are ready to start coding the logic for both the new classes in Visual Studio, but there is still one more step. Usually, a new project would not have all the needed modules loaded; we have mentioned this before. While we are working, we will need to add several modules. Take the Paper2D module as an example; we added it during the process of building the player.

Now, we need to add the AI module, as it is not loaded by default with any project. If you still remember, you can do it through the project Build.cs file, which is Billz.Build.cs in the case of my project, and set it within the required modules:

```
PublicDependencyModuleNames.AddRange(newstring[] { "Core",
"CoreUObject", "Engine", "InputCore", "AIModule", "Paper2D"});
```

Now, we have everything set up and are ready to write the code. I would like to split it into two main parts: the part where we write the EnemyAIController and the other part where we write the Enemy class.

EnemyAIController

I want the main job of this class to set the values for the **Blackboard** asset, adjust the rotation of the enemy, and use the navigation mesh.

EnemyAIController.h

Just like all the other header files, we have to start with the includes. There is nothing fancy to include here, except the header file of the base class:

```
#include "AIController.h"
#include "EnemyAIController.generated.h"
```

Also, define the class name, the inheritance, and the constructor. The three of them are made by default while creating the class, and probably, you don't have to change any of them:

```
UCLASS()
class BELLZ_APIAEnemyAIController : publicAAIController
{
  GENERATED_BODY()

public:
  AEnemyAIController();
```

As we discussed earlier, the **Blackboard** asset is like a data holder asset and the AIController will be setting its data; it is essential to create a blackboard component in order to use it as a reference for the required blackboard.

In the same way, will be creating a behavior tree component. Later, inside the editor, we will assign the behavior tree we've created to it.

This way, we will make sure that any communications we need between the `AIController` and the assets we've created are going to be easy through this class.

```
UPROPERTY(transient)
  UBlackboardComponent* BlackboardComp;

UPROPERTY(transient)
  UBehaviorTreeComponent* BehaviorComp;
```

As we are inheriting our class from the `AAIController` base class, there are several virtual functions that have their own functionalities and we need to override them here. We will be overriding the `Possess` function, which is responsible for treating this class as an AI, and the `BeginInActive` state. But keep in mind, the possess function works differently in the case of a multiplier game, as it is a server authority, which means that it is not called on the clients:

```
virtual void Possess(classAPawn* InPawn) override;

virtual void BeginInactiveState() override;
```

The next thing is to add a couple of functions. The first one will be called `SetEnemy`. We will call it whenever we want to mark something as the enemy of our enemy, which means the player.

I named the other function `GetEnemy`. As the name implies, this one will be called to return the current enemy of our enemy, which again should be the active player:

```
UFUNCTION(BlueprintCallable, Category = Behavior)
void SetEnemy(classAPawn* InPawn);

UFUNCTION(BlueprintCallable, Category = Behavior)
class AGladiator* GetEnemy() const;
```

The last tree functions are mostly behavior-related, but not major behaviors, such as attack. These functions are more like the status of the AI. The first one is called `UpdateControllerRotation` and is responsible for updating the rotation of the controller to the walking direction (usually forward).

The second one is called `PawnCanBeSeen`. This one is essential to detect the player or in other words, it is essential to tell whether the AI can see its enemy (the player) or can't see it.

The last function I called is `OnSearchForEnemy`. As its name implies, its functionality will be searching:

```
UFUNCTION(BlueprintCallable, Category = Behaviour)
```

```
void UpdateControlRotation(float DeltaTime, bool bUpdatePawn);

UFUNCTION(BlueprintCallable, Category = Behaviour)
boolPawnCanBeSeen(APawn * target);

UFUNCTION(BlueprintCallable, Category = Behaviour)
void OnSearchForEnemy();
```

The last part of the header file is meant to define a few variables. These variables are there to get and store values in the blackboard:

```
protected:
    int32 EnemyKeyID;
    int32 EnemyPositionKeyID;
```

Now, you have understood everything related to the header file. I made some functions to serve several goals while some virtual functions were being overridden. Finally, I made a few variables in order to control the blackboard and store the blackboard itself and the controlling behavior tree. So, let's go ahead with the implementation of the source file for that class.

EnemyAIController.cpp

While this source file starts with includes, I have to include a lots of stuff, mainly to handle the behavior tree and call anything related to it:

```
#include "Bellz.h"
#include "EnemyAIController.h"
#include "Enemy.h"
#include "Gladiator.h"
#include "BehaviorTree/BehaviorTree.h"
#include "BehaviorTree/BehaviorTreeComponent.h"
#include "BehaviorTree/BlackboardComponent.h"
#include "BehaviorTree/Blackboard/BlackboardKeyType_Object.h"
```

Regarding the constructor, there wasn't too much to do except create the **Blackboard** component and the behavior tree, so I can assign them through the editor later and use their value within the coming set of functions:

```
AEnemyAIController::AEnemyAIController(/*const class
FPostConstructInitializeProperties& PCIP*/)
/*: Super(PCIP)*/
{
    // create blackboard and behaviour components in the constructor
```

```
BlackboardComp = CreateDefaultSubobject<UBlackboardComponent>(TEXT("Bl
ackBoardComp"));

BehaviorComp = CreateDefaultSubobject<UBehaviorTreeComponent>(TEXT("Be
haviorComp"));

   bWantsPlayerState = true;
}
```

Within the `Posses` virtual function, I decided to make sure first that the current `AIController` is the `Enemy` class type (I'll be discussing the `Enemy` class in a moment). If it was true, I'll be initializing the `Blackboard` component, getting the value from its variables, and assigning them to the local variables I've made within this class (the protected variables `EnemyKeyID` and `EnemyPositionKeyID`).

Last, but not least, I just started the behavior tree. It is necessary to do that, otherwise the behavior tree will remain offline, and the enemy will be stuck in his position:

```
void AEnemyAIController::Possess(APawn* InPawn)
{
   Super::Possess(InPawn);

   AEnemy* _tempEnemy = Cast<AEnemy>(InPawn);

   // start behavior
   if (_tempEnemy && _tempEnemy->EnemyBehaviorTree)
   {

     BlackboardComp->InitializeBlackboard(*_tempEnemy-
>EnemyBehaviorTree->BlackboardAsset);

     // Get the enemy blackboard ID, and store it to access that
blackboard key later.
     EnemyKeyID = BlackboardComp->GetKeyID("Enemy");
     EnemyPositionKeyID = BlackboardComp->GetKeyID("EnemyPosition");
     BehaviorComp->StartTree(*_tempEnemy->EnemyBehaviorTree);
     UE_LOG(LogClass, Log, TEXT("============>>>> Got the enemy and the
BT have been started"));
   }
}
```

The `SetEnemy` function is very simple, as it is going to check whether there is already a **Blackboard** component and it is not null. Then, it will set the value of its `Enemy` class to the one being passed through the function parameters. Finally, it will set the value of the enemy's position.

Doing this means that the blackboard has the latest data, which means that, when the behavior tree wants to use the player data or its position as an enemy for our AI, it will find valid and up-to-date data:

```
void AEnemyAIController::SetEnemy(class APawn* InPawn)
{
  if (BlackboardComp)
  {
    BlackboardComp->SetValue<UBlackboardKeyType_Object>(EnemyKeyID,
InPawn);
    BlackboardComp->SetValueAsVector(EnemyPositionKeyID, InPawn-
>GetActorLocation());
    SetFocus(InPawn);
  }
}
```

GetEnemy is even simpler than SetEnemy, as it will just get the enemy value from the blackboard. And as you can see, the function type is AGladiator, which means that the enemy of the AI must be the player!

```
class AGladiator* AEnemyAIController::GetEnemy() const
{
  if (BlackboardComp)
  {
    return Cast<AGladiator>(BlackboardComp-
>GetValue<UBlackboardKeyType_Object>(EnemyKeyID));
  }

  return NULL;
}
```

While the AI is navigating through the level, it will look weird, as it is only changing its position to traverse between the points, but adding a rotation to it will make it more realistic and as natural as anything walking or navigating. It does not only change position, it also changes direction.

I made a vector called TheCenter to store the center of the player. Then, I processed the whole logic if it is not 0 and the player is valid.

I used a simple math calculation to calculate the direction and store it in a vector called Direction. Then, I did the math clap to blend the rotation between the current value and TheNewRotation based on the Direction component detected:

```
void AEnemyAIController::UpdateControlRotation(floatDeltaTime,
boolbUpdatePawn)
{
```

```
// Look toward focus
FVector TheCenter = GetFocalPoint();
if (!TheCenter.IsZero() && GetPawn())
{
    FVector Direction = TheCenter - GetPawn()->GetActorLocation();
    FRotator TheNewRotation = Direction.Rotation();

    TheNewRotation.Yaw = FRotator::ClampAxis(TheNewRotation.Yaw);

    SetControlRotation(TheNewRotation);

    APawn* const _tempPawn = GetPawn();
    if (_tempPawn &&bUpdatePawn)
    {
        _tempPawn->FaceRotation(TheNewRotation, DeltaTime);
    }

}
}
```

Finally, by the end of the class, I did the search function, which is the longest yet in this class.

The search function will check whether the AI is a valid pawn; if it is, it will proceed in the process; otherwise, it will just stop.

Then, the use of a `for` loop and `GetPawnIterator` allows me to get all the pawns within the world and go through all of them.

Within the `for` loop, I will test whether the index of the pawn is from the player class named `AGladiator` or just another enemy that is based on the `AEnemy` class.

Then, if it is really not an enemy, I will do a final check to catch whether that player is still alive or not using the method `GetIsStillAlive` we built in *Chapter 2, Setting Up Your Warrior*. If it is not dead, it means that I can set it as an enemy for the AI:

```
void AEnemyAIController::OnSearchForEnemy()
{
    APawn* _tempPawn = GetPawn();
    if (_tempPawn == NULL)
    {
        return;
    }

    const FVector _tempLocation = _tempPawn->GetActorLocation();
    float BestDistSq = MAX_FLT;
```

```cpp
   AGladiator* PlayerPawn = NULL;

   //foreach all pawns in world
   for (FConstPawnIterator It = GetWorld()->GetPawnIterator(); It;
++It)
   {
     if (PawnCanBeSeen(*It))
     {
        AGladiator* TestPawn = Cast<AGladiator>(*It);

        AEnemy* const _testEnemy = Cast<AEnemy>(TestPawn);

        if (_testEnemy)
        {
          //it is just another enemy, not player
        }
        else
        {
          if (TestPawn && TestPawn->GetIsStillAlive())
          {
            UE_LOG(LogClass, Log, TEXT(" ====================>>>>>  ENEMY
SEEN %s "), *GetNameSafe(*It));
            const float _distanceSq = (TestPawn->GetActorLocation() -
_tempLocation).SizeSquared();
            if (_distanceSq < BestDistSq)
            {
              BestDistSq = _distanceSq;
              PlayerPawn = TestPawn;
            }
          }
        }

     }
   }

   if (PlayerPawn)
   {
     // We saw someone, so set him as target.
     SetEnemy(PlayerPawn);
     UE_LOG(LogClass, Log, TEXT(" ====================>>>>>  Set
Target"));

   }

}
```

Now, we have completed the AIController; only one more note to go. You might find me using lots of UE_LOG methods, but this is just to test and keep a nice log while playing just in case something went wrong. I can track it faster than throwing some break points.

Now, let's go ahead and break down the code for the Enemy class itself.

Enemy

This class is very different, as it is not playing the controller role as the previous one. Here, we will be adding a component in order to build the enemy character itself, static mesh, triggers, and so on.

This is not just the building process for the enemy, but also the main and core functionalities, such as the attacking logic or what happens before and/or after an attack takes place.

Also, we include the attributes of the enemy, such as the attacking range, its health, or even the variables that will be controlling some animations, such as the status of life or dead.

Enemy.h

As usual, we will start with the set of the default header files to be included and then the name of the class and its base:

```
#pragma once
#include "GameFramework/Character.h"
#include "Enemy.generated.h"

UCLASS()
class BELLZ_APIAEnemy : publicACharacter
{
  GENERATED_BODY()
```

Then, I managed to create three different components; all of them will be working as triggers. A huge one will be at the middle of the AI that will be taking the damage from the player. Alongside will be two other trigger spheres. Each will be parented to the palm of a hand and both will cause damage to the player when the AI attacks:

```
UPROPERTY(VisibleAnywhere, BlueprintReadOnly, Category = Triggers,
meta = (AllowPrivateAccess = "true"))
  classUSphereComponent* bodySphereTrigger;

UPROPERTY(VisibleAnywhere, BlueprintReadOnly, Category = Triggers,
meta = (AllowPrivateAccess = "true"))
```

```
class USphereComponent* leftHandTrigger;

UPROPERTY(VisibleAnywhere, BlueprintReadOnly, Category = Triggers,
meta = (AllowPrivateAccess = "true"))
    class USphereComponent* rightHandTrigger;
```

Then, there is a set of default methods that is included in the code by default; this includes `constructor`, `BeginPlay`, `Tick`, and `PlayerInputs`. You are free to use any of them, but you can also ignore any or all of them as long as they are not serving any purpose for your logic:

```
//The constructor
AEnemy();

//Override the PostInitializeComponents()
virtual void PostInitializeComponents() override;

// Called when the game starts or when spawned
virtual void BeginPlay() override;

// Called every frame
virtual void Tick( float DeltaSeconds ) override;

// Called to bind functionality to input
virtual void SetupPlayerInputComponent(classUInputComponent*
InputComponent) override;
```

I wanted to declare some variables to help me while writing the logic — `TotalHealth` to represent the health of the AI, `AttackRange` to define the attack range of this AI, `AttackDamage` to tell how much damage it causes the player when it attacks him, and a Boolean `IsDead` to tell whether the AL is dead or not, as this will affects the animations. Or finally, another Boolean named `IsAttacking` to define whether it is really attacking; this will affects the animations too:

```
//The health of the enemy
UPROPERTY(EditAnywhere, BlueprintReadWrite, Category = "Enemy
Behavior")
float TotalHealth;

//The range for the enemy attack
UPROPERTY(EditAnywhere, BlueprintReadWrite, Category = "Enemy
Behavior")
float AttackRange;

//The power of the enemy attacks
```

```
UPROPERTY(EditAnywhere, BlueprintReadWrite, Category = "Enemy
Behavior")
float AttackDamage;

//Check if the enemy is dead or alive
UPROPERTY(EditAnywhere, BlueprintReadWrite, Category = "Enemy
Behavior")
bool IsDead;

//Check if the enemy is dead or alive
UPROPERTY(EditAnywhere, BlueprintReadWrite, Category = "Enemy
Behavior")
bool IsAttacking;
```

Then comes one of the most outstanding components of the Unreal Engine, called the **sensing component**. This is basically a component used with AI in order to give the characters the ability to hear or listen to anything around them:

```
//The sensing component used to see or hear the player
UPROPERTY(VisibleAnywhere, BlueprintReadOnly, Category = "Enemy AI")
class UPawnSensingComponent* PawnSensor;
```

Then there is the behavior tree component. Yes, we have created the behavior tree asset. Later, we will be building its logic, but the AI needs to know which behavior tree is driving its behaviors. That's why we will be adding it in the form of a component to the Enemy class:

```
//The used BT with that enemy
UPROPERTY(EditAnywhere, Category = "Enemy AI")
class UBehaviorTree* EnemyBehaviorTree;
```

Then, I've declared three major attacking functions. One will be called to perform the attack itself, with all an attack means. The other two play a very major role; one will be called before the attack in order to prepare for it and the other one will be called after the attack to clean up after it.

I've used this approach basically to control the trigger, because if the functions are enabled all the time, they will be registering too many hits to the player. But with this approach, I guarantee that one enemy hit will register once within the physics engine:

```
//Perform attack
UFUNCTION(BlueprintCallable, Category = "Enemy AI")
void OnPerformAttack();

//Applied before performing an attack
```

```
UFUNCTION(BlueprintCallable, Category = "Enemy AI")
void OnPreAttack();

//Perform attack done
UFUNCTION(BlueprintCallable, Category = "Enemy AI")
void OnPostAttack();
```

As we have used a sensing component in order to hear and see through the environments, I've decided to create two main functions, one for hearing and one for seeing, but both are based on the sensing component:

```
//Hear the player's noise using the sensing component
UFUNCTION()
void OnHearNoise(APawn *OtherActor, constFVector&Location, float
Volume);

//See the player's by sight using the sensing component
UFUNCTION()
void OnSeePawn(APawn *OtherPawn);
```

Now, because I've created triggers for the hands, I want them to affect the player in several ways, such as decreasing his health, displaying a screen shake, and so on. That will be done when I'm able to detect the trigger overlap:

```
UFUNCTION()
void OnHandTriggerOverlap(classAActor* OtherActor,
classUPrimitiveComponent* OtherComp, int32 OtherBodyIndex, bool
bFromSweep, constFHitResult& SweepResult);
```

Finally, just in case I want to get the trigger of the whole body (not from the hands' ones), I will set it within its own `getter` function to return it anytime:

```
FORCEINLINEclassUSphereComponent* GetBodySphereTrigger() const {
return bodySphereTrigger; }
```

Now, as everything is well declared within the header file, let's go ahead and work on the implementation of the code within the source file itself.

Enemy.cpp

The `Enemy` source file might look complex the first time you open it. But when you break it down into pieces and refer each piece to the header file description, you'll find that all the logic is easy and makes sense in terms of our goals.

As with any of the other source or header files, this one has to start with the include statement for the different header files. While you might be familiar with all of the included header files, here, I've presented new one, `PawnSensingComponent.h`, which is used for the sensing of AI:

```
#include "Bellz.h"
#include "Enemy.h"
#include "EnemyAIController.h"
#include "Gladiator.h"
#include "Perception/PawnSensingComponent.h"
```

The constructor looks huge and even larger than the constructor of the player itself, but this is because we have to construct several components and the majority of them are triggers to attack the player and get them damaged:

```
AEnemy::AEnemy()
{
  //Tick needed or no, it's a default from UE
  PrimaryActorTick.bCanEverTick = true;

  //Set the AI Controller class.
  AIControllerClass =AEnemyAIController::StaticClass();

  //Set the enemy behavior values
  TotalHealth = 100;
  AttackRange = 100;
  AttackDamage = 10;
  IsDead = false;
  IsAttacking = false;

  //Because the enemy have to rotate to face the running direction,
The Yaw rotation needed!
  bUseControllerRotationYaw = true;

  /*Build the sensing component, and set the required values for it.
You can publicate some
  variables to control those values, but for my AI within this game,
it is fine to just set some base values here*/
  PawnSensor = CreateDefaultSubobject<UPawnSensingComponent>(TEXT("Pa
wn Sensor"));
  PawnSensor->SensingInterval = .25f; // 4 times per second
  PawnSensor->bOnlySensePlayers = true;
  PawnSensor->SetPeripheralVisionAngle(85.f);

  bodySphereTrigger = CreateDefaultSubobject<USphereComponent>(TEXT("B
odyTriggerSphere"));
```

```
bodySphereTrigger->SetSphereRadius(150.f);
bodySphereTrigger->AttachTo(Mesh);

FColor handsTriggersColor = FColor (0, 0, 255, 255);

leftHandTrigger = CreateDefaultSubobject<USphereComponent>
(TEXT("LeftHandTriggerSphere"));
leftHandTrigger->SetSphereRadius(70.f);
leftHandTrigger->AttachTo(Mesh, "hand_lf",
EAttachLocation::SnapToTarget);
leftHandTrigger->ShapeColor = handsTriggersColor;
leftHandTrigger->bGenerateOverlapEvents = 0;

rightHandTrigger = CreateDefaultSubobject<USphereComponent>
(TEXT("RightHandTriggerSphere"));
rightHandTrigger->SetSphereRadius(70.f);
rightHandTrigger->AttachTo(Mesh, "hand_rt",
EAttachLocation::SnapToTarget);
rightHandTrigger->ShapeColor = handsTriggersColor;
rightHandTrigger->bGenerateOverlapEvents = 0;

//Just make sure to not use the Enemy::Character capsule as the
navigation collision, and use the agent and set its radius to
something fits the enemy size
//the main goal is to avoid as much as possible the cases when the
enemy meshes intersecting with each other, or with the environment
GetCharacterMovement()->NavAgentProps.AgentRadius = 400.f;
GetCharacterMovement()->SetUpdateNavAgentWithOwnersCollisions(fal
se);

}
```

Everything starts with defining the value of the variable `AIControllerClass` and setting it to the `AEnemyAIController` that we have just created. I managed to set some of the default values, such as the `health` and `damage` values. You still can change them from within the editor, but I decided to test values and put some of them here as defaults.

Because the AI has to keep rotating toward the movement direction (forward), I managed to set the value of the Boolean `bUseControllerRotationYaw`, which is a default bool within any character-based class, to `true`.

Then came the time to create the very interesting seeing component we named `PawnSensor`. I created it using `CreateDefaultSubobject` and then set some of its default parameters, such as `SensingInterval` to define the interval of searching and `bOnlySensePlayers` to `true`, to make sure no other AI creatures will be detected.

After this, I started to build the triggers. As we discussed earlier, there will be three triggers, one for the body and two for the hands. So, I used `CreateDefaultSubobject<USphereComponent>` in order to create all of them. Then, I set the radius for each of them and finally, attached them to a target. Sometimes, the main character mesh was the target, while with the hands I was targeting skeletal bones, such as `hand_lf` or `hand_rt`.

To make sure that my hand triggers will be generating overlaps that will be affecting the player capsule, I managed to set `bGenerateOverlapEvents` to `0`.

To make everything look a lot clearer in the editor, I've created a color variable, named it `handsTriggersColor`, and set its value to the hand triggers via the `ShapeColor` member variable, so I can differentiate them from all the other triggers.

The last and the most effective part of the constructor was related to the navigation mesh. I managed to set the `NavAgentProps.AgentRadius` radius to a value that fits my bear character, and disabled it, using the character collision for the navigations. Using the agent is more effective and this was done by switching off `SetUpdateNavAgentWithOwnersCollisions`.

I left the default functions, such as `BeginPlay` and `Tick`, as they are, as none of my logic will yet that targets them. I didn't manage to delete them, as I might need them to expand my system in the future, but it was enough to switch of the `Tick` function from the constructor.

```
//Called when the game starts or when spawned -> Default by UE
void AEnemy::BeginPlay()
{
  Super::BeginPlay();
}


//Called every frame -> Default by UE
void AEnemy::Tick( floatDeltaTime )
{
  Super::Tick( DeltaTime );

}


//Called to bind functionality to input -> Default by UE
```

```
void AEnemy::SetupPlayerInputComponent(classUInputComponent*
InputComponent)
{
    Super::SetupPlayerInputComponent(InputComponent);


}
```

I used `PostInitialize`, as it is required here in order to register the delegate functions for seeing and hearing, These functions come from `Perception/PawnSensingComponent.h` that we've included at the top of this source file. Then, I registered `OnBeginComponentOverlap` to the local function we made in the header file.

So, using the `PostInitialize` was a good choice, as it takes place before `BeginPlay`:

```
void AEnemy::PostInitializeComponents()
{
    Super::PostInitializeComponents();
    PawnSensor->OnSeePawn.AddDynamic(this, &AEnemy::OnSeePawn);
    PawnSensor->OnHearNoise.AddDynamic(this, &AEnemy::OnHearNoise);

    // Register to the delegate of OnComponentBeginOverlap
    leftHandTrigger->OnComponentBeginOverlap.AddDynamic(this,
&AEnemy::OnHandTriggerOverlap);
    rightHandTrigger->OnComponentBeginOverlap.AddDynamic(this,
&AEnemy::OnHandTriggerOverlap);
}
```

Then, the most important part about this enemy is attacking. The `attacking` method itself is kind of useless, because the way I decided to go with this AI made the `PreAttack` and the `PostAttack` methods the most important ones.

The plan is at the behavior tree; the AI will be moving toward the player. Once it reaches the player, it will attack.

The attack itself is just an animation tick that will be played, no more. But the idea here is that, when the attack starts, we call the `OnPreAttack` function, and by the end of the animation we will call the `OnPostAttck` function. Both functions work only on enabling and disabling the attacking triggers, which are both in the hands of the AI. Later, by the end of the chapter, I'll discuss how we will call both through the animation notifications:

```
void AEnemy::OnPreAttack()
{
    leftHandTrigger->bGenerateOverlapEvents = 1;
```

```
    rightHandTrigger->bGenerateOverlapEvents = 1;

    FString message = TEXT(">>>>>>>>>>> Attack just going to start
<<<<<<<<<<< ");
    //GEngine->AddOnScreenDebugMessage(-1, 2.f, FColor::Red, message);
}


void AEnemy::OnPostAttack()
{
    IsAttacking = false;

    leftHandTrigger->bGenerateOverlapEvents = 0;
    rightHandTrigger->bGenerateOverlapEvents = 0;

    FString message = TEXT(">>>>>>>>>>> Attack just finished
<<<<<<<<<<< ");
    //GEngine->AddOnScreenDebugMessage(-1, 2.f, FColor::Red, message);
}
```

After enabling the triggers for the hand from the OnPreAttack function, if the player was still in his position and didn't move, it means that the triggers from those hands will be touching the player's collider 9 capsule and that will trigger an Overlap event.

That was the whole point. We will check when the hand trigger is active (from the OnPreAttack function) and it is touching the player, which is the AGladiator type of class. Then, the function OnChangeHealthByAmount of the player will be called with a specific amount in order to decrease the player's health. Anything else will happen from the player side, as in the previous chapter, for the shake or claw display on top of the screen.

Most importantly we need to disable the triggers again, so they do not keep decreasing the player's health:

```
    void AEnemy::OnHandTriggerOverlap(classAAActor* OtherActor,
    classUPrimitiveComponent* OtherComp, int32OtherBodyIndex,
    boolbFromSweep, constFHitResult&SweepResult)
    {
      AGladiator* const _tempGladiator =  Cast<AGladiator>(OtherActor);
      if (_tempGladiator)
      {
        FString message = TEXT("=== HIT PLAYER WITH HAND ==== ");
```

```
    GEngine->AddOnScreenDebugMessage(-1, 2.f, FColor::Red, message);

    //in case it hit the player, it is good idea to disable the
triggers, this way we'll make sure that the triggers will not over
calculate with each single hit
    leftHandTrigger->bGenerateOverlapEvents = 0;
    rightHandTrigger->bGenerateOverlapEvents = 0;

    _tempGladiator->OnChangeHealthByAmount(5.f);
  }
}
```

Now, both classes are running fine. You can keep adding more logic to fit your design and idea, but remember, once you're done, do compile the code either from the editor or from Visual Studio. This is the only way to get the new code to work!

Building the behavior tree

The behavior tree is just a bunch of scenarios and calls for various functions. The core function we have already written into the C++ classes, but we will never be able to just directly use them within the behavior tree. That's the reason behind having the other supportive assets, such as the task, blackboard, and service. So, in order to build the BT, we need to prepare the other assets.

- **Blackboard**: After you open the blackboard, you'll find it looks empty, and as it is a data holder asset, we will need to add some data that matches the data we wrote about within the AIController class. You can simply add data using the **New Key** button in the top-left corner of the blackboard editor.

Now, you can keep adding the keys (variables) and changing their names and types in order to fit the C++ code we have already done. Personally, I ended up with these three, and while we need only two, I made one more just while trying to expand my AI functionalities.

Now, the last thing we need from the blackboard is to assign the base blackboard of the behavior tree. So, you can double-click to open the behavior tree asset we made. On the right-hand side, there is a huge **Details** panel that usually holds one option, which is the **Blackboard Asset**. From its selection drop-down menu, choose our blackboard asset.

- **BTService**: If you double-click to open the service blueprint we made earlier, you will find it holds a method called `EventRecieveTick`. This is just like a normal `Tick` method, but this one could be changed to not call every frame. That's one of the difference, between `Services` and Tasks. This is basically the reason behind using this blueprint type.

  Now, with a simple cast to get to owner actor, we can check whether it is an EnemyAIController-based class or no. If it is, then we just call the function `OnSearchForEnemy` from the C++ code.

That's all this service is going to do.

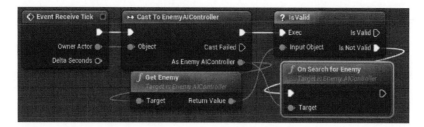

- **BTTask**: Within the task, we will be doing almost the same thing as the service. But the difference here is that we will be just calling OnPerformAttack from the C++ code.

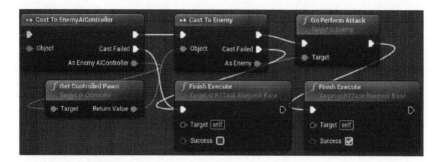

Still, there are few differences you have to bear in mind. They are as follows:

- Because a task is not called all the time like the service, the logic is connected in EventRecieveExecute.

- After the casting is successful to AIController, we can check for the Enemy class and cast for it, because the method we want to execute is inside the Enemy class.

- There is a node called FinishExecute. You have to put it at the end of all the logic branches, because without this node things will go weird. But using it will guarantee that the behavior tree will continue after a task is done.

Now, with all the supporting assets done, you can easily assemble the behavior tree. There aren't too many types of nodes that you can use inside a behavior tree, and this makes it easy to construct it. Anything you need will be found on the right-click context menu.

Now is the time to build the actual behavior tree itself, and while we spend some time building its component, we only need task and service, and we have already assigned the blackboard to it and filled the blackboard with the data we want to keep up-to-date. At the same time, we built the C++ logic that is essential for the enemy behaviors. Building the tree itself is a matter of putting in some composites, nodes, and decorators.

Now, all you have to do is to build the behaviors logic. All the types we discussed before are inside the right-click menu.

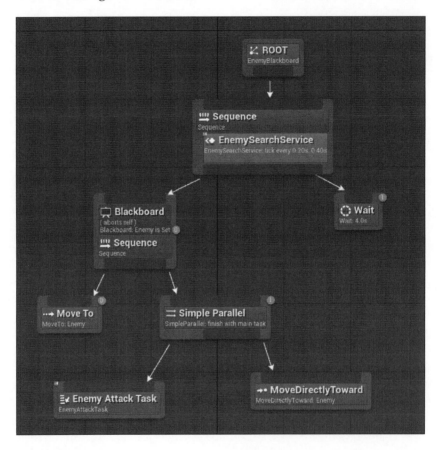

My tree will start itself from the C++ code, after the `posses` function is called. That's what is called the **ROOT**. Then I used the following sequences:

1. I used a sequence, which means that all its children will be an ordered series and you can tell that from the numbers at on the right of the nodes. Then, I set a service for it; this service is the one we created as a `BTService` asset, which is responsible for searching the player.

2. The sequence itself of the previous node is one of two things: either wait for a specific time or run another sequence.

3. The other sequence is going to use the enemy data from the blackboard to move the AI to the player (enemy here means the enemy of the AI, which is the player).

4. Then, the other part of that last sequence is something called simple parallel, which is basically an execution of different things at the same time. But it will only get executed when the previous one (move to) is done, which means that we are already at the player's position.

5. The simple parallel holds the `enemy attack` task and a `MoveDirectlyToward` behavior node, which has the enemy (the player) as its target.

6. Finally, the whole thing will keep redoing itself!

Creating the blueprint

As we discussed earlier in *Chapter 2, Setting Up Your Warrior,* when we finish creating the C++ code, it is not usable until we build a blueprint based on it. That's in the majority of cases, and it's the case here.

In order to put an instance of the `Enemy` class into the level, we have to have a blueprint based on it first, in the same way you used to create blueprints. But this time, the base class will be `Enemy`, as this is the main class we want to use for it.

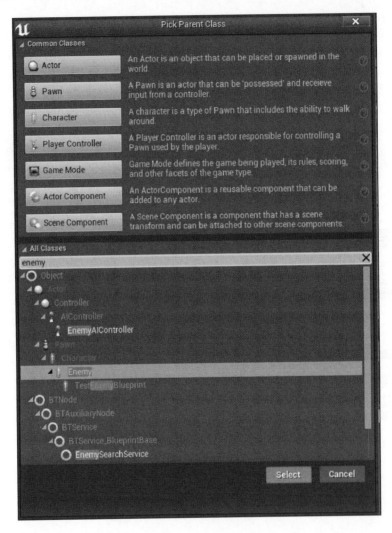

But as you remember, we will always need to change default values. Despite this, you can set almost all the values within the constructor of the class, but still some values will be faster to set within the editor itself.

I've changed some settings, such as the animation blueprint value I've set to use the **Bear_animationBlueprint** that I've created especially for the bear enemy.

Because the blueprint we are finishing here is for an AI, there are even more values we have to set. For example, my `Enemy` and `AIController` code has a reference for the used behavior tree. I've listed it to be within a category named `Enemy AI`. Then, simply browsing for the BT is essential, otherwise the enemy will not start following any BT.

Because the enemy is based on a character, with lots of premade logic to fit different behaviors, and that's a default from Unreal, I worked on disabling the unneeded behaviors from the **Movement Capabilities** section.

To be honest with you, leaving these will not have any effect, as for example the enemy will never jump until you define that in code, add it to a task, and set it inside the behavior tree. But the point is, what if a designer or another colleague is looking into the whole thing? If the jumping capability was marked `true`, he would think the enemy is not jumping, because the code has some errors. But marking it as `false`, means it is not used here, or in the code!

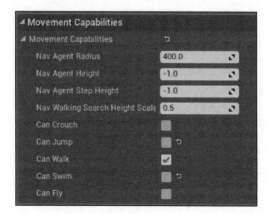

One last thing; we have created an AIController-based class that is called `EnemyAIController`, but this class is not used yet. We didn't create a blueprint based on it. We didn't reference it within the `Enemy` C++ class. But then, how this is going to work and how will the most important function of it (dedicated to searching for the player or storing data within the blackboard) be done?

Well, any pawn, by default, has an option to set `AIControllerClass`. If you left it to none, it means that the pawn is not an AI; but if it is the AI that is going to navigate, then you have to set a value here.

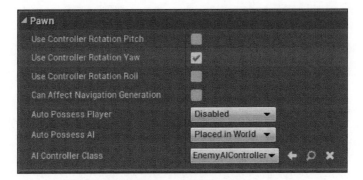

Finally, with all in place and with the triggers we have created through the C++ code and animations in place, this is how my enemy sample looks and it is ready to be spawned in the map:

Adding notifies

Remember a few pages ago, when we created the animation blueprint? Or, to be more precise, when I showed my animation blueprint setup and you used the knowledge you have from *Chapter 1*, *Preparing for a Big Project*, and *Chapter 2*, *Setting Up Your Warrior*, to build your own animation blueprint setup for your AI?

There was one more thing that I didn't want to add to the animation blueprint at that time, as it is was more dependent on the C++ code. It is the animation notifies.

We have discussed before the importance of notifications and how accurate they are when it comes to executing something at the exact moment.

Within the C++ code, we have written two important functions and the loss of gameplay logic will count on these two functions; it was the `OnPreAttack` and the `OnPostAttack` methods. Both the functions do handle each other; the `OnPreAttack` method works on preparing the enemy to do an attack and the `OnPostAttack` method works on returning everything to normal.

But when we decide that the attack is about to happen, can we prepare for it? And, when we decide that the attack is done, can we reset things to normal?

Well, it is simply through the animations!

At the start of each attack animation, we can call `OnPreAttack`, as this is exactly the moment where the attack will start. And so, at the last few frames of the attack animations, we can call `OnPostAttack`, as this implies that the attack animation was already completed.

This said, the only thing left to do is just put the two notifications within all the attack animation clips that I have.

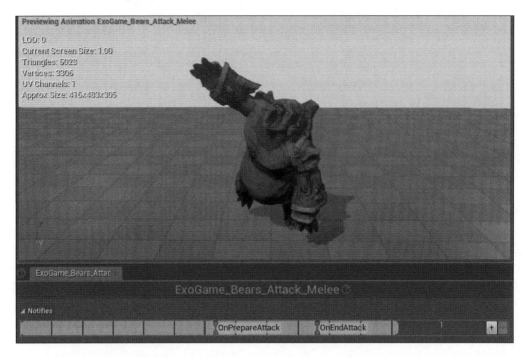

Then, from within the animation blueprint, it is simple to just call `OnPostAttack` and `OnPreAttack` from the C++ code and apply them to the notifications.

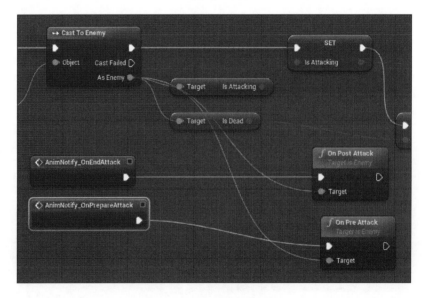

What else?

Well, when we create an AI for a game, we keep updating it within each update, not only for the sake of bug fixing, but also adding new features, making it more accurate and more live!

Now, I would recommend you to do two main things. First, go ahead and add more and more tasks, services, and code to it to make your AI decide more, I'm limited by the page count, but don't be limited by your imagination; go ahead and imagine more behaviors and add them to your enemies.

I would also recommend you to gather all what learned so far and try to build a new class that is responsible for spawning enemies; some games have enemies already in their maps, but the majority of the games spawn enemies at runtime, so why not build such a small system?

Otherwise, you can drag and drop instances of the enemy blueprint within the scene at the positions that you want them to start in, and they will do the rest once the game starts!

Summary

Now, you have created the most complex and funny part of this game and game development in general.

You have got an idea about how huge AI systems are built and how inheritance usually goes for the different AI classes. Even if your AI is going to be simple enough, it is good to understand how huge projects handle it.

The AI system within Unreal Engine has several different assets, all of them have to be used in order to create a complete AI system; you can ignore some, but using them will empower your work. Blackboards are essential to save data for the AI, while services and tasks work as procedures for the AI, but each does that in a different manner. All of the previous asset types have to be handled within the amazing BT editor, within a BT asset, and you have learned how to do that. Not only what the BT is and how to use it and its editor, but also you've learned how to use the most interesting parts of it, such as decorators and composites; you now have mastered them.

The animation blueprint is essential for any animated entity within your game; the more complex your blueprint gets, the more life it gives for your characters and entities, and you have practiced in using them here again.

The AI core C++ logic is the soul of everything the AI can do; all the assets and behavior trees take their orders from here and now you have done one more practice in coding complex things within Unreal Engine. Regardless of the base class of your enemies, you have learned that any AI needs an `AIController` class to drive it; that's how navigations works, and you have done it perfectly.

Creating the blueprint is always the last step, just to make an instance of your class to be used within the game. Regardless, you will be directly throwing it inside the map or spawning it at runtime; you must create at least a blueprint based on the class and set all its parameters to match your design.

What if we want to call some parts of the code at a certain moment, but we are not so sure when this moment will come? Well, animation notifications have always been the trick, and you have now done them in a very wide form, such as giving orders to the AI before and after doing attacks; this is a good skill in its own right, not because of something more than that usually the blueprints handled by the artists, and the code handled by the codes, but this is the gray area between black and white, it is done in the asset side, but it needs coding skills, and you understood it perfectly now.

With all of these in place, play your game, fix what needs to be fixed, and let's go ahead and take another C++ coding challenge: in-game collectables.

5
Adding Collectables

What is the point of playing a game without being able to win?! It is the main purpose of a game, that you win, right? But how do you win?

Well, winning varies depending on the game's genre, but there is one thing in common between all genres: almost all games have collectables.

Now the equation is simple: in order to win, you have to collect some stuff. Take *Super Mario* as an example; this was my first time learning about the importance of collectables, and this game was all about collectables. Yes, of course, if you run out of time, you lose, but you can collect time as an item to increase that limit.

Even in an *AAA* shooter, or a similar hardcore game, you would never make it to the end of the level without getting some health pickups, or food in the most recent games.

So in a nutshell, collectables are essential. Regardless of the genre, you'll find yourself ending up with having at least one type of collectable item in your game. That's what we are going to discuss.

By the end of this chapter, you'll be able to:

- Understand the different ways of building a collectables system
- Construct a collectables hierarchy
- Create a `Coin` class based on the Base pickups class
- Build the blueprint of a collectable
- Use `overlap` events to detect the surrounding actors
- Increase a variable amount based on the collections

Now, let's get started. Open your game, or your Bellz, and let's add some collectable items to it!

The idea behind collectables

If you are following this book chapter by chapter, that means you have already completed the AI chapter, and you already have an idea about how things should be constructed. But let's be more specific here.

There are different ways, methods, and approaches that we can use in order to build a collectables system. The variation comes from the fact that not all games are made the same way, and engineers do not necessarily work using similar methods. But the two most common methods I've found that we can use are as follows:

- We build a base collectables class, and then we build some classes inherited from it, each new subclass serving a different type of collectable item. For example, we could have the main `PickupBase` class for the general behaviors shared between all pickup items, and then derive several classes from it, such as `money`, `health`, `food`, and so on, where each type of collectable will behave differently.

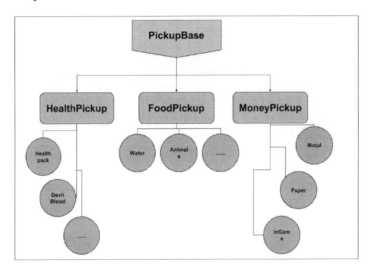

- On the other hand, we could have just one collectable class. Based on something (let's say a tag or object instance name), we could apply a different scenario after the item is picked up.

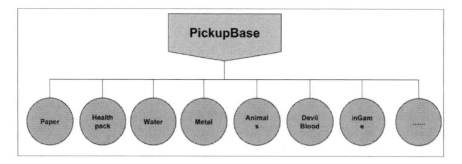

Despite this, there are unlimited ways by which you can classify such a thing, but these are the two most common methods I have found within projects. It's interesting that these methods are in two different directions; while one tends towards a detailed control over each type, the other just puts all collectables into one plot. Each has its own advantages and disadvantages that you can learn by experience!

While I usually like to use the first method, you will mostly find yourself using the second one, as it requires less implementation, fewer classes, and usually less typing. But to be honest with you, what makes good code better than bad code is not the code quality or amount as much it is about the code design and structure, and how extendable and flexible it is. Flexibility is something you get from the first method.

While we followed one approach while building the enemies, let's use a different technique for the collectables: let's have a base class and child classes.

The base class

The base class will hold the major behaviors and instructions for all the collectables. Go ahead and create a new class based on the Actor class and name it PickupBase. Once Visual Studio opens, let's write some code for it.

PickupBase.h

As all we have to do (so far) for this class is based on the Actor class, I didn't have to include something special for its header file. At the same time, write the code for the defining the constructor and the class:

```
#pragma once

#include "GameFramework/Actor.h"
#include "PickupBase.generated.h"
```

```
UCLASS()
class BELLZ_API APickupBase : public AActor
{
  GENERATED_BODY()

public:
  // Sets default values for this actor's properties
  APickupBase();
```

Then you can remove the definition set of the default two functions, but I kept them just in case I need them in the near future:

```
// Called when the game starts or when spawned
  virtual void BeginPlay() override;


// Called every frame
  virtual void Tick( float DeltaSeconds ) override;
```

As the coin pickup (or any other pickup) will have a static mesh to represent it inside the game world, I made a get function called `GetMesh` to return a type of `UStaticMeshComponent`, just in case it is needed:

```
//Return the static mesh of the pickup instance
  FORCEINLINEclass UStaticMeshComponent* GetMesh() const { return
ThePickupStaticMesh; }
```

Because these pickups have to be collected, at some point a pickup needs to be hidden. I did this by adding a Boolean called `IsActive` that holds the activity status, and a method called `SetActive` that takes a Boolean as its parameter, in order to set the activity at any given moment:

```
//The pickup active or not!
  UFUNCTION(BlueprintPure, Category = "Pickups")
    bool IsActive();


//Change the active status from the outside
  UFUNCTION(BlueprintCallable, Category = "Pickups")
    void SetActive(bool NewPickupState);
```

Now that picking up and switching activities are mentioned, I decided to add the function that will be responsible for picking up the collectables. I called it `OnGetCollected`, and then I created the virtual `OnGetCollected_Implementation` function that will be used with the inherited child classes (such as the `CoinPickup` class):

```
//When the pickup gets collected, this function should be called
UFUNCTION(BlueprintNativeEvent)
```

```
void OnGetCollected();
virtual void OnGetCollected_Implementation();
```

Finally, I managed to create a `UStaticMeshComponent` component and named it `ThePickupStaticMesh`, and this is where we will be holding the collectable mesh and/or its visual representation:

```
//The static mesh of the pickup, to give it visual looking, you can
replace it with Sprites if it is a 2D game
UPROPERTY(VisibleAnywhere, BlueprintReadOnly, Category = "Pickups",
meta = (AllowPrivateAccess = "true"))
class UStaticMeshComponent* ThePickupStaticMesh;
```

Now the header file is complete. As you can see, there isn't anything unusual, just methods to be used when the pickup is actually collected, or methods to inquire about things. While all this is fresh, let's go to the source file and start the implementation of this stuff.

PickupBase.cpp

As always, it all starts with the set of included header files. But nothing very important was added here, other than the default ones:

```
#include "Bellz.h"
#include "PickupBase.h"
```

After that, it's time to add the constructor. Remember, I might be able to use the constructor to add a mesh, or a certain type of physics, but I always prefer to keep those types of parameter within the editor. I mean that the parameters that I will need to set once and for all I prefer to do in the editor; otherwise, if the parameter needs some tweaks, it is better to set it here, in the constructor.

I also managed to set `PrimaryActorTick.bCanEverTick` to `false`, as I have no intention of using the `tick` method for any logic; thus it is better to disable it.

Last but not least, I initialized and created the `ThePickupStaticMesh` variable of the `UStaticMeshComponent` component type and set it to the root of the object:

```
// Sets default values
APickupBase::APickupBase()
{
  // Set this actor to call Tick() every frame. You can turn this off
to improve performance if you don't need it.
  PrimaryActorTick.bCanEverTick = false;
```

```
  // All pickups start active
  bIsActive = true;

  // Add the static mesh component
  ThePickupStaticMesh = CreateDefaultSubobject<UStaticMeshComponent>(T
EXT("PickupMesh"));
  RootComponent = ThePickupStaticMesh;
}
```

The two main methods, `BeginPlay` and `Tick`, are left as is. If you want to remove them, just remember to remove them from the header file first; otherwise, there is no effect on the performance, especially because I have disabled the `Tick` method from within the constructor:

```
// Called when the game starts or when spawned
void APickupBase::BeginPlay()
{
  Super::BeginPlay();

}

// Called every frame
void APickupBase::Tick( floatDeltaTime )
{
  Super::Tick( DeltaTime );

}
```

Then, the small simple method to return the active status of the object was made. It is important, in some cases, just to make sure the coin/collectable is active before collecting it:

```
// Getter to the active status
bool APickupBase::IsActive()
{
  return bIsActive;
}
```

The last and most important part of the coin code is `OnGetCollected_Implementation`, where we can execute any necessary code once the item has been collected. For now, it is enough to print a message to the screen, but this is the place that will be used to spawn some particles later:

```
void APickupBase::OnGetCollected_Implementation()
{
  //Display to screen
```

```
  FString message = TEXT(" == Successfully Picked up == ") +
GetName();
  GEngine->AddOnScreenDebugMessage(-1, 2.f, FColor::Red, message);
}
```

The coin class

The coin class is a child class, derived from the base class, and it will only hold the behaviors and instructions required for coins. Go ahead and create a new class based on `PickupBase` class, and name it `CoinPickup`. Once Visual Studio opens, let's write some code for it.

CoinPickup.h

As the coin has nothing special to do except hold its own value, the amount of increase that it will give to the player when it is collected, I managed to just add the override for the virtual function `OnGetCollected` from the base, and a float named `CoinValue`. We can set its value either in the constructor or in the editor:

```
#pragma once

#include "PickupBase.h"
#include "CoinPickup.generated.h"

/**
 *
 */
UCLASS()
class BELLZ_APIACoinPickup : publicAPickupBase
{
  GENERATED_BODY()

public:
  // Sets default values for this actor's properties
  ACoinPickup();

  // The Override for the Virtual of the base class
  void OnGetCollected_Implementation() override;

  //Access the Coin value
  float GetCoinValue();
```

```
protected:
    //The value that the coin adds to the collected items, you can make
a Special coins with higher values or so...
    UPROPERTY(EditAnywhere, BlueprintReadWrite, Category = "Coins", Meta
= (BlueprintProtected = "true"))
    float CoinValue;



};
```

While we have some kind of value, I managed to add a basic getter function, GetCoinValue, that will return the value of this coin, just in case I need it.

CoinPickup.cpp

As the class header doesn't have much to implement, it was enough to do the following in order:

- Give a base value for the coin CoinValue in the constructor

- Return the CoinValue within the getter function GetCoinValue()

- Finally, write down the override of the virtual OnGetCollected from the parent class and add a simple actor called Destroy() in order to destroy itself when it is collected

```
...
#include "Bellz.h"
#include "CoinPickup.h"


//Set default values
ACoinPickup::ACoinPickup()
{
    //the base value of the coin
    CoinValue = 20.0f;
}


void ACoinPickup::OnGetCollected_Implementation()
{
    // Use the base pickup behavior
    Super::OnGetCollected_Implementation();
    // Destroy the coin
    Destroy();
}
```

```
// return the value of the coin
float ACoinPickup::GetCoinValue()
{
    return CoinValue;
}
```

Making it collectable

Now we have a collectables base class, and we have a type of `pickup` item, which is the golden coin. But if we created an instance of it as a blueprint based on the `CoinPickup` class, it will not be collected, because there is no code to make the character (the `Gladiator` class) able to recognize the collectables.

So, inside the `Gladiator` class, I will be adding one function, `OnCollectPickup()`, and it will work as follows:

1. The most important thing is that we'll be using the `GetOverlappingActors()` method of the gladiator collider in order to pick up anything that collides with the character right away. However, in order to store the data found, we will need something like a container for it.

2. So, the first thing to be done is creating an array of `Actor` called `CollectedPickups`.

3. Then, access the `CapsuleComponent` component of the `GladiatorCharacter` class (`AGladiator`) using the word `this` in order to refer to the current instance.

4. By using the array we made as a parameter for the member function `GetOverlappingActors`, we will be able to store all the collisions.

5. Then, a typical for loop, in order to loop between all the collided objects, we get through `GetOverlappingActors`.

6. Now it is just a matter of making sure the actor in this loop iteration is the one we want.

7. And to make sure of that, I checked that it is `APickupBase`, and not going to be destroyed, and is still an active instance.

8. If all this is `true`, then I proceed and then call its `OnGetCollected` function (all the pickups will have it).

9. Finally, make sure it is a coin by comparing it to `ACoinPickup*` `const _tempCoin`.

10. If it is, then I'll just increase the coin's final value variable of the `Gladiator` class, which is called `CollectedCoinsValue`, and also count how many coins been collected.

11. The last important part is to disable and hide this pickup by setting its activity to `false`. This way we make sure the coin will not be over-calculated. Remember, we made ourselves safe when we added the `Destroy` call inside the `OnGetCollected_Implementation` method of the `CoinBase` class.

12. Finally, I print to the screen using `GEngine`, which is used in the entire game, just to test it:

```
...
void AGladiator::OnCollectPickup()
{
  //Lets make a temp array to hold the overlapped coins
  TArray<AActor*> CollectedPickups;

  //let's check if something overlaps the player capsule, and then
save the result at the temp array
  this->CapsuleComponent->GetOverlappingActors(CollectedPickups);

  // loop within the overlapped items
  for (int32 c = 0; c < CollectedPickups.Num(); c++)
  {
    // Cast the actor the base pickup
    APickupBase* const _tempPickup = Cast<APickupBase>(CollectedPi
ckups[c]);
    // If cast is done, then let's make sure that it is active
    if (_tempPickup && !_tempPickup->IsPendingKill() && _
tempPickup->IsActive())
    {
      //call the internal OnGetCollected
      _tempPickup->OnGetCollected();
      //Then cast to a coin, to make sure it is a coin, you can
add different scenarios for the different types of collectables
      ACoinPickup* const _tempCoin = Cast<ACoinPickup>(_
tempPickup);
      if (_tempCoin)
      {
        //if it is really a coin, then lets add 1 to the amount of
collected coins, and then add the value of this coin to the score
        CollectedCoinsValue += _tempCoin->GetCoinValue();
        CollectedCoins += 1;

        FString message = TEXT("Collected another coinCoin --->
Total of ") + FString::FromInt(CollectedCoins) + TEXT(" And all
value now is") + FString::FromInt(CollectedCoinsValue);
        GEngine->AddOnScreenDebugMessage(-1, 2.f, FColor::Blue,
message);
```

```
        }
    // Disable the pickup item
    _tempPickup->SetActive(false);
      }
   }
 }
```

One thing to keep in mind, you'll need to add a couple of extra headers into the `include` statements of the `Gladiator` class, `PickupBase` and `CoinPickup`, in order to be able to access their member variables. Keep in mind that there is nothing called a finished class. Sooner or later, you'll be jumping between classes, in order to connect them with each other:

```
#include "PickupBase.h"
#include "CoinPickup.h"
```

Don't forget to define the function inside `Gladiator.h` (the header file):

```
//Called when we collecting a pickup
UFUNCTION(BlueprintCallable, Category = "PickupSystem")
void OnCollectPickup();
```

Building the blueprint

Now, creating the blueprint is very simple, as always. Just create a new blueprint, but this time base it on the `CoinPickup` class.

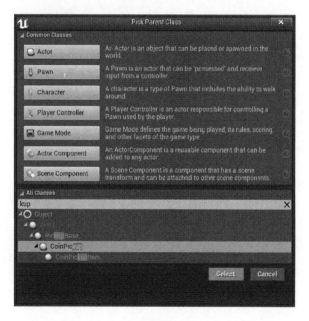

Name it whatever you want, it will not make a difference. The method we followed is not affected by naming. After creating it, open the blueprint editor, and set the coin mesh as the mesh asset you have (feel free to get the one I made from my project by following the `Migrate` assets from *Chapter 1, Preparing for a Big Project*).

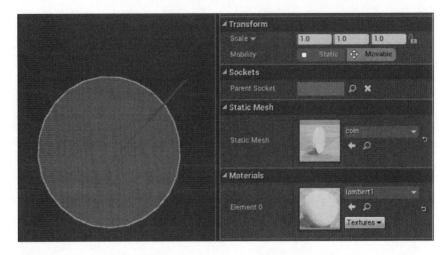

Now it's time for the last step before throwing it into the map. Just change **Collision Presets** to **OverlapAll**. This way we make sure it is not an obstacle for the AI, and doesn't block the player.

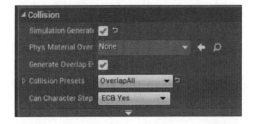

Throw some coins onto the map, in different places, and then hit **Play**. You'll notice that once you touch any coin with the gladiator, the coin will disappear right away; and its value will be added to your stock, and it will all be printed onto the screen.

Going forward

Now that you have a base pickup class with one type of pickup, I suggest you do two more things: first, keep building different pickups that affect the character differently, for example, a weapon pickup, a health pickup, and so on.

Secondly, I would suggest you write a small class that places the pickups around the level. As you know, lots of games are based on randomness, but the majority of them are based on the design of the level. I mean, some games force us to put the collectables one by one around the levels at certain places, while other games are based on an algorithm or a system that places pickups all around the level.

Go ahead, find the best for you and do it. In Bellz, I was trying to show you the way, and I found it is enough to create the pickups. decide how to place them around in a level, and investigate. Go ahead and do it.

Summary

Now you understand one of the cornerstones of any game. All games have pickups, and they are essential for many aspects of the game. Having them is important, but we have to know how to add them, and you've gained this skill.

Building a few more C++ classes, and getting more and more used to the workflow of coding for Unreal games, is something you spent a lot time on in this chapter.

After creating a class, it has to end up as a blueprint to be used in levels, and you learned how to do that.

Collectables without player interactions are not collectables. It is better to describe them as items. But in order to collect them, the player has to interact with and touch them, and you learned how to trigger overlap between them.

Now, I think that this is enough code. We have been writing code for the last couple of chapters. Let's take a break, and let's go for some eye candy. If you are done here, and feel that you have practiced pickups enough, let's go ahead and make some particles to give some life to our game.

6
The Magic of Particles

While the game (Bellz) looks amazing right now, if you keep playing it several times, you will always have the feeling that there is something not right. Something is going wrong, or more accurately, something is not in the right place. Despite that, the game still has no music or sound effects, which will give that feeling of being disconnected from the reality of the game world. However, what we are missing here, and what we need right now, is particles.

Is it right to leave the character running without getting some dirt out of the ground, based on foot-drag and interaction? Or even hitting the bears with an axe without getting some blood out of their bodies? It is not only dirt or blood that we need, but even the simplest particle systems that we can throw around the map will make a difference, and will make it pop with life.

Unreal Engine appreciates that desire to make things more detailed via particles, and takes really good care of the concept of particle systems. It is not only about giving particles their own types of assets to be made and used, but also about having a huge and independent particle system editor, called Cascade. Not only that, but this editor has full support for animation curves, which is enough to take us to a whole new world of particle behaviors.

And that's our mission now: get into the particles system workflow inside Unreal, master it, and support out game example with some particle systems.

By the end of this chapter you will be able to do the following:

- Understand the structure of a particle system's assets
- Master the usage of the particle editor (Cascade Editor)
- Build any particle system you have in mind, regardless of its complexity

- Use animation curves with particle systems in order to have more control over them
- Spawn particles at runtime in different ways
- Change particle parameters at runtime

Now, while we have what looks like an interesting plan, let's open the editor, and let's get started!

The particles editor

As you might already know, Unreal Engine is built in a way that makes it looks like it is a composition of several mini editors: an editor for character animations, another for materials, one for physics, and one more for the particle system, and so on.

Cascade is the proper editor inside Unreal Engine that is responsible for creating and editing particle system assets. Accessing Cascade is as easy as any other asset-based editor, like Material Editor for example. Just by double-clicking on a particle system asset from the content browser, you will be able to launch Cascade in a second:

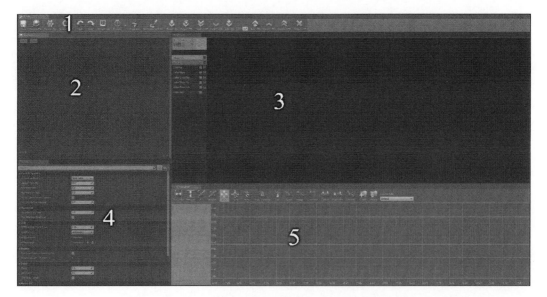

Once the particles editor is opened, you'll find it is designed in the same way as all other Unreal editors, with different areas that give you easy access to all the needed functionalities to achieve the goal of that editor. The good thing about Unreal is that all you want is just in front of your eyes, and you don't have to navigate through tons of huge menus with tons of submenus. The main areas that make up the Cascade editor are:

- **1**: Toolbar
- **2**: Viewport panel
- **3**: Emitters panel
- **4**: Details panel
- **5**: Curve editor

As each section is a huge corner of the editor on its own, let's get more detail about those sections, and let's dive into each part, as each parameter you can change, or each value you can enable, will have a huge impact on the final result or on the process of building particle systems.

Toolbar

This contains lots of buttons for the most commonly used tools, functionalities, and visualization orders, which you'll need all the time. Some of the buttons might be hidden at the UI due to the screen size, but in general the toolbar always contains the following:

All the buttons you find at this bar come in handy when you start the building process; while the Cascade Editor supports lots of keyboard shortcuts, sometimes it is faster to hit the buttons around the bar while you are already holding the mouse! The following are the options available on the toolbar:

- **Save**: This saves the changes into the particle system.

- **Find in CB**: This points to the current particle system asset at the content browser.

- **Restart Sim**: This restarts the simulation at the viewport panel.

- **Restart Level**: This restarts the particle system in general, which means not only at the viewport, but also all the instances inside the level.

- **Undo**: This undoes the previous operation.

- **Redo**: This redoes the previous undone operation.

- **Thumbnail**: This saves the current frame from the viewport panel's camera as a thumbnail image for the particle system to be displayed at the content browser.

- **Bounds**: Thus toggles on/off the display of the bounding shapes of the current particle system at the viewport panel.

- **Origin Axis**: This toggles on/off the origin axis at the viewport panel.

- **Background Color**: This changes the color of the viewport panel's background. It is black by default, but it is very useful in case your particle system itself is black; by changing the background color, you'll be able to get a better understanding.

- **Regen LOD, Duplicating Highest**: This regenerates the lowest LOD by duplicating the highest LOD.

- **Regen LOD**: This regenerates the lowest LOD by using values that are a preset percentage of the highest LOD's values.

- **Lowest LOD**: This loads the lowest LOD.

- **Lower LOD**: This loads the next lower LOD.

- **Add LOD before current**: This adds a new LOD before the current one.

- **Current LOD**: This selects the current active LOD, if you have set up LODs.

- **Add LOD after current**: This adds a new LOD after the current one.

- **Higher LOD**: This loads the next highest LOD.

- **Highest LOD**: This loads the highest LOD.

- **Delete LOD**: This deletes the current LOD.

The viewport panel

Just like any visual tool within Unreal Engine, such as the Material Editor, keep it a rule of thumb that, whenever you have to make an artistic visual piece of asset, you must have a small viewport inside its asset editor in order to display up-to-date changes while creating them.

It is just a small viewport that is meant to give you a real-time visual feedback of the final look of the particle system. As you know, changing values, colors, and settings, even with the least amount of change, could have a huge impact on the final result.

As with any other viewport inside the engine, it has some viewing options listed inside the top buttons, just like the main level viewport inside Unreal Editor. Also, it is responsive to the shortcuts, which means you can still navigate inside it in the same way you'd navigate inside your level, by using the mouse buttons or even some shortcuts, such as hitting *F* to focus on the particle system:

The viewing options include the following:

- **ViewOverlays**: This toggles between the different data readouts, which gives you lots of information about the current particle system:
    - **Particle Counts**: This shows how many particles are being emitted from each emitter at the current particle system
    - **Particle Event Counts**: This shows how many events have been triggered within each emitter at the current particle system

- º **Particle Times**: This shows how long each emitter of the current particle system has been active
- º **Particle Memory**: This toggles a display of particle system memory usage, both for the template and for each instance

- **View Modes**: The different options inside this menu allow you to switch between the different draw modes in the viewport panel. They are mostly the same as the ones inside the Level Editor viewport:
  - º **Wireframe**: The **Wireframe** view mode shows a wireframe of the particles. If the emitter uses sprites, you will see the two polygons which make up each sprite.
  - º **Unlit**: The **Unlit** view mode shows the result of the particles without lighting or post processing.
  - º **Lit**: The **Lit** view mode shows the result of the particles with lighting and post processing.
  - º **Shader Complexity**: **Shader Complexity** displays feedback on how many instructions are required for a particular shader. Green is the lowest value, and red is the highest value.

- **Detail Modes**: The **Detail Modes** submenu allows you to switch the viewport window between low, medium, and high detail. These correlate to engine detail modes, allowing you to see how a particle system will appear at each different mode. If you are using any but the high mode, you will see a visual text in the left corner of the viewport, telling you that you are looking at a specific one, just to save you from thinking that you are seeing the best quality right now:
  - º **Low**: This previews the particle system as it would appear when the system detail mode is set to low
  - º **Medium**: This previews the particle system as it would appear when the system detail mode is set to medium
  - º **High**: This previews the particle system as it would appear when the system detail mode is set to high

- **Background Color**: This opens the color picker where you can change the color of the viewport panel's background. It is the same as the one you find on the toolbar.
- **Orbit Mode**: This toggles camera behavior between orbiting around the particle system and moving freely in the viewport pane.

- **Origin Axis**: This toggles visibility for the origin axis gizmo. Works like the one you also find on the toolbar. The origin axis is always located in the lower-left corner.

- **Vector Fields**: This toggles on/off any vector fields applied to the particle system.

- **Grid**: This toggles on/off the viewport grid. It makes it easy to define the particle system in space.

- **Wireframe Sphere**: This shows a wireframe sphere representing the spherical radius of the particle system.

- **Post Process**: This toggles visibility of the global post process. Not always useful, but sometimes it makes you understand how it would look in case your game has some post processing effects.

- **Motion**: This toggles between on/off if the particle system remains stationary or revolves around the center of the grid.

- **Motion Radius**: Use its input field to set the radius of revolution for the Motion setting.

- **Geometry**: This shows or hides the default test mesh.

- **Geometry Properties**: This brings up the **Geometry Properties** window, where you can adjust the properties of the default geometry, adjusting placement, swapping out the mesh used, and many other options.

- **Bounds**: This toggles on/off for the particle system bounds, just like the one on the toolbar. These are shown as both a bounding box and a bounding sphere.

- **Set Fixed Bounds**: If you activated it, this fixes boundaries for the particle system and automatically sets the values to the largest setting.

Now, let's look at the timing options:

The timing options include:

- **Play/Pause**: This plays or pauses the simulation for the current particle system.
- **Realtime**: If checked, the simulation plays in real time. Unchecked, the simulation only plays when something updates the viewport panel.
- **Loop**: Either the particle system plays once, or it should restart once it reaches the end.
    - ○ **AnimSpeed**: With its submenu, you will be able to adjust playback speed percentage between **100%**, **50%**, **25%**, **10%**, and **1%**

The emitters panel

You have to know the difference between the particle system and the particle emitter. The particle system is the actual asset itself, which means it is an asset you can create in your content browser, and it is the final look of what you are building inside Cascade and the one used inside the game. The emitter is the unit used to create a system, which means the particle system could be made out of one particle emitter, five emitters, or even an unlimited amount of emitters!

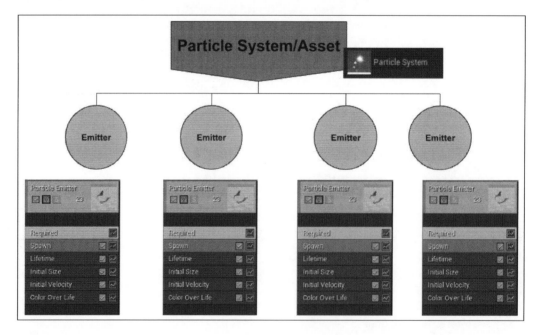

As a particle system is made up of one or more particle emitters, this is the place where you can add, select, edit, and arrange your emitters. Think about it as a graph area like the one with the Material Editor, or even like the Blueprint graph. This is where you put the actual content!

As it is just an area for all the emitters, you can call it **The emitter list**, as lots of people do:

It contains a horizontal arrangement of all the emitters within the current particle system and, regardless of the amount of emitters you decided to go with, this horizontal list will keep expanding for you.

Each column represents a single particle emitter, and each is made up of an emitter block at the top, followed by any number of module blocks, which are the parts used to define the behavior and look of that emitter.

The emitter block at the top contains the basic properties of the emitter, such as the name, editor color, details amount, and the type of the emitter; is also used to quickly enable/disable the emitter or even solo it to see it only at the viewport panel. The modules beneath it each control various aspects and behaviors of the particle:

Required, **Spawn**, **Lifetime**, **Initial Size**, **Initial Velocity**, **Color Over Life**, **Initial Rotation**, **SubImage Index**, **Sphere**, **Drag**, and **Size By Life** are all modules that control the emitted particles' behaviors.

Each module has three major ways to be controlled:

- Click the module inside the emitter to highlight it, and then start changing its values from the **Details** Panel.

- Click the checkbox at the module itself to enable or disable it quickly so you can get a better understanding of its effect over the whole emitter.

- Click the little graph icon at the right of each module to start controlling its value with a curve that you will be drawing inside the curve editor. As you can see, some of the modules have a colored strip at the far left (red or green); this tells us that the module already has a curve controlling it.

Creating a particle emitter from scratch, not giving you an empty emitter as an expected behavior for a modular particle systems editor. But, in fact, a base emitter must have the raw modules that control its particles with minimal requirements. As everything here is up to you, those initial modules could be removed totally if you want. But...they are essential in most cases!

But what if you want to add more modules?

Well, adding modules will give you control over the behavior and final look of the emitter or particle system. So, by right-clicking at the top of the emitter top, you are going to display a huge context menu of modules provided by Epic. The emitter context menu includes some parameters related to the emitter itself, but most importantly it contains all the modules that could be used:

Now think about it like this: the modules are the main unit that builds the emitters (while the emitter itself is the main unit for building the whole particle system), and modules are used to control the various aspects of the particles that are released by an emitter. How simple now?!

Once you realize the importance and the job of modules and emitters, you'll be able to build any system regardless of its complexity!

There are different modules that can be added to the particle emitters. Those modules are broken up into various categories based on their usage. The supported categories are as follows:

- **Acceleration**: These modules control the particle acceleration effects, such as drag forces and constant acceleration force
- **Attraction**: These are modules which control particle movement by attracting particles to various points in space
- **Camera**: These modules control the motion of the particle according to the camera space
- **Collision**: These modules help you handle collisions between particles and geometries
- **Color**: These modules control the color of the particles
- **Event**: These modules control the triggering of particle events, which can in turn cause a variety of in-game responses
- **Kill**: These modules control particle destruction
- **Lifetime**: These modules control how long particles should live
- **Light**: These modules govern particle lights
- **Location**: These modules control where particles will be born relative to the location of the emitter actor
- **Orbit**: These modules allow for screen-space orbital behavior to add extra motion to effects

- **Orientation**: These modules allow for a rotational axis of the particles to be locked
- **Parameter**: These modules can be parameterized or controlled via external sources such as Blueprints and Matinee
- **Rotation**: These modules control rotation of particles
- **RotationRate**: These modules control the changes in rotation speed
- **Size**: These modules control the scale of particles
- **Spawn**: These modules add specialized particle spawn rates, such as spawning particles per unit
- **SubUV**: These modules allow an animated sprite sheet to be displayed on a single particle
- **Velocity**: These modules control the velocity of each particle

Those are all the categories that you can find inside the Cascade module's context menu; feel free to start using the diffident ones from each category in order to learn about the slight difference between them. Also, checking the particle system reference guide from Epic's homepage is a good way to learn about the finer differences between each module.

The details panel

This is just like any other details panel you could find around the different editors of the Engine. And as is the habit with all other Unreal Editors, by default, if you are not selecting any of the emitters inside the emitters list area, this panel will display the overall properties for the particle system itself.

But, as a sensitive window, it will automatically change its content and its set of options and parameters, based on your selection. Go ahead and try to select the emitter itself to see what it can display, or even try to select between the different modules, and you'll notice that it always changes its content and shows you different settings and parameters. Here is exactly where the majority of the magic happens. That is, adding the correct module for the required situation is the trick, but it is trickier when it comes to setting the parameters of the module itself:

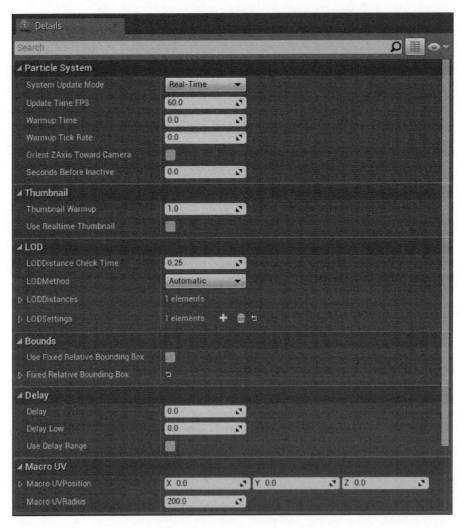

Now, after understanding how the details panel works, let's start to breakdown all the parameters that you can find there... almost all of them, starting with those related to the whole particle system, and then the ones relates to the particle emitter. The modules are different and the parameters for each are completely different, but there are a couple of attributes that are always the same within all the modules.

Particle system

A particle system is a complete particle effect made from one or more particle emitters. By allowing multiple emitters in the system, you'll be able to create particle effects that all belong to a single particle system. Then, you can use that particle system by spawning or inserting it into the level.

A particle system contains the following public parameters:

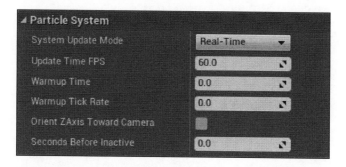

- **System Update Mode**: This defines the method the particle system should use to update all its emitters:

  - **Real-Time**: This updates the emitters in real-time.

  - **Fixed Time**: This updates the emitters at a fixed time step. This will lock the system to the update time of the game and is performance-dependent. By setting the value of **Update Time FPS**, you'll be able to control it. A lower frame rate lowers the update time of the system, which means a slower particle system, while a higher frame rate speeds it up. Try not to use this method a lot; it is best used when the particle system should give a certain behavior that is tied with something else that could get slower or faster than the rest of the game, for example, tying the emitter to an animation clip!

- **Update Time FPS**: This is the time-step to use when operating in **Fixed Time**.

- **Warmup Time**: This is the amount of time to warm up the system at launch. It will allow you to set an emitter to start at its behavior peak. While it is very useful in multiple cases, it can also affect performance, so use it sparingly, especially at high values. It is there to be used with particle systems you want to have started while the map initially loads, like a fire that is already there.

- **Warmup Tick Rate**: This controls the time step for each tick during system warmup (at the previous parameter). Increasing its value will improve the performance, and a value of **0** means the default tick time.

- **Orient Z Axis Toward Camera**: Setting it to `true` will force the local Z-axis of the particle system to be oriented towards the camera at all times.

- **Seconds Before Inactive**: This represents the number of seconds that, if the particle system is not rendered for it, it will go inactive and no longer be ticked. Using the value of **0.0** will prevent the system from ever being forced to be inactive:

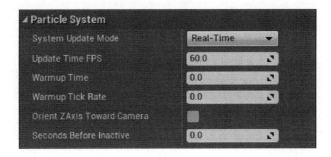

Thumbnail

Thumbnail consists of the following parameters:

- **Thumbnail Warmup**: The amount of time to warm up the system before capturing the thumbnail render when **Use Realtime Thumbnail** is checked.

- **Use Realtime Thumbnail**: If true, the thumbnail displayed in the content browser for the `ParticleSystemH` asset will be automatically captured using the default camera position and reflect the current settings and appearance of the particle system instead of using the saved thumbnail. Using real-time thumbnail rendering can slow down the performance of the content browser:

LOD

Here's what LOD consists of:

- **LODDistance Check Time**: This is how often, in seconds, the particle system should perform a distance check to get the LOD level

- **LODMethod**: This list contains options to define the method the system should utilize for selecting appropriate LOD levels:
    - ° **Automatic**: This sets the LOD level based on the LOD distance and checks the time automatically
    - ° **Direct Set**: The game will set the LOD level for the system to use directly
    - ° **Activate Automatic**: LOD level is determined at activation time, then left alone unless directly set by gameplay logic

- **LODDistances**: An array of distances you define in order to determine which LOD level to utilize while setting the **LODMethod** to **Automatic**

- **LODSettings**: An array of values to determine a few settings to use for each individual LOD:

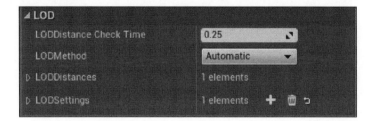

Bounds

Bounds consist of the following parameters:

- **Use Fixed Relative Bounding Box**: If true, the logic will utilize **Fixed Relative Bounding Box** as the bounds for the particle system.

- **Fixed Relative Bounding Box**: This allows you to set bounding boxes for the particle system. This is a good choice to make in order to reduce the overhead of performance while performing bounds updating each frame. You might need to right-click on the **Toggle Bounds** button on the toolbar and fill in this dialog box with the currently-used values of the dynamic box in Cascade; that will give you some values that you can use to start tweaking your **Min** and **Max** values in **Fixed Relative Bounding Box**:

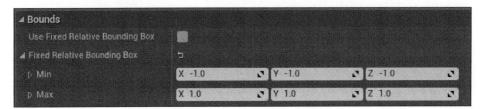

Delay

Within this section of parameters, you can set some custom timing values to control particles:

- **Delay**: The amount of time in seconds the particle system should wait before it gets active. It also represents the highest value of the range to use for choosing a random delay value when the **Use Delay Range** option is active.

- **Delay Low**: The lowest value of the range to use for choosing a random delay value when **Use Delay Range** is active.

- **Use Delay Range**: If true, a random value between **Delay Low** and **Delay** is chosen for the actual delay value to use:

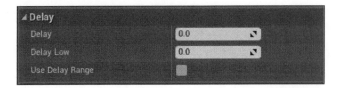

Macro UV

Using the **Macro UV** section, you can set more details for the particles' UV texturing:

- **Macro UVPosition**: The local-space position relative to the particle system used as the center point to generate the UV texture coordinates for the `ParticleMacroUV` material expression.

- **Macro UVRadius**: The world-space radius that determines the distance from the macro UV position where the UV texture coordinates generated for the `ParticleMacroUV` material expression will begin tiling:

Occlusion

Sometimes it is necessary to make sure particles that are out of the bounds get occluded, and within this section you can set the parameters for occluding particles:

- **Occlusion Bounds Method**: The method to use when calculating the occlusion of the particle system:
    - **None**: Occlusion is not calculated for the particle system
    - **Particle Bounds**: The bounds of `ParticleSystemComponent` are used for calculating occlusion for the particle system
    - **Custom Bounds**: **Custom Occlusion Bounds** (the coming value) values are used to calculate occlusion for the particle system

- **Custom Occlusion Bounds**: The bounds to use for calculating occlusion when using the **Custom Bounds** occlusion bounds method:

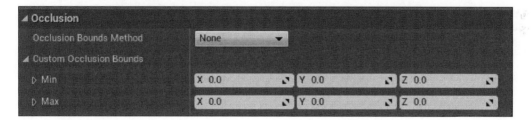

Materials

Here you can set an array of the materials used for particles.

- **Named Materials Slots**: An array of named material slots to be used by the emitters of this particle system. An emitter can use this array of materials rather than its own material:

The particle emitter

A particle emitter is the unit used to build a particle system. The particle emitter contains the following parameters.

Particle

Here we list the settings that you can set for each particle. Be aware that changing some values here might have an effect on performance:

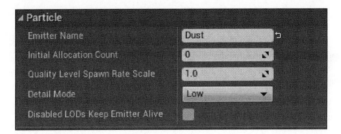

- **Emitter Name**: The name of the emitter.
- **Initial Allocation Count**: This value allows you to declare the number of particles that should be allocated at initialization of the emitter. If it is **0**, the calculated peak count is used.
- **Quality Level Spawn Rate Scale**: You can use this value to scale down the spawn rate of the emitter when the engine is running in the **Medium** or **Low** detail mode. It could be used to optimize the particle draw cost in split-screen mode.

- **Detail Mode**: Choose a detail mode to be applied; the **Low** option will cause give better performance; you've spawned several clones of the particle system, while the **High** detailed mode will cause more performance hits. The three modes are as follows:

  ○ **Low**

  ○ **Medium**

  ○ **High**

- **Disabled LODs Keep Emitter Alive**: Set it to `true` if your current LOD is disabled and you want the emitter to be kept alive and not considered as completed.

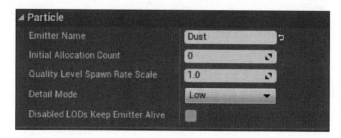

Cascade

Here you can find a few options, mostly used for display mode within the particle editor itself (Cascade). If you have lots of particle emitters within one particle system, it will be easier to differentiate them by colors defined in this section:

- **Emitter Render Mode**: The method to use when rendering the emitter's particles:

  ○ **Normal**: This renders the emitter's particles as intended

  ○ **Point**: This renders the emitter's particles as a 2x2 pixel block without scaling

  ○ **Cross**: This renders the emitter's particles as a cross of lines

  ○ **None**: The emitter's particles are not rendered

- **Emitter Editor Color**: The color of the particle emitter block when collapsed in the curve editor and debug rendering modes, as well as the strips at the emitter's title when it is not collapsed.

- **Collapsed**: Set to `true` in order to collapse the particle emitter in the Emitter List in the editor. Double-clicking on the particle emitter block gives the same result:

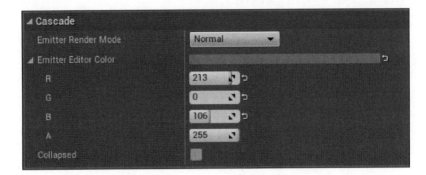

Particle modules

A particle module is the base of all modules (regardless of the type or functionality, each module has its own parameter list and the Cascade parameter list). This means that all modules will contain the following properties.

Cascade

This contains the following options:

- **3D Draw Mode**: If `true`, any 3D visualization helpers for the module, for example, wireframe geometry depicting the extent of an **Initial Location** module, will be displayed.

- **Module Editor Color**: This is the color the module will utilize in the graph editor:

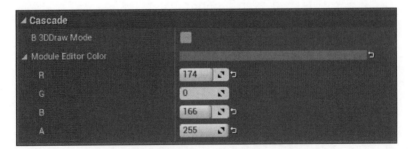

Curve Editor

To be honest with you, creating particles, or anything with a constant value, has always been tedious. But things started to change when the concept of curve editors and curve-based values came into the process.

Now it's different, and rather than saying the X value is going to be 1 all the time, you can say that the X value is going to start at 0.5 and reach 1.0 by the end of the lifespan of that particle; this could have a huge impact on behaviors!

One of the most powerful features of the Cascade Editor is the typical Unreal Editor Curve Editor panel (like the one used in Matinee Editor). At first glance, you might think it is not the proper place to have a Curve Editor! But once you know why it is there and how to use it, you'll definitely appreciate its existence:

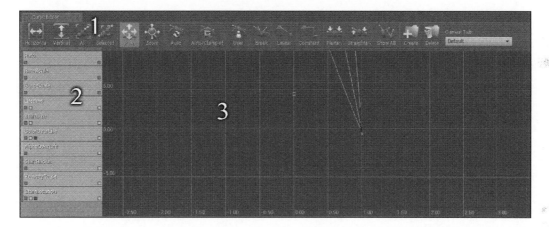

The curve panel allows you to adjust any of the module values that need to be changed along the life of a particle, or even along the whole life of an emitter. With this, you'll be able to have two types of values:

- Constant vales that will never be changed
- Dynamic values that always change over time

Any module property could be editable within the curve inside the curve editor, but the only condition is that the property must have a distribution type that can utilize a curve. A distribution type such as **DistributionFLoatConstantCurve** is used to control float values. As you can see in the preceding screenshot, the Curve Editor is simply divided into three main areas:

- Toolbar: A bar full of buttons that give you easy access to the important functionalities needed while drawing curves:

- ○ **Horizontal**: Horizontally fits the graph view to the current visible tracks
- ○ **Vertical**: Vertically fits the graph view to the current visible tracks
- ○ **All**: Fits the graph horizontally and vertically to the current visible tracks
- ○ **Selected**: Fits the graph horizontally and vertically to the selected points of the current visible tracks
- ○ **Pan**: Switches the Curve Editor into the **Pan** and **Edit** modes
- ○ **Zoom**: Switches the Curve Editor into the **Zoom** mode
- ○ **Auto**: Sets **InterpMode** (interpolation mode) for selected keys to the **Auto-curve** mode
- ○ **Auto/Clamped**: Sets **InterpMode** for selected keys to the **Auto-curve** mode
- ○ **User**: Sets **InterpMode** for selected keys to the **User curve** mode (user-modified tangents)
- ○ **Break**: Sets **InterpMode** for selected keys to the **Curve Break** mode
- ○ **Linear**: Sets **InterpMode** for selected keys to the **Linear** mode
- ○ **Constant**: Sets **InterpMode** for selected keys to the **Constant** mode
- ○ **Flatten**: Set selected keys/points tangents to be flattened horizontally
- ○ **Straighten**: Straightens selected keys/point tangents, if it was broken
- ○ **Show All**: Turn on/off the display of all key tangents

- ○ **Create**: Creates a new tab
- ○ **Delete**: Deletes the current tab
- ○ **Current Tab**: Allows you to choose the current tab if you've created multiple tabs

- **Track List**: A list of all the tracks you have within a particle system (In short list of the modules that is using curves to control its parameters):

This is the list where you find all of the curves currently loaded into the current tab. Each track in the track list has a name, representing the name of the property associated with the track. Also, each track in the list has a visibility switch button for each curve in the track and an overall visibility switch button to turn on/off all of the subtracks. In order to remove a track from the list, the easiest way is by right-clicking on a track in the track list; this will trigger the track list context menu, which has only two options:

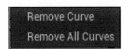

- ○ **Remove Curve**: Removes the current track from the Curve Editor
- ○ **Remove All Curves**: Clears all tracks loaded in the curve editor from all tabs

- **Graph**: The vast area with a vertical (value) and horizontal (time) axis on which to draw all your curves:

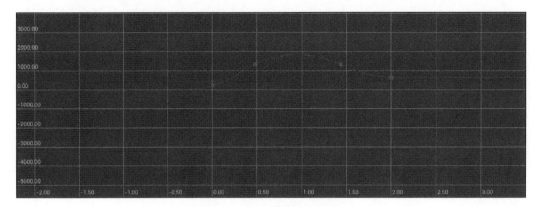

It is the most important and unimportant part of the curve editor panel! It sounds contradictory, but it is the truth. You can make an amazing particle system using Cascade without using graphs made by the curve editor at all, and it will still look amazing. But, at the same time, you might not be able to do anything without graphs! It depends on the visual look you are seeking, the game look, and the amount of complexity the particle system should have.

This area is a just a straightforward graphical representation of the value (the vertical axis) over time (the horizontal axis). The main unit that makes a curve is the **keys**; if you have one key only, then you don't have a curve, but if you have more than one key, then you have a curve. Keys are displayed as points (that is the reason you find me sometimes calling them keys, while at others calling them **points**), which can be selected and manipulated to visually edit the curve. Those keys could have different interpolation modes applied in order to directly change the key look, which will change the way that a key will lead on to the following one.

Right-clicking on the graph brings up the graph-sensitive context menu. While clicking on an empty area gives a general option on the context menu, clicking over a key/point will give you a whole different context menu. Right-clicking on empty space will display the following:

- ° **Scale All Times**: Scales the time values (horizontally) of all points on all visible tracks

- ○ **Scale All Values**: Scales the values (vertically) of all points on all visible tracks

Right-clicking over a key will display the following:

- ○ **Set Time**: Manually sets the time of the key
- ○ **Set Value**: Manually sets the value of the key
- ○ **Delete Key**: Deletes the selected key/keys

Interpolation modes

The interpolation mode buttons control the applied interpolation method that will be used at the curve point in order to allow a key on the curve to use that method to reach the next key. Some of these modes are a one constant result method, while others could be adjusted more freely. Methods such as `Break`, `Auto`, and `User`, will produce white handles for you; you can use those handles to take more control over the resulting curve between keys. The different interpolation modes supported by Unreal are as follows:

- **Auto**: Unreal will automatically define the interpolation between the keys and this might cause undesired behaviors:

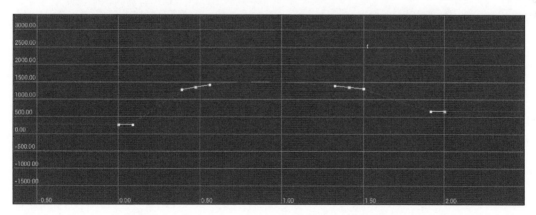

- **Auto Clamped**: The clamped are usually the best fit for you; it does a smooth interpolation between keys, while keeping things logical. For example, when you've two keys sharing the same value but at different times, the blend between both keys will be smooth without changing in values, which is missing in the **Auto Clamped** mode:

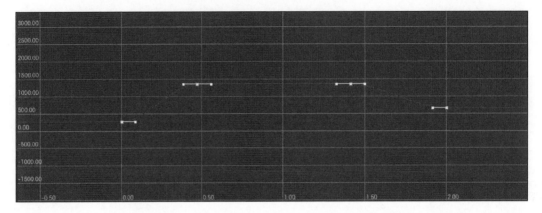

- **User**: This mode gives you the opportunity to adjust the look and feel of each key and curve:

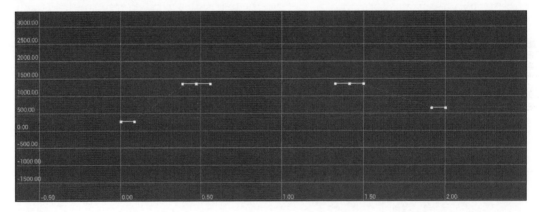

- **Break**: This mode is very special and extremely popular with lots of 3D packages. This mode will break each key into two separate handles; you can control each independently, and it is very good in the case of bouncy curves:

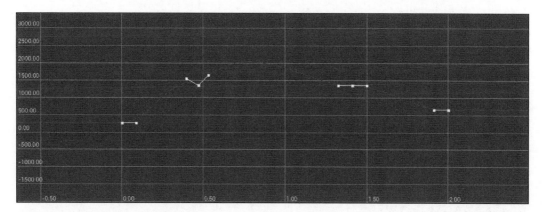

- **Linear**: This is one of the most used modes; the movements between keys are not smoothed at all, which means there isn't any type of ease in or out, and the interpolation will always be at one speed:

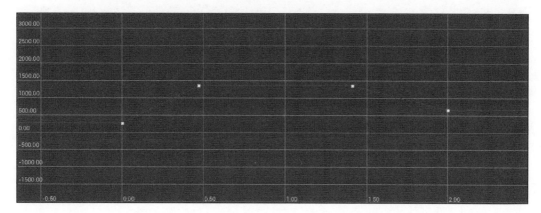

- **Constant**: This mode is mostly known as "Stepped" mode within the interpolation curve world. As you can see in the following screenshot, the interpolation just occurs at one frame, which means there isn't any type of interpolation at all, neither smooth nor linear. It is snappy:

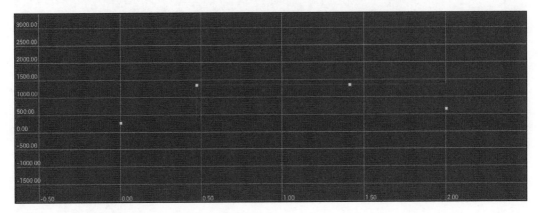

Organizing curves

We mentioned the importance of curves earlier in this chapter, and how they make results way more different and acceptable. But how could we force a value to use a curve rather than a constant value?

A few pages ago, while breaking down the emitter itself, and how it is constructed, we mentioned that there is a small button within each module that can make it controllable via curves.

This means that, to add a certain module to the curve editor, you just need to click on that green little box with a curve that appears on the far-left side of the module itself. This will produce a colored curve directly on the curve editor; you can remove it by simply pressing the button again.

Keep in mind that the color that is used to draw the curve is a randomly generated color, but you still can change it by selecting the module and editing its color from the **Details** panel, which is good for organizing stuff. Personally, I like to tag my curves in order to facilitate looking around them when things get more crowded!

Adding curves to the graph

Adding a curve is as simple as clicking on the previously mentioned curve icon in an emitter module; this will send any available curves for that module down to the curve editor.

Removing curves from the graph

In order to remove curves from the graph once you are done editing them, you just need to right-click over the block for the curve in the curve editor list, and choose **Remove Curve** from the context menu.

Organizing the curve editor with tabs

I have mentioned that we can change the colors of graphs in order to make things more organized. But that's not everything. The colors trick is good to differentiate between the different curves based on their goals. But what if you have to organize hundreds of curves?

There is more when it comes to being tidy here!

Have you ever thought about having around a hundred tracks inside one particle system that is made up of multiple emitters? Yes, it is possible, and in some cases, with the most complex systems, you might need to go beyond the first hundred. In that case, you can start adding tabs, which are mostly described as folders!

Just like adding folders inside the scene hierarchy in order to organize it, here you can add tabs as folders to include as many curves as you wish, and then give a general name for the tab.

Creating a new tab is easy; it can be created by pressing the toolbar shortcut button. Tabs can even be deleted with another shortcut button:

Spawning particles

Now Tabs ended up with particle system assets, basically inside the content browser—just an asset within a folder. But how can these be used inside the game or the map itself?

Well, when it comes to the usability, Unreal is the master, and as with anything else within Unreal Engine/Editor, there are various ways to help you achieve your goals. These are common and yet known methods that you can follow in order to use any particle system you have made:

- Drag and drop: This is the most common method, where you just drag the **Particle System** asset from the content browser, and drop it inside the map. But this method only comes into use when you are building the level, and you need to put some particles there by default, for example, when you need to put some fires around it.

- Animation notifications: This one of my favorite methods, as when we used it to call logic through notifications before, while building enemies and the player; the same approach could be applied here as well, and in fact the notifications menu has an option to spawn a particle. I usually use this method when the animation needs to be perfectly timed with the animations, something like footsteps, for example. Just choose the custom option called **PlayParticleEffect**:

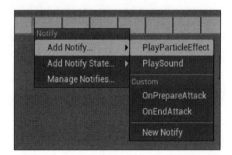

After that, and once you have the notification added to the animation timeline, you can select the notification, and that will open lots of parameters that you can set at the **Details** panel, not limited to but including the particle system itself:

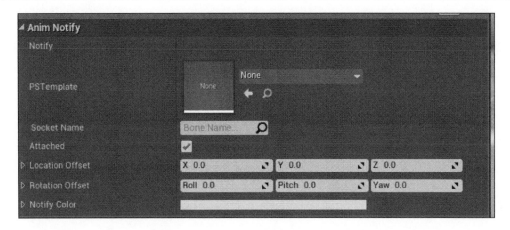

- Blueprint nodes: The other common method of spawning particles at runtime is by using a blueprint node. With the same approach you use for your gameplay logic, at any certain moment where you need to spawn a particle system, you can either call the **Spawn Emitter at Location** node, or **Spawn Emitter Attached**:

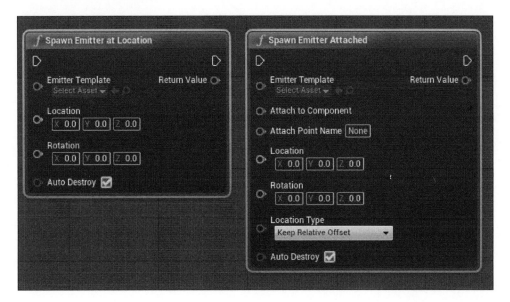

- C++ logic: As always, while there are methods to be followed in Blueprint, there must be methods to be followed with C++ code. At the end of the day, Blueprint logic is a visual form of the C++ logic. At any moment you need to write a magical line that spawns particles for you, you just either call the method `UGameplayStatics::SpawnEmitterAtLocation` or the method `UGameplayStatics::SpawnEmitterAttached`, which are basically just the equivalent of the blueprint nodes:

```
UFUNCTION(BlueprintCallable, Category="Effects|Components|Particle
System",
         Meta=(Keywords="particle system", WorldContext="WorldCon
textObject", UnsafeDuringActorConstruction="true"))
static UParticleSystemComponent * SpawnEmitterAtLocation
(
    UObject * WorldContextObject,
    class UParticleSystem * EmitterTemplate,
    FVector Location,
    FRotator Rotation,
    bool bAutoDestroy
)
static UParticleSystemComponent * SpawnEmitterAttached
(
    class UParticleSystem * EmitterTemplate,
    class USceneComponent * AttachToComponent,
    FName AttachPointName,
    FVector Location,
    FRotator Rotation,
    EAttachLocation::Type   LocationType,
    bool bAutoDestroy
)
```

Changing parameters at runtime

Sometimes a game forces you into strange situations. One of the situations I can remember in a game is when we needed to change the particle system color to match a certain color the player had collected. In such a case, it was not possible to define a color previously, and the particle system needed to be flexible enough to match the color the player already had, keeping in mind that every time the scenario is different and the player holds a different color.

Such a situation normally is not easy, but thankfully, with Unreal Engine, you can define the parameters that you might need to change at runtime. Then, changing its value is a matter of setting a new value to the tagged parameter. But how?

1. First you need to decide which value is going to be changed, and let's say I need to change the main color of the particle system. So, you simply go to the targeted module and to the desired value, and set its **Distribution** value to **Distribution Vector Particle Parameter**.

2. Now you need to give a name to the parameter, in the **Parameter Name** field. In my case, this is `theColorParameterRuntime`:

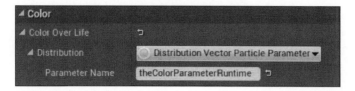

3. This given name is very important, as you are going to access the value using this name through the logic.

4. Now within the logic, once you have a reference to the particle, you can simply call a node such as `SetColorParamater`, in order to set the value, and don't forget to write down the parameter name:

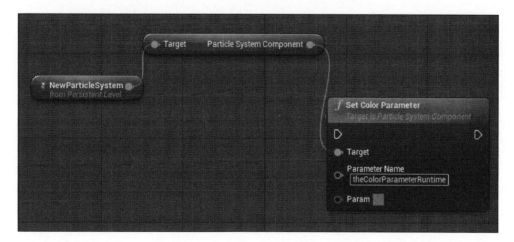

5. Keep in mind, I used the **Set Color Parameter** node, because the value I wanted to change was a color, but sometimes you need to change a `float` or `int` value, and there are plenty of those set nodes to serve the desired goal.

Summary

Congratulations, you have now got to grips with one of the most important and core parts that make Unreal an Unreal Engine. It is not only because of the importance of particles to the game's final look, but also because tons of artists and developers move into Unreal Engine, just for the sake of its powerful particle workflow. It is the best place to showcase a demo of 3D content!

You went through the particles editor step by step and understood all its sections, how to use each of them, and, most importantly, what each part is responsible for.

A particle system is an asset that is made out of several (or only one) particle emitters, and you've learned how to build any type of system you want.

A particle system asset is just another asset within the editor; you can have it already inside your maps, but it is more common to spawn it at runtime, and you have understood the several ways that you can use to spawn a particle at runtime. The engine provides more than one method, and you have to pick the one that is most fitting for the situation!

Sometimes, particles look better when you change them at runtime, and sometimes the story itself forces you to do that. You have just learned how to control any parameter at runtime, not only that, but also how to add an animation curve to support any value or parameter for the particle system.

Now I would recommend you go ahead inside your game sample, play it a couple of times, and try to notice what is going to familiarize yourself with particles. Come up with a list of required particles, and spend some time making them real, and most importantly, connect them after that with your game logic.

Once you are done, go ahead to the next chapter, and let's add some visual appeal to the final look of our map!

7
Enhancing the Visual Quality

Sometimes, building the game world and throwing some light sources in an artistic way is not enough to visualize the game world, and not even enough to support the game story.

As you know, working in a movie comes to a lot of editing, mostly in computers, using applications such as Adobe After Effects or Nuke. Using those apps has become essential for any media, as you can add some effects on the resulting movie or clip that lead to a huge dramatic effect and feel for the audience.

Games, as well, are a type of media, and games too can tell a story; even if the game has no story, the overall mode of the game can tell its own story. Color effects, or old screen effects using blur or such, and tons of other effects, can all deliver the content in a most appealing way.

And that's what we are going to do next. We are going to focus on the details of applying post processing effects and mastering the usage of the post processing volumes. We will also be looking into making lightmaps, in order to get the best out of lighting.

By the end of this chapter you'll be able to do the following:

- Create a friendly lightmaps environment
- Bake the lightmaps for better performance
- Understand the usage of the post processing volumes
- Master all the different post processing effects available within Unreal
- Use the reflection probes to enhance the reality of the levels
- Master the fog effects, and use them if needed

With all of this eye candy content are set in place, let's get started: open your game sample, and let's make it simply stunning!

The lightmass

Yes, you didn't read it wrong! Lightmass is the name Unreal engine usually gives to the term **lightmaps**. When it comes to baking the light data into maps (the lightmaps/lightmass), Unreal Engine has within its rendering toolset: the ability to bake the light data into this type of maps. These maps will be used later at runtime to light the level. The lightmass builds the lightmaps for the stationary light sources and the static light sources only.

And it is obviously clear why it does not supporting the dynamic (moveable) lights, as this type of lights can't be precomputed by any means.

The Swarm Agent

The process of building lightmaps is an automated one, which means there is no specific length of time that it will take. Based on your map or game and its complexity, building lightmaps could take too much time and performance from the machine.

But Unreal Engine is full of supporting tools that are built in such a way as to serve you by saving time and delivering the best content. There is a small C# tool that is connected to the Unreal editor, which plays the role of manager to handle the communications between the lightmass and the editor. That manager is called Swarm Agent.

Swarm Agent is autofired in order to perform its job and stay minimized (this means that you don't have to manually run it from somewhere); it was written to know the time that it has to start and finish its job and then shut down:

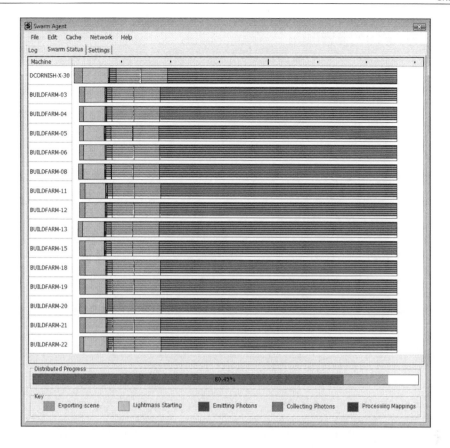

For more information about Swarm Agent, you can check the Unreal Engine 3 UDN documentation site, `http://udn.epicgames.com/Three/Swarm.html`, as Swarm was not well covered within Unreal Engine 4 now!

The ambient occlusion

We usually call the indirect shadow ambient occlusion. When lightmass gets built, it calculates the **ambient occlusion** (**AO** for short from now on).

Lightmass works by calculating AO, and then applying it to direct and indirect illumination, and finally baking it into lightmaps. The AO is enabled by default, but you can still disable it for your own artistic goals. Disabling it is very easy: you need to uncheck the checkbox **Use Ambient Occlusion** in **Lightmass Settings** of the **Lightmass** tab within **World Settings**:

Don't forget that you have to rebuild the lightmass in order to update it to the latest configurations you have changed (just hit the **Rebuild** button at the mid-top of the editor). A scene without AO really looks too different and less live than a scene with AO. You can check the difference between the following two images; while the first has the AO disabled, the second one has it enabled (check the edges' and corners' indirect shadowing):

That's how it will look when it is enabled. While those are just simple primitives, the shadowing around the corners, edges, and contact points makes them more acceptable and believable.

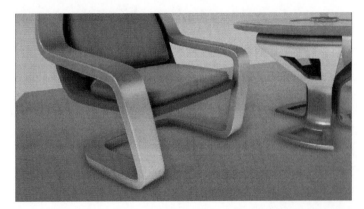

But as always, life is not a fairytale, and while there are advantages to something, there must be some disadvantages. The one and only disadvantage of AO is that it requires a high resolution light map in order to look as expected, and it never looks as expected as long as the quality setting is set to **Preview Quality**.

AO settings

For some people, AO is just an option to enable, and this is partly true. But sometimes, even enabling it will not give you the desired look, and then you have to start adjusting and tweaking some values to achieve the best visual fidelity:

- **Use Ambient Occlusion**: Enables and disables the feature.

- **Visualize Ambient Occlusion**: This is useful for seeing exactly what occlusion changes you made and comparing the effects of different settings as it works by overriding the lightmaps.

- **Max Occlusion Distance**: Maximum distance for an object to cause occlusion on another object.

- **Fully Occluded Samples Fraction**: Fraction of samples taken that must be occluded in order to reach full occlusion. Note that there is also a per-primitive **Fully Occluded Samples Fraction**, which allows control over how much occlusion an object causes on other objects.

- **Occlusion Exponent**: Higher exponents increase contrast.

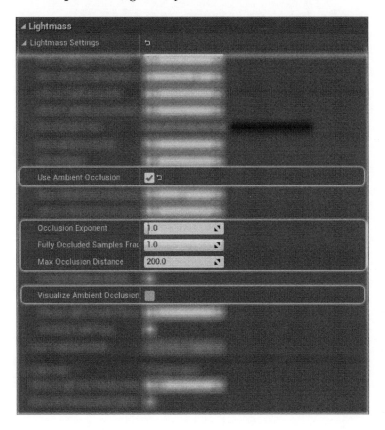

Lightmass settings

In order to get full control over Lightmass's final results, Unreal Engine gives you lots of attributes that you can adjust. Unfortunately, not all of them are in one place and they are scattered around the editor, which means there isn't one panel where you can adjust all the parameters related to Lightmass, and that is due to the wide modularity of the engine.

So if you are going to use Lightmass (which everyone does nowadays), you will need to adjust the settings for the level itself, as well as meshes, brushes, materials, light sources, and finally, the **Lightmass Importance Volume** value.

World Settings

The global **Lightmass** settings can be found under the **World Settings** window, within the **Lightmass** section:

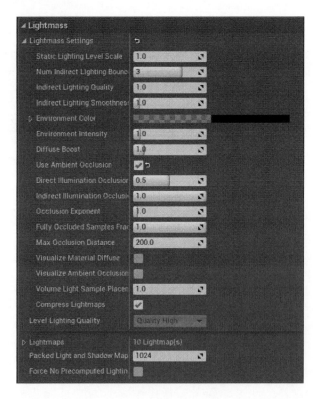

The various settings are as follows:

- **Static Lighting Level Scale**: While one Unreal Unit = 1 cm, this value represents the scale of the level relative to the scale of the engine. It is usually used to decide how much detail to calculate in the lighting. Logically, the smaller scales will increase build times.

- **Num Indirect Lighting Bounces**: The number of times light is allowed to bounce off surfaces, starting from the light source, with **0** being direct lighting only, and **1** being one bounce.

- **Indirect Lighting Quality**: This scales the sample counts used by the **Lightmass GI solver**. Higher settings result in fewer solver artifacts but longer build times.

- **Indirect Lighting Smoothness**: The higher the values, the more smoothing will be applied, which can hide solver noise but also causes detailed indirect shadows and AO to be lost.

- **Environment Color**: Color that rays which miss the scene will pick up.

- **Environment Intensity**: Scales the previous value to allow an HDR environment coloring.

- **Diffuse Boost**: Scales the diffuse contribution of all materials in the scene. Increasing **Diffuse Boost** is an effective way to increase the intensity of the indirect lighting in a scene. The diffuse term is clamped to 1.0 in brightness after **Diffuse Boost** is applied, in order to conserve the material energy (meaning light must decrease on each bounce, not increase). If raising the diffuse boost does not result in brighter indirect lighting, the diffuse term is being "clamped", and the light's **Indirect Lighting Scale** value should be used to increase indirect lighting instead.

- **Use Ambient Occlusion**: Enables static AO.

- **Direct Illumination Occlusion Fraction**: How much of the AO to apply to direct lighting.

- **Indirect Illumination Occlusion Fraction**: How much of the AO to apply to indirect lighting.

- **Occlusion Exponent**: Higher exponents increase contrast.

- **Fully Occluded Samples Fraction**: The fraction of samples taken that must be occluded in order to reach full occlusion.

- **Max Occlusion Distance**: The maximum distance for an object to cause occlusion on another object.

- **Visualize Material Diffuse**: Override normal direct and indirect lighting with just the material diffuse term exported to lightmass. This is useful when verifying that the exported material diffuse matches up with the actual diffuse.

- **Visualize Ambient Occlusion**: As discussed earlier, this is useful for seeing exactly what occlusion changes you made and comparing the effects of different settings, as it works by overriding the lightmaps.

- **Volume Light Sample Placement Scale**: While volume light samples are computed via the lightmass, that value will scale the distances at which volume lighting samples are placed. Using the larger scales will end up with fewer samples and less memory usage, and will reduce the indirect lighting cache update time.

- **Compress Lightmaps**: Enable or disable the texture compression. Disabling this will result in an increase of memory size and disk size, and will also produces a tidier texture with fewer artifacts.

- **Level Lighting Quality**: This reflects the current level's lighting build quality settings.

- **Lightmaps**: The list of Lightmaps textures.

- **Packed Light and Shadow Map Texture Size**: The maximum size for the packed light textures and the shadow maps.

- **Force No Precomputed Lighting**: Allows you to force the lightmaps and the other precomputed lighting to not be created even when the engine thinks they are needed. It is a useful choice for improving the iteration in level with fully dynamic lighting and shadowing.

Importance volume settings

Lots of your level parts are mostly there for the sake of having them; some parts are not visible to the player at all, while other parts are visible but are either unreachable (such as distant mountains, for example), or are not playable elements in interaction with the player.

Only the actual playable area needs high-quality lighting. While the lightmass emits photons based on the size of the level, the background and unused objects and meshes will be there just to increase the number of photons that need to be emitted! That will end up in higher lighting building time.

Here comes one of the most outstanding tools within Unreal Engine, **Lightmass Importance Volume**, which is meant to control the area that lightmass emits photons in, and allows you to concentrate the lightmass efforts. Any area outside the Importance Volume gets only a lower quality one bounce of indirect lighting.

As you can see this is a map of Bellz. At the first image you see the size of the full map, but actually what the player needs is the central part, which is in the second image.

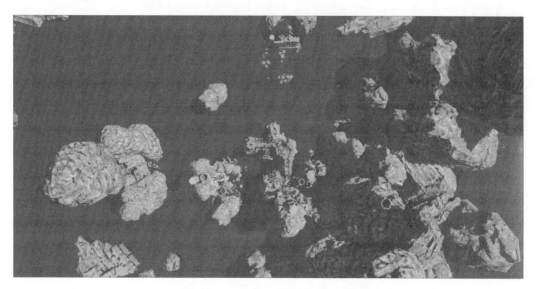

But while the focus area of the gameplay is a lot smaller, and centered in the middle of the map, there are lots of decorative assets far away, and background elements that the player will never reach. We have to put the Importance Area on the area of focus.

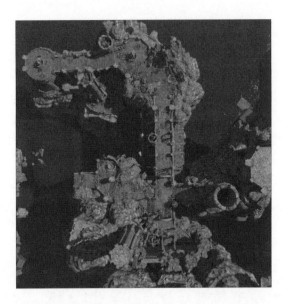

Adding the Importance Volume to the level is done the same way you add any other volumes. You just drag and drop them into the level, and you just need to know where to find them inside the **Modes** panel.

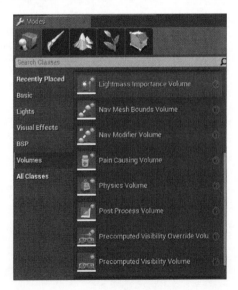

This is not the only way you can do that; actually, any brush shape within Unreal Engine could be used as an Importance Volume. You just need to convert the brush into the **Lightmass Importance Volume**, by selecting the actor and choosing the type of actor to be converted:

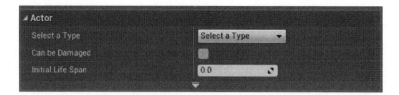

Then select the proper type from the list. This method is not only used to convert brushes into Lightmass Importance Volume, it could also be used to convert a brush into any of the types listed in the drop-down list. We used it a lot in *Chapter 3, Designing Your Playground*, while building the playground:

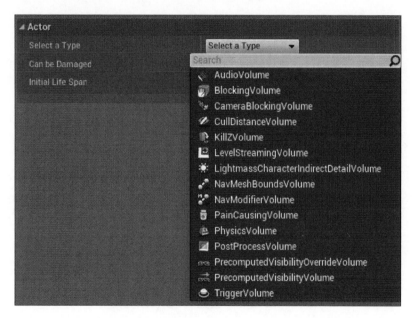

Once you've inserted the light source into the map, on selecting it, you have access to all its attributes and parameters within the **Details** panel. This set of settings not only indicates the light color and look, but also some **Lightmass** options related to the light shape itself:

- **Light Shape Settings**: Any light source that could be found within the Unreal Editor has some lightmass parameters that are listed inside the **Lightmass** section within its **Details** panel:

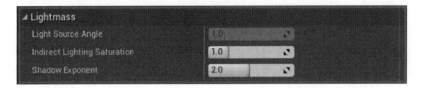

This consists of the following:

  ○ **Light Source Angle**: Determines the angle that the light's emissive surface extends relative to a receiver (but only for directional light sources)

  ○ **Indirect Lighting Saturation**: A value of **0** will result in indirect lighting being completely de-saturated; **1** will be unchanged

  ○ **Shadow Exponent**: Controls how fast areas change from fully lit to fully shadowed, or in a more technical sense, it controls the shadow penumbras falloff value

- **Material Settings**: Even a material asset has its own **Lightmass Settings** to be adjusted. To access them, you have to double-click the material in order to open it inside the Material Editor, then select the base node of the material, and finally find **Lightmass Settings** under the **Lightmass** section of the details panel:

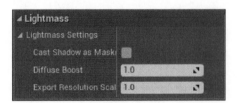

These settings consist of the following parameters:

  ○ **Cast Shadow as Masked**: Works with the translucent materials, as it is meant to treat the material as if it is masked for the purposes of shadow casting!

- ° **Diffuse Boost**: Scales up the diffuse contribution of this material to the static lighting

- ° **Export Resolution Scale**: If you needed to add more details to a surface using this material, then scaling up this value will scale up the resolution that this material's attributes are exported at

- **Brush Settings**: After adding a brush, you might need to apply some changes to it in order to be able to see its **Lightmass Settings** inside the **Details** panel:

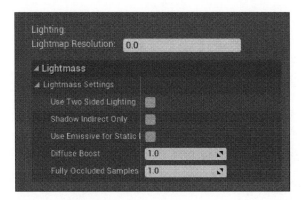

These settings consist of the following:

- ° **Lightmap Resolution**: The resolution of the lightmap.

- ° **Use Two Sided Lighting**: Setting it to true makes this object lit as if it receives light from both sides of its polygons.

- ° **Shadow Indirect Only**: If checked, this object will only shadow indirect lighting. This is useful for grass, since the geometry that is rendered is just a representation of the actual geometry and does not necessarily cast accurately shaped shadows. It is also useful for grass because the resulting shadows would be too high frequency to be stored in precomputed lightmaps.

- ° **Use Emissive for Static Lighting**: Setting this to `true` will allow you to use the emissive for static lighting.

- ° **Diffuse Boost**: Scales the diffusion of all materials applied to this brush.

- ° **Fully Occluded Samples Fraction**: This value allows you to control how much occlusion an object causes on other objects.

The post process project settings

Remember in *Chapter 1, Preparing for a Big Project*, while we were setting up the project and setting some of the major settings there, there were some parts that we left to be changed later, such as the post processing settings. Now it is time to change them.

As Unreal Engine was designed to give the best quality ever, there are already-activated post processing effects that your game/project will have by default, and you will be able to get their results inside your editor window while working once a project been made.

Those effects are there to give you a nice look, but are not mandatory; for example, if you are building a 2D game within Unreal that does not require any of the heavy bloom effects, or others, you can still disable or enable any of them upon your request.

You can access the effects from the **Rendering** section underneath the **Project Settings** window from the **Edit** menu. Pull all the way down to **Default Postprocessing Settings**, and then pick what you want and leave the rest:

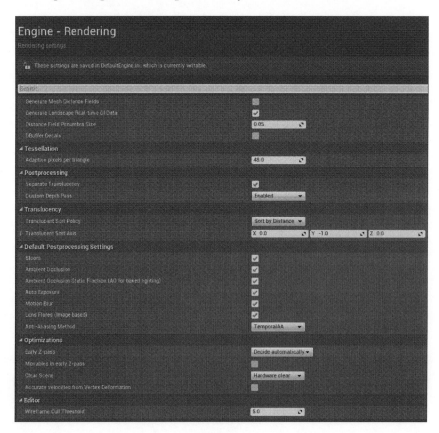

The post process volume

While you can have an overall post processing setting set up inside **Projects Settings**, you can still add more details and even apply post processing effects to a certain area within a map.

Just like all the other awesome features of Unreal Engine, this is handled by using a primitive, cubes, which is usually called volumes, to control it at runtime (or even at edit time, just as in this feature). The post process volume could be added to a level and then its position or size could be changed, which might be a reason for getting different results.

These types of volumes are the only possible way to manipulate post processing parameters. While other engines handle post processing by connecting them to the camera as components or something else, Epic decided a long time ago to go for it with regard to volumes. Why?

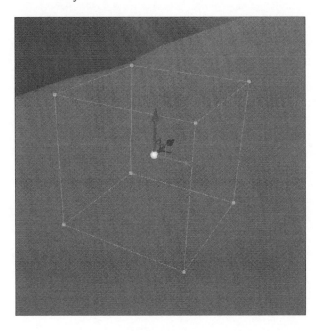

While the answer to that question is known only by the engineers who built the engine, it is very obvious that extendability is the reason behind most of the decisions made for the engine.

Let me go into more detail. If the volume is working as an attachable component or attribute to the camera, that means it will affect the overall look of the camera all the time, but the volumes within Unreal are different. They mostly affect the camera as long as it exists inside that volume... BRILLIANT!!!

That means you can have different blur types within the scene, just based on the spread of your volume. For example, if you have a character underwater, and he/she gets out of the water, you can apply two different volumes, one for the water area and the other outside. Both have different blur values; both have different color correction. Unreal will make the transition, while your character/player navigates between both. Brilliant, isn't it?

After all, Unreal still adds a default post processing class/struct into each camera, so you can set up the different post processing effects per camera too, if that makes you consistent with whatever background you came from:

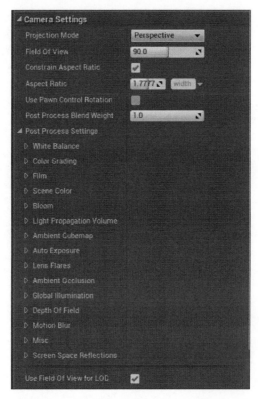

Each post processing volume within Unreal Engine works as a blend layer, while other blend layers might be a result of something else, like another post process volume or UI, for example. Each layer could have a weight, so you can blend between the different effects with a linear interpolation curve (that is, **lerp**). As mentioned earlier, the reason behind having volumes is that it makes sense that the post process volume will only be applied and blended when the camera is within its bounding box, unless the **Unbound** property is checked (check the next paragraph, don't just wonder!).

Epic's team was very smart when designing that system within the **Rendering** toolset. What if the designer wants to give one color tine, one mood, and one bloom value for the whole level? Does it make sense to have a GIANT post processing volume to affect the whole level, and just scale it up? Or does it make sense to just keep putting volumes all over the level?

What they found makes sense was actually what I really feel makes sense. They just put a property within the post processing volume that is set to either `true` or `false`. That attribute, called **Unbound**, if checked, means that the post processing volume will affect the entire scene, regardless of its size, and regardless of the camera's position within it.

What made that make really perfect sense is that it fits the concept of the level blueprint; while there is a normal blueprint per object or per actor, there is a global blueprint for the entire level. It is the same here: if you just set that small property, then the volume will be a global effector for the level.

The properties

Here is a list of the normal properties found in the post process volume, regardless of which effect you are going to use, meaning that those are the normal minimum requirements for a post process volume:

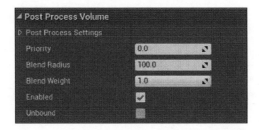

Here you go:

- **Post Process Settings**: This is an expandable list that contains **Post Process Settings** for all the effects for that volume:

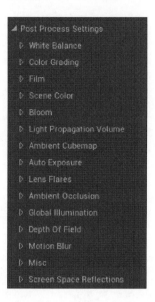

- **Priority**: The order when it comes to blending multiple volumes. The volume with the highest priority value will take precedence over all other volumes overlapping with it.

- **Blend Radius**: Distance measured in Unreal units around the volume at which blending with the volume's settings takes place.

- **Blend Weight**: The amount of influence the volume's properties have. A value of **1** means it is a full effect, while the value of **0** means there is no effect.

- **Enabled**: Shows if it is working or not.

- **Unbound**: Remember, that's the local VS global option! It defines whether the bounds of the volume are taken into consideration or not. If the value is `true`, the volume affects the entire level, regardless of its bounds or position from the camera. If it is set to `false`, the volume only has an effect within its bounds and on the camera inside those bounds.

  One thing to mention is that if the volume is going to be **Unbound**, the **Blend Radius** value will be disabled as it makes no sense to use it any more.

The available effects

Unreal Engine has lots of different post processing effects in order to guarantee your full control over the final look of each pixel in your games. As it is not only one effect or one parameter: the following is a list of all the support post processing effects in detail for each one of them. Just keep in mind that they are not ordered with their priority or with a certain rendering order, but are just ordered as they are found on a **Post Processing Volume** details panel.

While the effects used to be arranged within the settings panel in a different order, as the engine keeps upgrading, Epic keeps adding new effects and arranging the whole menu in a different way. The available effects include:

- **White Balance**
- **Film**
- **Anti-Aliasing** (AA)
- **Bloom**
- **Color Grading**
- **Depth Of Field** (DOF)
- **Auto Exposure** (Eye Adaptation)
- **Lens Flares**
- **Post Process Material**
- **Scene Fringe**
- **Vignette**
- **Grain**
- **Screen Space Reflections**
- **Light Propagation Volume**
- **Ambient Occlusion**
- **Global Illumination**
- **Motion Blur**
- **Screen Percentage**

There may be a few more effects that could not be listed, or could even be classified as color corrections (but there is not an actual list or tab named color correction). I decided to include a list of the available post processing effects, as the menu is not super clear. For example, **Anti-Aliasing** is a world standard post processing effect nowadays, but there is not an actual menu or tab with that name, and the AA options are listed under a **Misc**. menu.

It is the same for the popular **Fringe**, **Vignette**, and **Grain**. As the three of them are super popular and famous world standard effects, they are tabbed under one menu, named **Scene Color**. So, the preceding is just for your reference to let you know what you have and can achieve with the post processing volumes.

Go ahead and keep enabling and disabling the different effects, keep changing values, to understand how the end result will look. The effects' names are self-explanatory, but believe me, the best practice here to learn all of them is by enabling and disabling them to learn about their effect.

One rule of thumb I would give is that when you change any value for a certain effect, try the highest and the lowest values; both will give you an idea of what you could achieve in between!

Reflection Capture

Sometimes, by design, the map or level has to reflect something. Having a mirror, water drops, or metallic parts around will never look real without reflecting some parts of the environment. And that's when it is time to use **Reflection Capture**.

Reflection Capture is not only the name of an actor you use inside the editor, but also the functionality itself at the same time. While having real-time reflections is really costly performance-wise, it is possible to reduce that cost using **Reflection Capture**.

Simply, it is the same concept as lightmaps; you can bake those things earlier in a sort of a map and use them later at run-time. Unreal Engine has inside its toolset what is called **Reflection Environment** via the **Reflection Capturers**.

The **Reflection Environment** toolset provides efficient reflections in all the directions of the scene, just like metal surfaces (the idea is to have objects that have materials with a high and noticeable specular and a low roughness values, so it is not only metals!). While it sounds like an awesome feature, the only con for it is that it does not provide reflections of moveable (dynamic) objects or sharp reflections, which usually could be achieved using other Unreal methods, just like **Screen Space Reflections**.

By setting up some light sources and building the lightmass once, you are ready to start setting up the reflection environment. You will never be able to build it without having a prebuilt lightmap, as its calculations are based on having indirect diffuse lighting around the scene.

Setting up the reflection environment is super simple. It is done usually by inserting the **Sphere Reflection Capture** actor into the scene (mostly we use the sphere shape, but still there is a cube one, and we will discuss the differences later):

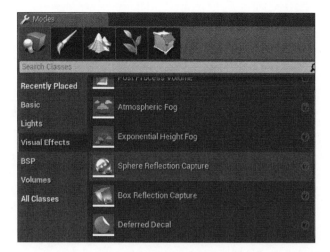

Reflection captures acts a lot like lightmaps. It needs to be baked several times, and all the time, as it is not always kept up to date. That means that if you added a new object into the scene, moved an object, or even made any change to the scene's look, those changes will not be captured.

Only loading a map or building lighting will update the reflection captures. So anytime you make a change and you want it to be included and captured, you have to select a capture and click **Update Captures** in order to capture the latest changes:

As with all the other optimizations you are going to make with Unreal, there is always a way to visualize and review the changes you make. While you are able to display the indirect light cache, you are able to display what is being captured by the **Sphere Reflection Capture** actor by enabling the **Reflection Override** view mode. And you'll see how reflective the surfaces that you have are:

The way the reflection environment mechanic works is very simple. It works on capturing the static objects of the scene at different capturing spots and then projecting them as a reflection onto simple surfaces like spheres; that's the reason behind the spherical shape of the capturer actor.

The capturing spots are manually selected by you; by just placing the **Reflection Capture** actors, you ask for Unreal to define this area as a reflection capturing area. And as long as you are inside the editor and building up your levels in **Edit** mode, the reflections on the spherical shape will keep updating in real-time during the editing process. But once you hit **Play** or package your project into a game, then the reflections will be static during runtime.

Reflection Capture actors

There are two reflection capture actors supported by Unreal Engine. You can find both of them listed in the **Modes** panel:

The main difference between them is the shape of the capturer itself, as the shape of it is the most important element of this process. The shape works by defining which parts of the scene are captured into the cubemap and then which part of the scene can receive reflections from that cubemap. The supported two shapes are as follows:

- **Sphere shape**: The sphere shape is the most useful one as it has no corners (discontinuities) and it is hard to match the reflected object.

  As you can control the radius of the effect, smaller captures will override larger ones, so you can provide refinement by placing smaller captures around the scene. Imagine that you have a room, putting a large one in the middle while putting smaller ones in the corners will be your best solution to get it all perfectly done.

  Using the orange gizmo surrounding the sphere shape that is visualizing the radius, you can control which pixels can be affected by the cubemap:

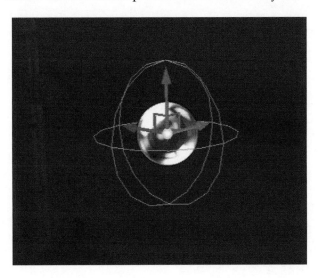

- **Box shape**: It is easier to call it the useless shape, or the limited one, as it only works well when it is used with rectangular rooms, but still, lots of people use the sphere shape for that situation too! Lots of people just don't trust it for the sake of being a cube, as it produces lots of artifacts due to the projection onto a box shape:

As is the case with the sphere, the box has a gizmo that displays its range too (also in an orange color).

The fog effects

While all other engines support only the **Fog** feature, Unreal Engine's team decided to give us two types of fog, based on the targeted usage; each type has its own parameters that could be used to define its look. The two supported fog types are:

- **Atmospheric Fog**
- **Exponential Height Fog**

Atmospheric Fog

Atmospheric Fog gives you an approximation of light scattering through a planetary atmosphere:

Adding it

By adding an actor from the visual effects section of the **Modes** panel, you will have the **Atmospheric Fog** type installed into your level directly:

Here's how to add it:

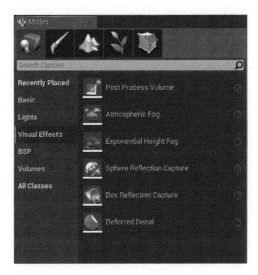

In order to be able to control the final visual look of the recently inserted fog, you would have to make some tweaks to its properties attached to the actor:

- **Sun Multiplier**: An overall multiplier for the directional light brightness. Increasing this value will not only brighten the fog color, but will also brighten the sky color as well.

- **Fog Multiplier**: A multiplier that affects only the fog color (not the directional light).

- **Density Multiplier**: A fog density multiplier (not affecting the directional light).

- **Density Offset**: A fog opacity controller.

- **Distance Scale**: A distance factor compared to the Unreal unit scale. This value is more effective with very small worlds. While the world size increases, you will need to increase the value too, as larger values cause changes in the fog attenuation to take place faster.

- **Altitude Scale**: The scale along the z axis.

- **Distance Offset**: The distance offset in KM in order to manage large distances.

- **Ground Offset**: An offset for sea level (normally the sea level is **0**, and while the fog system does not work for regions below sea level, you need to make sure that all terrain is above this value in order to guarantee that the fog works).

- **Start Distance**: The distance from the camera lens that the fog will start.

- **Sun Disc Scale**: The size of the sun disc; keep in mind it couldn't be 0, as before, there was an option to disable the sun disc, but in order to keep it real, Epic decided to remove that option and keep the sun disc, but gives you the chance to make it as small as possible.

- **Precompute Params**: Recomputation of precomputed texture data:

    ○ **Density Height**: Fog density decays height controller. The lower the values, the denser the fog will be, while the higher the values, the less scatter the fog will have.

    ○ **Max Scattering Order**: A limit on the number of scattering calculations.

    ○ **Inscatter Altitude Sample Number**: Number of different altitudes where inscatter color will be sampled:

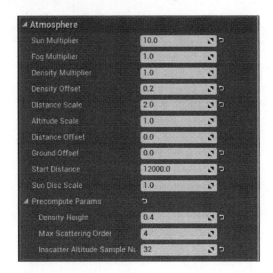

Exponential Height Fog

That is a special type of fog, which has some requirements in order to work perfectly. While the **Atmospheric Fog** type can be added anytime or anywhere and it works, the **Exponential Height Fog** type requires a special type of map where there are low and high points, as its mechanics include creating greater density at the low places of a map and less density at the high places of the map, and there will be a smooth transition between both areas.

One of the most interesting features of **Exponential Height Fog** is that it has two fog colors, the first one is for the hemisphere facing the dominant directional light, and the second one is for the opposite hemisphere:

Adding it

As before, adding the volume type is very simple: from within the same **Visual Effects** section of the **Modes** panel as before, you can select the **Exponential Height Fog** actor, and finally drag and drop it into the scene. But as you can see, even the icon infers the high and low places from the sea level!

In order to be able to control the final visual look for the recently inserted fog, you would have to do some tweaks to its properties attached to the actor:

- **Fog Density**: The global density controller of the fog.

- **Fog Inscattering Color**: The inscattering color for the fog (the primary color).

- **Fog Height Falloff**: The height density controller; this controls how the density increases as height decreases.

- **Fog Max Opacity**: The maximum opacity of the fog. A value of **0** means the fog will be invisible.

- **Start Distance**: The distance from the camera at which the fog will start.

- **Directional Inscattering Exponent**: The size of the directional inscattering cone.

- **Directional Inscattering Start Distance**: The start distance from the viewer of the directional inscattering.

- **Directional Inscattering Color**: The color for directional inscattering, used to approximate inscattering from a directional light.

- **Visible**: The fog visibility.

- **Actor Hidden In Game**: Enable or disable the fog in-game (it will not affect the editing mode).

- **Editor Billboard Scale**: The scale of the billboard components in the editor:

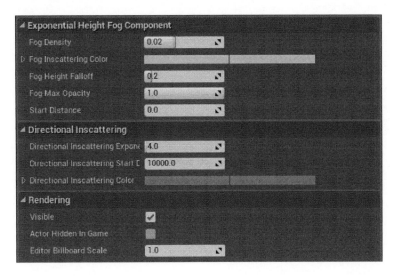

Summary

Congratulations! Reading the summary means that you reached the end of this chapter. Well done!

Having lights within a game is essential, and without light sources you will probably see nothing. But there should also be wisdom behind this process; adding too many light sources could come at a cost, and the game performance might get worse. But having something like lightmaps makes it easy to do all the lights you want, make the map look just like it should, and just bake the lightmaps, and that will save the day. You just learned not only this process, but also how to be prepared for it.

You have also gone through lots of fun, and specially through the post processing volumes, and how and why you would use them. All their parameters and the effects that can be achieved using them, all of that you went through from zero to hero and you have simply mastered it.

Sometimes the environment has to reflect something; it might be water doing it or even a mirror, but doing real-time reflections is always costly, and not recommended in games, but there is always a way around that. You have just mastered how to use the reflection probes to achieve such a result.

Fog is one important feature within any engine; it doesn't have to be used in the form of fog, but using it always has its own dramatic effect and impact over the story and the gameplay experience, and you just learned the different types of available fog and how to use them.

Now go ahead and keep tweaking the visual look of your maps, and once you are pretty satisfied, go ahead and take some screenshots; yes, you are in a great moment now, so share them on Twitter, and don't forget to use some hashtags to reach more of the Unreal and game dev community. Use things like #unrealengine or #ue4, #gamedev, and #indiedev, which are all active hashtags. Once you have done, go straight away to the following chapter, where we are going to learn how cinematics are made in games!

8

Cinematics and In-Game Cutscenes

Cinematics, what a wonderful thing we have in games nowadays. Regardless as to whether the game is based on a story or not, games usually have cutscenes. If it is not to tell a story, then it is to direct the player correctly through the game.

While some companies prefer to create their cutscenes within a third-party animation software such as 3dsMax or Maya, and pretender it, in order to get the best quality, other companies prefer to do the cutscenes in the engine itself, in order to get the smoothest experience. Both are fine, but the last one is the best. But why?

Well, creating cinematics and prerendering them outside the engine, will give an unexpected level of quality that is not consistent in the game, so the player experience will be like a zigzag; a player will enjoy a certain level of quality while playing, but a totally different quality while watching the cutscenes.

But using the in-engine solutions in order to create the cinematics will not only make sure that the player will be seeing all the game and its movies with a specific quality, but also once a cutscene ends, the player will move smoothly into the gameplay.

It is very common in some games that by the end of a cutscene, your character is holding a gun, but once you go back to the gameplay again, you find him holding another weapon; that's because of the predictions the designers made. But if the cutscene is being rendered in real-time in the engine, then whatever weapon or position your character has by the end of the cut scene, the gameplay will continue within the same flow!

Cutscenes or cinematics within an Unreal Engine are very easy to create, as long as you have, as the responsible editor, the basic knowledge of animations and key frames. Matinee is just like a curve or tracks editor; no more.

Keep in mind, while Matinee is the cinematic solution within Unreal right now, there are better and more powerful cinematic solutions being developed by Epic, one such solution being Sequencer. It is currently enabled for experimental usage. Which means that in the near future, within 4.12 or 4.13, you might start using Sequencer rather than Matinee.

By the end of this chapter, you'll be able to perform the following tasks:

- Understand and use Matinee
- Create cutscene actors in different ways
- Understand the difference between the tracks
- Use the Director to create a mix between cameras and actions
- Animate anything and add it to a cinematic
- Run the cinematic at certain moments
- Save the cinematics into a video format

With all that said, let's get started!

Matinee actor (cinematic actor)

Let's now stop referring to cinematic or cutscene, and let's call it Matinee, as this is how the Unreal Engine is calling it within the ecosystem. So just to make it clear, in case any of your maps include Matinee, that means you need to add a Matinee actor into this map. You can have endless amounts of Matinee actors inside one map; there is no limit, and it is back to your needs and story.

But you have to keep in mind that one Matinee can't call another one, which means you can't do half of the show inside one Matinee actor, and try to call another Matinee to continue the show. This is not going to work, and that's the reason behind the topic of Director, which will be discussed later in this chapter.

So, think about it in this way: one Matinee actor equals one piece of cinematic. Keep in mind, those Matinee actors are parts of the map, which means, they can't be part of the content browser, or to put it another way, they are not assets, they are just part of an asset, which is the map.

So, you can't create a Matinee inside the content browser and drag and drop it into the map; this will not happen. The only thing related to a Matinee that you can create at the content browser, is called Matinee data, which basically involves holding two attributes to be used within any Matinee, and you'll rarely need this!

Now, if we want to introduce the Matinee actor into the scene, in order to start creating some sort of in-game cinematic, there are two methods to create a Matinee:

- From the top menu bar, you can choose the **Cinematics** button, and this will give you two options, either to create a new Matinee through the **Add Matinee** button, or you will find a list of the current Matinee actors inside the current map, and clicking any will open it. Keep in mind, once you choose **Add Matinee**, the newly created one will be exactly at the center of the current view, not at the zero of the map as most people would expect.

- The other way is via the **Modes** panel; you can find the actor inside the **All Classes** section.

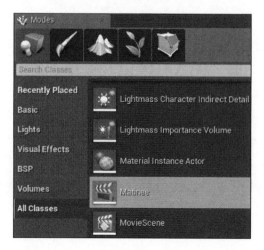

Whichever way you decide to follow, you'll have the Matinee inside the map, represented with this icon:

The Matinee Editor will launch right away for you. If it doesn't, then as you know, clicking the **Cinematic** button at the top bar will get it for you.

A Matinee actor, apart from being a special type of actor that is designed to create those fancy in-game videos, also has some default settings that you can tweak for a better result or specific result. By selecting **Matinee Actor**, you will activate its parameters set within the **Details** panel.

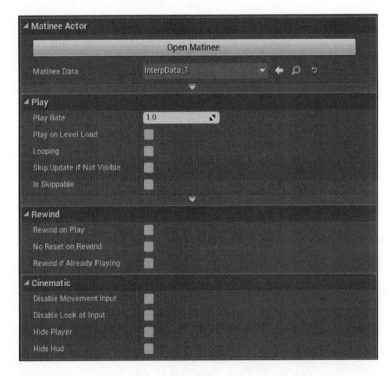

The various options are:

- **Matinee Actor**: This has the following options:
    - ○ **Open Matinee**: It is another way to open the Matinee Editor
    - ○ **Matinee Data**: As mentioned before, you can create the data asset and then refer to it here

- **Play**: This has the following options:
    - ○ **Play Rate**: The multiplier for playback speed.
    - ○ **Play on Level Load**: If this set to `true`, once the map is opened, the cinematic will run.
    - ○ **Looping**: Is it going to loop? However, be aware that if it is loopable, you have to stop it through the logic.
    - ○ **Skip Update if Not Visible**: A Matinee is just a set of animation tracks for some actors. Setting this option to `true` will skip playing Matinee, in a case where all the actors involved in this Matinee are not visible.
    - ○ **Is Skippable**: Is the player allowed to cancel this cinematic? This is good when some parts of the game are really important to the flow, while other parts are not essential to watch.
    - ○ **Is Playing**: It returns the current state of the Matinee.

- **Rewind**: This has the following options:
    - ○ **Rewind on Play**: Setting this to `true`, will force the cinematic to play in reverse, from the back to the start.
    - ○ **No Reset on Rewind**: When setting this to `true`, and the previous option is `true` as well, once the first play is completed, and this Matinee is going to loop, the animations will start from the last positions.
    - ○ **Rewind if Already Playing**: What if you gave a **Play** command to the Matinee while it was still playing? This option determines if it is just continuing or rewinding.

- **Cinematic**: This has the following options:
    - ○ **Disable Movement Input**: Disable or enable the player controller movement.
    - ○ **Disable Look at Input**: Disable or enable the player mouse or analog sticks.

      ∘   **Hide Player**: Hide the player or keep it as is.

      ∘   **Hide Hud**: Keep the UI or just hide it. But keep in mind that some UI like a UMG at the world space will still be shown.

The rest of the settings are the same ones shared between all actor types, such as **Transform**, **Rendering**, and **Actor**.

Matinee Editor

Once you open Matinee Editor, you'll find it split into four main sections. Those sections are as follows:

- **Toolbar**: It has the main controls that will allow you to insert the keys, play or stop, or even set some helpful values for display, such as the playback speed for instance:

- **Curve Editor**: Once you have done some animations, you have the chance to push it even further forward, but changing the ease of the movement in order to fasten or slow it down. All that could be done through the Curve Editor. By the way, this is exactly like any other curve editor within Unreal, such as the particles Curve Editor, for instance:

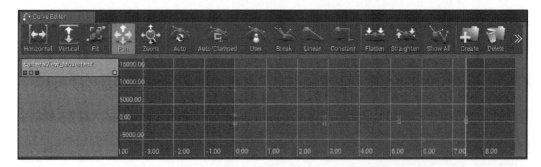

- **Tracks**: As we discussed earlier, a Matinee actor is just a set of actors with animated values. Those animated values have been set inside **Tracks**. Here in this section, you can add the actors and the tracks and keep them organized. For example, if you have a character that needs to move, apply animation. You'll probably be creating a folder named with the character name, and will add two tracks inside this folder, a track for the animations and a track for the positioning:

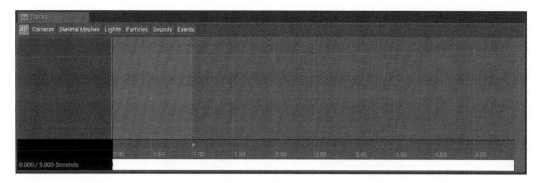

- **Details**: The **Details** panel shows the parameters that could be changed, just like any **Details** section of the Unreal Engine. But this panel usually is disabled. The only way to enable it is either by selecting a track from the **Tracks** section, or by selecting a key. In both cases, the **Details** panel will show only what could be changed:

Now you probably have an idea about what is the main goal of this editor, and what are the sections of it, and most importantly the functionality that each section serves. Now let's go ahead in more detail, and discuss the two major components that make a Matinee actor, namely the groups and tracks.

Groups

Groups exist in the **Tracks** area of the editor only. It is the Unreal way to make things organized and tidy. Think about a huge cutscene, where there are lots of characters and enemies, vehicles and weapons, and firing. Just think about creating a war cutscene! That will make the **Tracks** area super crowded. And here comes the solution of creating what is like a folder to contain some tracks. For example, one character in that war scene, will have at least three tracks: animation, movement, and animation blueprint. Multiplying this minimum amount by the amount of actors that need to be animated is crazy. But if you created one folder per actor that can host as many tracks as it takes, then life will be easier. And if you have 10 character fighting, then you'll have 10 groups/folders for each, regardless of the amount of tracks. You can then open or close, or hide or disable, each group/folder.

A group, by default, is a normal group. It has only one parameter, which is the group name. And here we see the extendibility of Unreal. Rather than giving us only one type of group, it gives us groups per actor type, so we can have a particles group, that has some options that could be applied for the particles, or we can have a camera group, that creates a camera inside it, and so on. But usually, and most of the time, you will need to create normal groups through **Add New Empty Group**. Here is a list of the supported groups you can find within Unreal Matinee:

Now if you want to assign any actor for the group you have created, all you need to do is the following:

1. Select the actor from the viewport.

2. Go back to Matinee.

3. Right-click on the group itself.

4. Choose **Actors** from the top of the menu.

5. Select the selected actor from the submenu:

Actors ▶	Select Group Actors
Add New Bool Property Track	Add Selected Actors
Add New Event Track	Replace Group Actors With Selected Actors
Add New Animation Track	Remove Group Actors
Add New Float Anim BP Parameter Track	SK_Enemy_FrostGiant_Captain(SK_Enemy_FrostGiant_Captain_4) ▶

Tracks

Once you have created at least one group, you will be able to create tracks, as tracks need somewhere to be hosted in. As tracks represent the animated value of the actors, you need to create actors first, or choose them. Choose an actor as you saw in the previous section, via the group right-click menu.

Once you've the group and actors inside (or even before putting actors inside), the right-click menu of the group will expose a huge list of the tracks that you can add.

Be careful in adding a track and fitting the type of actor you are animating. For example, you can't add a track to control the material color while the actor is **Light Source**.

So, you have to understand what each track is made for in order to be able to add them to the correct groups and actors. While the tracks' names are self-explanatory, this is the list of the tracks that you can add:

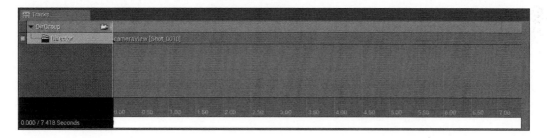

Now you understand the animation of the cinematics done inside tracks; those tracks control values of the actors, but not all actors, only the ones put inside groups. Finally, those groups should be inside a Matinee actor. This is the simple process of creating a cinematic, and in fact, the hard part of creating a cinematic is not here, it is in the direction and creation of the animations in the three-dimensional animation software. Apart from that, it is a very fun process. As it is fun, let's have a look at the Bellz cinematic.

Bellz cinematic

Now with Bellz, my goal is simple; once the player reaches a certain point, which is by the end of the map, I need to trigger a 5 seconds cinematic, where the player stops, a beast comes and turns, and there are some fancy camera animations.

Using the same tools, we discussed in the previous section, I was able to do this in a few quick steps:

1. Put the beast skeletal mesh in the map:

2. Create an empty group for the beast:

3. Add the beast as a skeletal mesh into this group, by selecting it from the map:

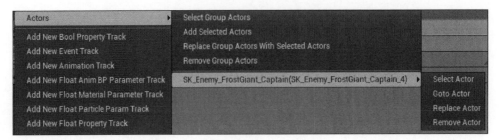

4. Create another group, the type of camera, and that will create a new camera in the map. Give the group a name; I named it `cameraView`:

5. Within the beast, add a new animation track:

6. Then at the first frame of the track, add a key, by pressing *Enter* (or the button at the top bar). I was then asked to choose an animation to insert:

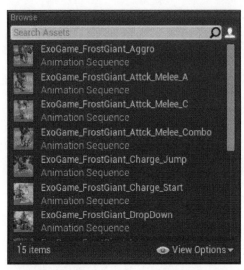

7. Now I've animated the beast.

8. Then choose the camera group.

9. I added a movement track, to be able to move the camera:

10. Then I started to set some keys for the camera, and move the camera in the viewport after setting each key:

11. By checking in the viewport, the camera will now have a yellow path that defines its movement:

12. But still the camera was not smoothing well. So I decided to go with a Curve Editor fixing.

13. In order to enable a curve for a selected track, you can just press the **Track** button in the curve:

14. Now you can keep changing the curve, until you are good with the speed:

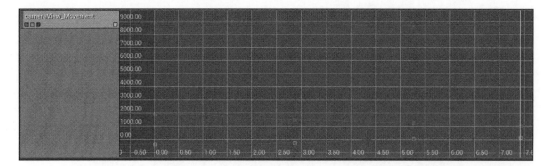

15. Finally, everything is good, but will not run as expected, as all this needs to be bundled within the Director because there is a different camera used other than the player camera.

16. So I added a Director group:

17. Now the Director asks which camera this track belongs to. I choose the cinematic camera, which is animated:

18. Now it is all right.

19. The last step is creating a trigger from the volumes and putting it in the area where I need the cinematic run on the player reach:

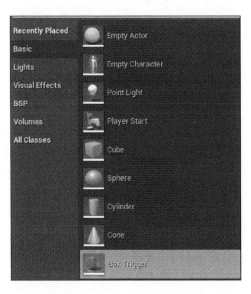

20. Finally, I set this simple logic that detects if the player (our Gladiator class) has entered this volume in which the cinematic will directly play:

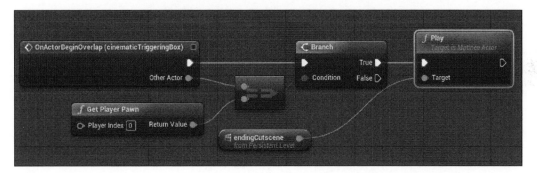

Now I've a cinematic piece of video that is rendered real-time inside the engine itself, and triggered by the character reaching some point, not only that but also showing some animations and fancy camera movement. That's amazing and was fast compared to other tools and engines in the market!

The animated fog

Almost like any other thing within Unreal Engine, you can do some animations for it. Some parts of the engine are super-responsive to the animation system, while other parts have a limited access. But speaking of the fog, it has a limited access in order to animate some values. You can use different ways and methods to animate values at runtime or even during the **Edit** mode.

Color

Height fog color can be changed at runtime using **Linear Color Property Track** in Matinee. We are going to dive deep inside Matinee in the next chapter, but here is the recipe in advance!

By following the given steps, you could change height fog color in-game:

1. Create a new Matinee actor.
2. Open the newly created actor within Matinee Editor.
3. Create a height fog actor.
4. Create a group in Matinee.
5. Attach the **Height Fog** actor from the scene into the group created in the previous step.
6. Create a linear color property track within the group.
7. Choose the **Fog Inscattering Color** or **Directional Inscattering Color** option to control its value (two colors is an advantage of that fog type, as we already discussed in *Chapter 7, Enhancing the Visual Quality,*...remember?).
8. Add key frames to the track, and set the color for them.

Animating exponential height fog

In order to animate exponential height fog, you can use one of two ways:

- Use Matinee to animate the **Exponential Height Fog** actor values
- Use a timeline node within **Level Blueprint**, and control the **Exponential Height Fog** actor values

So go ahead, and add some animation to your fog if you have any. Just as we did with animation for the characters and cameras, try your best to animate some fog colors.

Saving the cinematic as video

Sometimes, creating the cinematic is not a result of the need to play the game itself. Sometimes you want a piece of video for marketing or a best practice, or for creating a trailer or teaser. Then rather than running the game, and a recorder to capture the screen, Epic gives you the opportunity just to export it directly out of the engine, in a form that suits you; either a video or a sequence of images.

In case you want to process your cinematic that way, it is very simple, just open your Matinee actor inside the Matinee Editor. Then from the top-right corner, by the end of the toolbar, you'll find a button called **Move**. Click on it, and it will launch the **Render Movie Settings** window:

Within the window, you can choose either between a video or a sequence of images, and also the frame rate and the resolution. Those three options are the most important ones. Then you can define some compressions or a different directory to be used. It is all a self-explanatory set of parameters, which you are going to leave most of them as they are.

Once you are done, just hit **Capture Movie**, and the movie will start playing and saving at the same time. It will be slow, that's normal, as it has to write to the drive while playing. Depending on the duration and resolution, you'll get a different size, but don't be shocked if you find your video going beyond 5 GB; it is quite normal!

Summary

Now you have learned a whole new world of creativity that you can achieve only within the Unreal Engine, not only because of the visual quality, but also because of the ease of access.

You have learned what the Matinee actor is, how it works, and how to create it, but most importantly, how to edit it.

Matinee Data is one little type of asset, and you learned how to get it, and where to assign it for your Matinee.

A Matinee actor without the Matinee Editor is impossible. You've learned and mastered how to use the Matinee Editor, what are the essential parts of it, how to create curves, and what is the difference between the tracks and groups.

You have a piece of cinematic done, congratulations! But still, you've got to either run it or export it for it to be used for something else like a trailer or marketing. You also learned how to process your cinematic further.

Now before you go on to the next chapter, I would highly recommend you to create an outstanding cutscene and trigger it, or convert it to a movie. I focused on the movement of skeletal meshes, but this is because it is the most complex thing, with the same exact method. You can add audio and particles, so I recommend you try those too. In fact, go ahead and keep trying all the track types, it is going to blow your mind with new ideas! Once you're done, go ahead and progress to the next chapter.

9
Implementing the Game UI

A game without UI is something that cannot be made. Sometimes while playing a game, you can find there is no UI within the game while the gameplay is running. But even with those types of game, you must find a UI somewhere, at least in the game menus.

The game UI could be something simple, starting from a simple text on the screen HUD, or might be something more complex, such as 3D UI elements, or even a map as with FogOfWar.

The main functionality of the UI usually is not as a gameplay element, but it is a game play helper and a method for instant feedback. UI, as a helper, might be a map or a piece of text describing missions to the player, stating exactly what he/she should do or where to go.

However, it is mostly used as a feedback method, to tell the player about their current status, current health, damage, and what the player has earned, and what's been lost. A good player will always keep an eye on the entire game HUD, so as to learn on a regular basis about their progress.

This sounds as if the UI has a heavy load on its shoulders, and too much to deliver, but in fact the methods used to create the UI in the past made it an even heavier load on the developer. However, with the invasion of the current high-end engines, new tools and methods have been made, and creating a UI for a game has become as easy as arranging stuff inside Photoshop or a similar application. It is a matter of taste now more than a matter of coding. Even though there is some code to be added, or some blueprint logic, the process of constructing an intuitive UI that can fit any screen size is just a matter of taste!

By the end of this chapter, you will be able to:

- Understand the UMG concept and the editor
- Master the creation of the game UI by only using the UI widget actors
- Add and use animations to the UI elements
- Connect the UI widgets to your game using either C++ or blueprints

Having said that, let us get started!

UMG as Unreal's UI system

UMG is the UI system and the framework has been used for a while now. For not a long time, Unreal used to have a UI framework called **slate**. Slate is still being used underneath the UMG and the whole editor UI.

While slate was a little hard to deal with as a system and was neither super-friendly nor productive, Epic took a huge step to create the UMG system.

UMG stands for **Unreal Motion Graphics**, and you can understand from its name that it is not only a UI solution, but also indispensable in creating tons and tons of other stuff. It is possible to produce things like ads and motion graphics with UMG and Matinee. I've seen lots of people pushing the engine boundaries and creating ads and motion graphics using the Unreal Engine, which used to be made with packages such as Adobe After Effects.

The power within UMG is not only in its great performance, there are a few points that actually make it an amazing UI system. Let's look at them:

- UMG has its own editor, the **UMG Designer**, which give the player ease of access to create advanced UI systems with a few clicks.

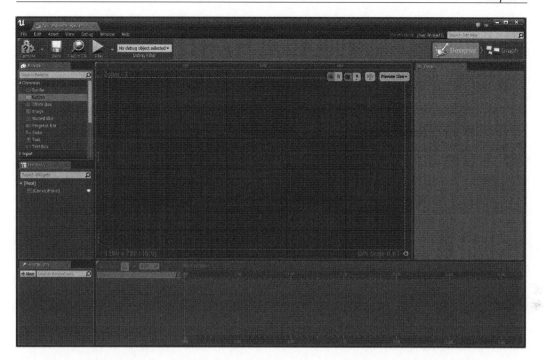

- UMG allows users to create animation, not only static components but also animated UI components. Which means either the game UI or the product motion graphics will be juicy.

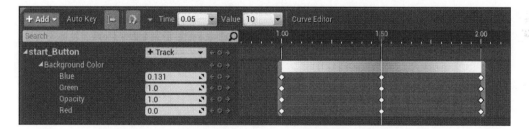

- UMG is completely integrated with all types of inputs, which means that you can navigate through the UI using a gamepad, mouse or keyboard, by just using a simple node to enable navigating between the UI buttons or sliders with a controller or keyboard rather than a mouse.

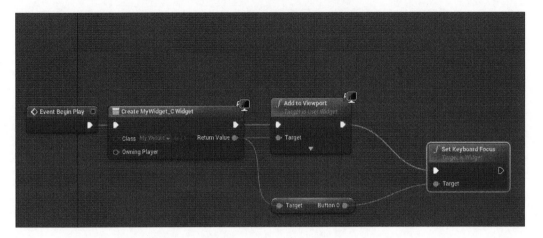

- UMG's performance is super stable.
- UMG can be used to create a world space UI or screen space UI. This means that you can have a UI attached to an actor inside the world, and not just a HUD component.

The game UI widget

Within UMG the UI screens or panels are called **UI widgets**. A widget can have an unlimited amount of UI elements, which include subpanels. But think about a widget as a container for UI elements.

The UI widget is an asset type, just like any other asset within Unreal. It is better to think about it as a blueprint, but a different type of blueprint. However, it shares the same methodology, which includes a designing part, where you can assemble some elements, and a logic part, where you can add logic or code for those designing parts.

Now, let's create a UI widget, which is as simple as creating an actor blueprint and can only be created from the content browser just like any other blueprint. You can pick a widget blueprint from within the **User Interface** submenu.

 I created mine, and just named it `InGameUI`. After creating it, do a double-click in order to open the UMG designer editor.

Remember to be very organized! The project is getting bigger with time, and things might get out of control, only because you were unorganized at an early stage. Try to make a directory for similar things, and for the UI widgets I've created a `UI` folder within the `Blueprints` folder, as they are blueprints asset types at the end of the day, but a different type of blueprint.

Now, as you have seen in the previous screenshot, there is an asset type called **Font** and it is tagged as **User Interface**, meaning that you can create and import font files to be used as your UI font for the game.

For Bellz, I have downloaded one of the free fonts online, and by just dragging and dropping it into the content browser, Unreal has detected its type and converted the font file into an Unreal font asset.

Keep in mind that usually the fonts you need might be TTF or OTF file formats.

UMG Designer

The UMG Designer is very interesting, as from the first time you open it, you will have the feeling that it somehow does not look like all the other editors within the Unreal Engine. And that's true, as it has tools that you'll be seeing for the first time.

The UMG Designer is exactly like the blueprint editor, not in how it looks but in its goal and objective, as both are not only used to create logic, but also to visualize and construct the actor, whatever the type of actors a UI or in-game item has (like an in-game object or character).

Now let's look at the main parts that create the UMG Designer.

The Toggle mode

At the top left corner of the UMG Designer, you will be find a **Toggle** button that allows you to switch the designer interface to two different types. They are:

- **Designer**: This is the default view of the UMG Designer, and it is the place where you'll be constructing your UI and putting things together
- **Graph**: This is the place where you'll be binding buttons and UI events and adding logic to control the different UI items

Palette

The UI is just a bunch of text, images, sliders, and few other types of controls. Here, within **Palette**, you will find all the control types supported by the Unreal Engine.

If you are familiar with the Windows form for Visual studio, or something like QT, you will understand the term here.

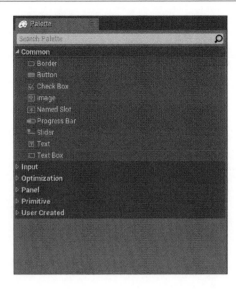

The hierarchy

Adding items to the UI widget could be done through the canvas or **Hierarchy**, but using any method, the added item will exist on both sides. This means that you can drag and drop items from **Palette** to the canvas or to **Hierarchy**, but in both cases, the dropped items will exist in **Hierarchy** and the canvas.

Animations

Sometimes you will need to add animation for the UI items, like pop-up windows or sliding panels and so on, and this is the place to do that. You can't import animations from third-party applications such as May or Flash, as any UI-related animations must be created within Unreal in this panel.

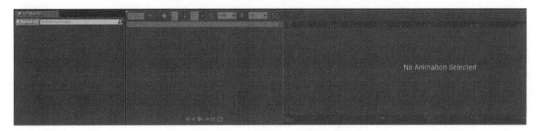

Canvas

The canvas is the area of action. This is where you'll be "drawing" and "putting together" all the UI elements. The canvas is like a grid, where you can place and align items. It has information for you, such as the screen aspect ratio you are using for the game.

The Details panel

The **Details** panel works like any other details panel within the Unreal Engine. It is the place where you can set and adjust the different parameters for the currently selected item. Once you add a UI item to the canvas, you will be able to adjust all its parameters from here. For example, adding text will let you change its size, color, the text itself, the anchoring, the text scale, and much more.

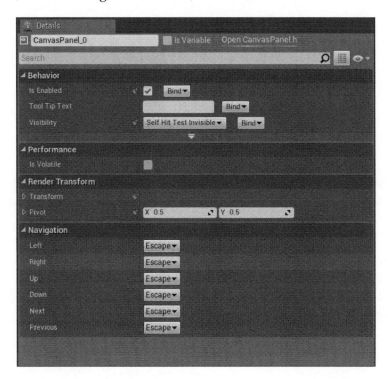

Constructing the UI

So, how does this work?

Well, it is very simple. In order to add content, you have to pick what you want from the **Palette** panel, and drag it, and then you can:

- Drop the item within the canvas
- Drop the item within **Hierarchy**

The last step is to adjust the size, name, or scale of each item you have placed.

Whether you're working in a team, or even alone, you should have a UI design mockup before you start putting things together within Unreal. For Bellz, in order to always include the player in the gameplay, I came up with this simple and standard game UI design.

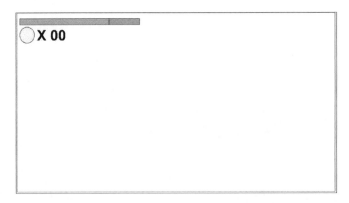

Simply, the player will be seeing all the gameplay UI in the upper-right corner of the screen, in order to save lots of space for the player to focus on the game, enemies, and the objective itself.

The UI will display all the information the player needs, and the values we have for the most important gameplay variables (health, coins count, and so on). As we worked on adding a system for the AI to hit the player and affect his health, the player needs to be aware of the current health status, in order to take the decision to keep on fighting or running away to look for a health pack or such.

Also, we have presented a collectables system, and we have added some logic for the player to allow him to do the collecting process, and increase the collected coins count. It is good to show the player how much he has got.

So, the conclusion is, we need:

- A progress bar that can change the value to match the player's health
- An icon for the coin to distinguish the value being displayed next to it
- A static text, x to be added next to the coin icon
- A dynamic text that will always be changing to match the number of the collected coins

Now, let's drag and drop items from **Palette** into the canvas, ordering them the same. One good tip is to use the **[Horizontal Box]** component, as it is good way to align things horizontally.

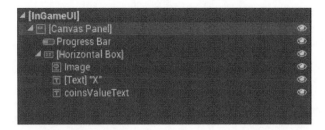

As you can see, the **[Canvas Panel]** component is my default root for everything. I've added a scroll bar and a horizontal box. Within the horizontal box, I've added the icon for the coin, and the two pieces of text. Isn't it so simple and quick? By adjusting some colors, and scales, it looks like this:

Now, one very important thing to keep in mind is that if you tried to use this UI in a different screen size (not 16:9) like the one being used while constructing the UI, probably things will get messed up, and you'll find items have been moved to different positions, and are no longer connected to the upper-left corners.

Here we come to the **Anchors** feature. By selecting any item, or parent item, you will find it is displayed like an anchor icon, which looks almost like a star.

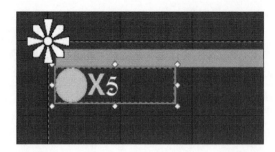

This star represents where the selected item is attached, and in case the screen size and the aspect ratio have been changed, it indicates how the item will be interacting and where it will be kept positioned and aligned to.

Changing the anchor has usually been done in code and used to be a tedious process for the UI programmers, but within UMG, Epic has presented the anchors set where you simply can choose one of the screen corners to attach an item to, and then everything else will be done under the hood.

By selecting an item from the canvas, you will see that the first option inside the **Details** panel is **Anchors**. By simply clicking on it, you will have a drop-down list of all the possible positions on the screen. Pick the one you want, and the one that fits your needs. I have picked the top left corner for all my controls, as this is where I need them in all aspect ratios.

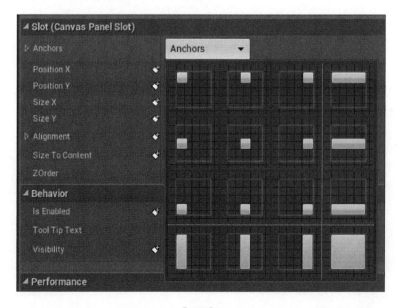

Now the UI is perfect and ready to be used. However, I would like to add one more thing in order to push it further and to make it more pumping with life, and at the same time, to experience all the UMG capabilities. Let's add some animations.

Adding animations to the UI

Animations can be complex, but for the UI it is usually simple positioning over time, and this is usually triggered at a particular moment, and is not running all the time. Having animations in the UI might distract the player, that's why you've to be very careful while creating UI animations, as they have to be only informative, and not distracting.

So, what am I going to animate here?

Well, my plan is to create an animation clip to the value of the coins (the text component) in order to show to the player where the collected coin value went, and what values in the UI have been increased. It is this type of effect that you usually see in RPG games.

Now, from the **Animations** section, all you need to do is to create a new animation using the **+Animation** button and give it a name.

If you've noticed, the whole animation panel was grayed out (disabled) until you created a new animation clip, which will enable the animation toolbar button.

From within the animation toolbar, you can hit the **+Add** button, in order to get access to all the available items in your canvas. All those items can be animated.

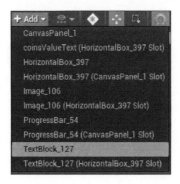

Select the item that you want to animate. For me, I used the coins text, as I mentioned before that the animation clip will be about driving the player's attention to the increased value of the coins.

Choosing a component to be animated will add it to the **Animation** panel, and display to you a **Track** selection button.

The **Track** selection button will be displaying a list for you; this list contains all the parameters that you can animate for the current selected item.

The animation we want to create is about increasing the size of the text, which means we need to scale the item. I will be selecting the **Transform** track to be animated.

The animation is simple and made of only three frames. Within the **Scale** parameter of the **Transform** track, I managed to set three keys, the first and the last have the same value, which is a value of **1** to both axes, **X** and **Y**. The middle key has a higher value, in order to scale up the size.

That's it. I have now animation that I can play and trigger anytime. Keep trying to add different animations for different objects, try to explore all the available tracks to be animated, and don't be afraid of trying things. Remember that any new animation clip you create, Unreal will be adding it as a `public` variable of the blueprint, so you can call it, play it, or stop it at any moment.

Connecting the UI with the game logic

Now, though we have UI widgets being built, we still can't see anything when we hit **Play**, simply because the UI widget needs to be spawned to the player. Its content needs to be connected to some logic in order to change the health bar value or to change the collected coins count.

In order to be able to go ahead, we have to make sure of a few things. Visual Studio will not allow us to write anything related to UMG without having things set up beforehand. So within the `Bellz.h` header file of the game, make sure that we are using the engine itself, not the minimal version of it.

```
#ifndef __PUREGAME_H__
#define __PUREGAME_H__
```

```
//I replaced the EngineMinimal.h, in order to get access to lots of
other things...Mainly was to enable the on screen debugging messages!
//#include "EngineMinimal.h"
#include "Engine.h"

#endif
```

Now, there is one more step to go. Inside the `Bellz.Build.cs` file, where we enabled some modules and where we enabled the AI and Paper 2d, let's add two more modules, the UMG and the slate (slate and slate core):

```
using UnrealBuildTool;

public class Bellz : ModuleRules
{
  public Bellz(TargetInfo Target)
  {
        PublicDependencyModuleNames.AddRange(newstring[] { "Core",
"CoreUObject", "Engine", "InputCore", "AIModule", "Paper2D", "UMG" });

    //PrivateDependencyModuleNames.AddRange(new string[] {  });

    // Uncomment if you are using Slate UI
    PrivateDependencyModuleNames.AddRange(newstring[] { "Slate",
"SlateCore" });

    // Uncomment if you are using online features
    // PrivateDependencyModuleNames.Add("OnlineSubsystem");
    // if ((Target.Platform == UnrealTargetPlatform.Win32) || (Target.
Platform == UnrealTargetPlatform.Win64))
    // {
    //     if (UEBuildConfiguration.bCompileSteamOSS == true)
    //     {
    //         DynamicallyLoadedModuleNames.Add("OnlineSubsystemSteam");
    //     }
    // }
  }
}
```

The most important part now is **GameMode**. As you will recall from *Chapter 1, Preparing for a Big Project*, *Chapter 2, Setting Up Your Warrior*, and *Chapter 3, Designing Your Playground*, we were creating the base of the player and AI, and we had a look at **GameMode** which is called `BellzGameMode`. As the game mode instance will exist within each map or level you load, adding the main logic for the game UI within the game mode will be the best strategy to follow.

Now open the header file `BellzGameMode.h` and make sure to:

- Add an event begin play function override
- A `UserWidget` variable to be used as the game's main UI instance and another variable of the same type, to be published within the **Details** panel, which will be holding the UI widget that we made

```
#pragma once
#include "GameFramework/GameMode.h"
#include "BellzGameMode.generated.h"




UCLASS(minimalapi)
class ABellzGameMode : publicAGameMode
{
   GENERATED_BODY()

public:
   ABellzGameMode();

   virtual void BeginPlay() override;

protected:
   //The game UI widget blueprint that been designed in UMG editor
   UPROPERTY (EditDefaultsOnly, BlueprintReadWrite, Category =
"UI", Meta = (BleprintProtected = "true"))
   TSubclassOf<classUUserWidget> GameUIWidget;

   //The in game instance of the UI
   UPROPERTY(EditDefaultsOnly, BlueprintReadWrite, Category = "UI",
Meta = (BleprintProtected = "true"))
   class UUserWidget* GameUIInstance;
}
```

Now within the CPP file, you will not be able to add any related logic without adding the header `Blueprint/UserWidget.h` in order to be able to control the `UserWidget` variable.

Now within the `Begin Play` method, all what we have to do is, to make sure that the game mode has an assigned instance of the game UI widget, and then use it to spawn a widget within the game, and add it to the player viewport.

```
#include "Bellz.h"
#include "BellzGameMode.h"
```

```
#include "Gladiator.h"
#include "Blueprint/UserWidget.h"

ABellzGameMode::ABellzGameMode()
{
  //set the gladiator based blueprint as the default pawn class of the
gamemode. Also we can assign it directly within the editor
  staticConstructorHelpers::FClassFinder<APawn>
PlayerPawnBPClass(TEXT("/Game/Blueprints/GladiatorCharacter"));
  if (PlayerPawnBPClass.Class != NULL)
  {
    DefaultPawnClass = PlayerPawnBPClass.Class;
  }
}


void ABellzGameMode::BeginPlay()
{
  Super::BeginPlay();

  if (GameUIWidget != nullptr)
  {
    GameUIInstance = CreateWidget<UUserWidget>(GetWorld(),
GameUIWidget);
    if (GameUIInstance != nullptr)
    {
      GameUIInstance->AddToViewport();
    }
  }
}
```

Now everything is good on the C++ side. Do compile and jump to the editor. Once the compilation is complete, create a blueprint based on the Bellz game mode and assign the GameUIWidget variable to it. Then hit **Play**, and you will see that the UI appears once the game has started.

So, how do we do the same thing in blueprints?

Well, it is easier and does not require much C++-based work. When you want to do the same thing in blueprints, you'll not need to include any header files or such, as everything will be on the editor side. All you need to do is to add a **Create Widget** node to the player, and choose the targeted widget for it. Finally, add this newly created widget to the viewport. Just the same steps, but via nodes and with fewer complications.

Both ways work fine, and lots of people tend to do this step in the blueprints side, as it is easier to keep making changes or switching between the different widgets faster!

Now we have the UI, and it is connected. But neither the animations nor the values of the progress bar and the coins are changing at all. And that's because we haven't connected the logic yet.

Connecting the logic for something is a fairly simple process, as long as we already have the logic to calculate the value itself, which means all we needs to do on the widget blueprint side is to display a specific value, and this is usually done through bindings.

For example, by selecting the progress bar we have, you will find a **Bind** button right away, next to its percentage value. By pressing it, it will take you right away to the graph, with a new bind being added for it.

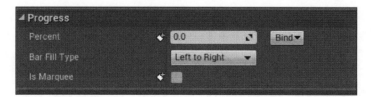

In the binding area, all you need to do is to get the correct value. As the health value has been stored and mated by the C++ code we made in *Chapter 2*, *Setting Up Your Warrior*, all I've got to do is just to get this value using a simple casting to the gladiator. However, keep in mind, getting the health value alone will not work, as you have to divide it by 100, which represents a percentage value.

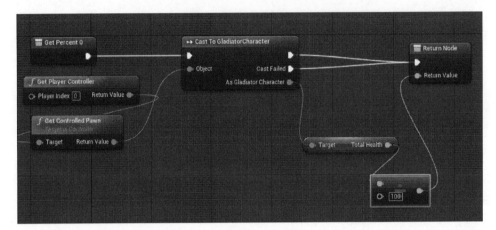

Now let's go ahead and bind the value of the collected coins text. After selecting the text from the canvas, you will find another similar **Bind** button as before, but this time it is next to the **Text** attribute of the text component.

In the binding area, with a similar casting to get the **Gladiator/Player** blueprint, we can get the **Collected Coins** value and convert it to a text variable to be returned and used with the text component.

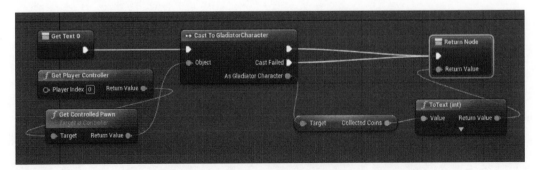

Now running and playing the game will have the expected experience; you will be able to collect coins, and the value of the coins at the UI will change. Also, you will be getting attacked by the enemies, and this will affect your progress bar or health. But still there aren't any animations for the UI. The one we made is to be used when coins get collected.

Let us open the coin blueprint, and do a simple process in order to get and play the animations we made:

1. Add a reference to the C++ method we made, the one called OnGetCollected.

2. Get the current **GameMode** used with the map, and cast it to **MainGameMode**.

3. After getting the game mode, we can get the value of the **GameUIInstance** that we made a few minutes ago in C++.

4. Finally, we can call the **Play Animation** node, by using the **CoinValueChange** variable of the UI widget as the used animation.

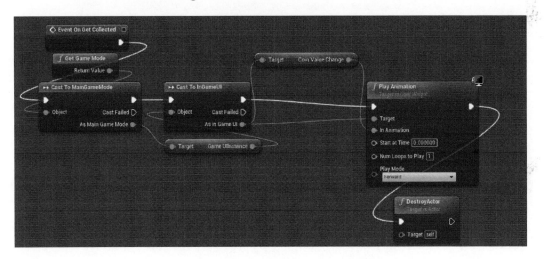

Now play the game once more, and try to collect coins, and see what happens. Exactly, the collected coins' animation effect will play on the UI.

What else?

Now, as you can see, I have created a main menu widget for the game. It is simple enough, and only has two buttons, one, to start the game and another one to quit. Go ahead and figure out how to connect them to the game and how to make them the first thing a player sees, and based on them, the player can either start playing or quit.

As you can see, Bellz's menu has only two buttons, but the bigger the game, the bigger its menu will be: you might have more buttons such as options, leader boards, and so on. However, those two options are quite enough to get you even more into the process.

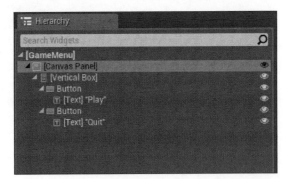

Don't be afraid to try new things, add animations for the buttons, change their colors based on the mouse events, and so much more. Keep trying and remember whatever you have in mind, you will be able to achieve somehow!

Summary

Now you have gone through one of the most important processes of the game creation journey. Creating the UI is not only something interesting, but it could be one of those things that distinguishes your game. Not only do fancy sound or amazing visuals or models makes a game perfect, but the UI can leave a perfect impression on the players about the way it works, the way it looks and the way it animates. All that could change the player's experience by 180 degrees.

In this chapter, you have learned a lot about the UMG and what makes it better than slate, and even the best UI solution yet within Unreal Engine since its first release.

UMG has its own editor/designer, and you have seen the main parts of its editor, and how or where to add things.

Making sure that a game fits all of the available screen size has always been complicated. However, using the **Anchor** points within UMG, makes this super easy, and you just learned how to anchor stuff.

The UI could be just perfect based on the assets used, but adding animations to the UI makes it more live and intuitive. You not only learned how to create animations for the UI elements, but also you learned how to play with them whenever you want.

Displaying the different UI widgets is a simple process, which could be achieved by using C++ or blueprints. You not only saw how to do this using both methods, but also you have learned what are the essential steps, headers and modules needed for a C++ project in order to make the UMG adjustable using code.

Now go ahead, and spend some time implementing the main game menu, add some fancy animations or even add more to the game UI itself. Try to add a map, notifications, missions, and so on. And once you feel good and friendly with the process of creating widgets and animations, then go ahead and find more in to the next chapter, where we will have a little chat about how to save and load values.

10
Save the Game Progress

Now that we have an almost complete player experience, you can hit **Play** and enjoy running from enemies, hitting them and collecting some coins, and most importantly, the player will have instant feedback through the UI.

However, the experience will be lacking some industry standards. Think about a power cut while playing, or even consider that your player may be feeling bored and wants to close the game for now. What should happen?

Exactly… The game progress should be saved. This is what we are going to do next.

Saving a game could be tricky, and could involve too many techniques in order to properly save the player data for all the supported platforms in a well-locked file format. Fortunately, Unreal Engine gives us an interface for its complex save system, and all that we have to do is to initialize that save system and save or load the data. All the underlying mysterious logic has been put under the hood, starting from creating the file format, to writing in binary and organizing the saved data in a well-managed way.

By the end of this chapter, you will be able to:

- Build a SaveGame class to be used for game loading and saving
- Save and load any game data using C++
- Understand the save and load workflow, and where to find the save files
- Use or open the saved data files
- Save and load data using blueprints

With that said, let's get started, and learn how to save and load!

Building the SaveGame class

While most of the classes we have built so far have been based on the actor class, there are some functionalities that are not supported by the actor class and saving the data is one of those.

In order to make a class that can be used as an instance to manage the game save and load, you'll need to create a class based on the SaveGame class.

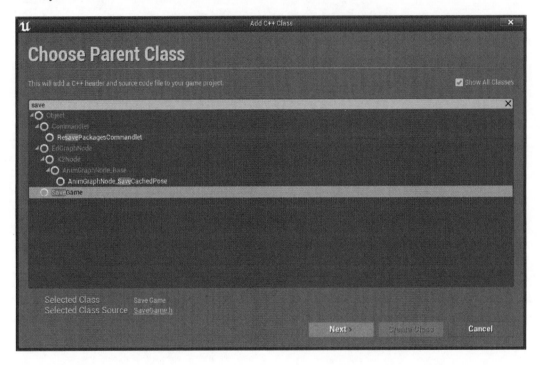

I have created mine for Bellz, and named it BellzSaveGame. Choose a name that suits you and just create it. Once the Visual Studio opens, go ahead and open the Bellz.h file or, in other words, the main header for your game (your game might not be named Bellz).

Within the header file Bellz.h, we will be including some extra header files in order to be able to use the save functionality within any class instance. We will be including:

- BellzSaveGame.h
- Kismet/GameplayStatics.h

But make sure that the new header files are added under the `Engine.h` file, otherwise you'll get an error.

```
//I replaced the EngineMinimal.h, in order to get access to lots of
other things...Mainly was to enable the on screen debugging messages!
//#include "EngineMinimal.h"
#include "Engine.h"
#include "BellzSaveGame.h"
#include "Kismet/GameplayStatics.h"

#endif
```

Once you have completed this, let us get back to the newly created `SaveGame` class, and open its header file. This way, saving data is simple. For any value you need to save, you will have to add a variable for it within your header file. So, if we consider that I need to save the player health value, which is float, that means I need to add a `float` variable to hold this value.

```
UPROPERTY(VisibleAnywhere, Category = SavedValues)
    float PlayerHealth;
```

And so on and so forth. For Bellz, I'll be saving health and collected coins, but you can save pretty much anything and everything in your game, as long as you are going to save the data or state of the entity. As we are still within the header file, it is a good opportunity to add a couple of extra variables:

- An integer to hold the current player index
- A string to hold the save slot name (the save file name)

This means that the header file should look like the following:

```
#pragma once

#include "GameFramework/SaveGame.h"
#include "BellzSaveGame.generated.h"

/**
 *
 */
UCLASS()
classBELLZ_APIUBellzSaveGame : publicUSaveGame
{
  GENERATED_BODY()
```

```
public:
  UPROPERTY(VisibleAnywhere, Category = SavedValues)
    FString SlotName;

  UPROPERTY(VisibleAnywhere, Category = SavedValues)
    uint32 PlayerIndex;

  UPROPERTY(VisibleAnywhere, Category = SavedValues)
    uint32 CollectedCoins;

  UPROPERTY(VisibleAnywhere, Category = SavedValues)
    float PlayerHealth;

  UPROPERTY(VisibleAnywhere, Category = SavedValues)
    uint32 lastUsedWeaponIndex;

  UPROPERTY(VisibleAnywhere, Category = SavedValues)
    FString PlayerName;


  UBellzSaveGame();


};
```

Isn't this simple and straightforward? A slot name holder variable, and a player index variable are both essential to complete the save process. All other variables, such as player health, collected coins, and weapon index, are variables to hold values that I'll be saving for my game.

Now, let's open the source .cpp file, in order to complete the integration of the BellzSaveGame class.

```
#include "Bellz.h"
#include "BellzSaveGame.h"

UBellzSaveGame::UBellzSaveGame()
{
  SlotName = TEXT("CoinsSaveSlot");
  PlayerIndex = 0;
}
```

Within the source file, the only needed logic is to add the player index value, which is 0 as the game is for a single player, and as for the name of the save slot, I just named it with the coin's name. Name it anything you want, I could have named it playerData or something but I just went with CoinsSaveSlot.

It looks like we have just added couple of lines, but in fact we have completed the job! Yes we have. Saving data within Unreal and C++ is a very simple process compared to the blueprints. Now all that we need, is to use UGameplayStatics::CreateSaveGameObject in order to save any value, or use UGameplayStatics::LoadGameFromSlot in order to load any value.

For example, I would like to save the value of the player health and load it anytime the player starts the game, as long as it is not 0.

Saving and loading game data in C++

As we already have included the needed header files within the main game header file, we will be able to access the SaveGame methods from anywhere.

So, within the AGladiator::OnChangeHealthByAmount(float usedAmount) method of the player controller, I'll be adding a logic to save the health value any time it gets changed.

```
void AGladiator::OnChangeHealthByAmount(floatusedAmount)
{
  TotalHealth -= usedAmount;
  FOutputDeviceNullar;
  this->CallFunctionByNameWithArguments(TEXT("ApplyGetDamageEffect"),
ar, NULL, true);

  //A message to be printed to screen
  FString message;
  //Creating an instance of the bellz save class
  UBellzSaveGame* BellzSaveGameInstance = Cast<UBellzSaveGame>(UGamepl
ayStatics::CreateSaveGameObject(UBellzSaveGame::StaticClass()));
  //Change the health value of the save class to match the current
health value of the gladiator
  BellzSaveGameInstance->PlayerHealth = TotalHealth;
  //Store the health value to the save file
  UGameplayStatics::SaveGameToSlot(BellzSaveGameInstance,
BellzSaveGameInstance->SlotName, BellzSaveGameInstance->PlayerIndex);
  //update the message that will be printed
  message=TEXT("The health been Saved ---> ") +FString::SanitizeFloat
(TotalHealth);
  //print a message to the screen
  GEngine->AddOnScreenDebugMessage(-1, 2.f, FColor::Green, message);
}
```

So, to break it down easily, it starts as we have done before while building the gladiator, with the value change based on the passed variable usedAmount to the function. Then follow these steps:

1. Create an FString message string to hold a message that will be printed to the screen.

2. Create an instance of UBellzSaveGame named BellzSaveGameInstance and, by a simple CreateSaveGameObject, we can instantiate the class instance.

3. Now we can change the value of the member variable PlayerHealth of the newly created instance to match the current player health.

4. Then confirm the save, by calling the method SaveGameToSlot, which usually takes three parameters:

   ° The save game instance, which is BellzSaveGameInstance

   ° The saving slot name, which is BellzSaveGameInstance->SlotName

   ° The current player index, which is BellzSaveGameInstance->PlayerIndex

5. Finally we just print a message on the screen, to make sure everything went all right.

That was the save part, which involved simply saving a value. Now let's load it at the correct time. At Begin Play of the same class I'll check whether there is already a saved value, and if there is I'll be loading it as long as it is not 0, otherwise, I'll give the player full health.

```
//Creating an instance of the Bellz load game
  UBellzSaveGame* BellzLoadGameInstance = Cast<UBellzSaveGame>(UGamepl
ayStatics::CreateSaveGameObject(UBellzSaveGame::StaticClass()));
  //Access the correct slot and use the correct player index
  BellzLoadGameInstance = Cast<UBellzSaveGame>(UGameplayStatics::Load
GameFromSlot(BellzLoadGameInstance->SlotName, BellzLoadGameInstance-
>PlayerIndex));
  //get the needed value and store it in a loacl variable
  float loadedPlayerHealth = BellzLoadGameInstance->PlayerHealth;

  FString message;
  if (loadedPlayerHealth != 0.f)
  {
    TotalHealth = loadedPlayerHealth;

    message=TEXT("The health been loaded ---> ") +FString::SanitizeFlo
at(TotalHealth);
```

```
    GEngine->AddOnScreenDebugMessage(-1, 2.f, FColor::Green, message);
}
else
{
    message=TEXT("---- No HEALTH value been found on save files ");
    GEngine->AddOnScreenDebugMessage(-1, 2.f, FColor::Red, message);
}
```

This way, I am able to save and load the player health at any time in the game. Now go ahead and repeat the same process for the coins or anything else, keep saving the different values, and try to load them. You will find it easy and funny as well.

The *.sav file

The file format that is used by Unreal Engine in order to store the saved data is the *.sav file. You can find all the save files (files named with the slot names you use within the C++ code) in the SaveGames directory, within the game or the project.

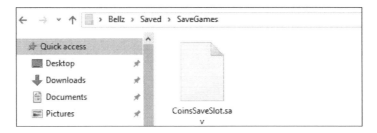

As you can see, Bellz's save game directory contains only one file, which is called CoinSaveSlot.sav, the name of the slot I defined earlier. That means you can not only save multiple values within one save file, but you can also save more than one save file. So you can think of a single save file as a table of values, and the save directory as the container of all the tables. And while you've got the chance to save unlimited amounts of save files, it always better to keep things organized within one file or even a few save files, in order to avoid any corruption or complications. Check any *AAA* game (the *Batman Arkham* series, for example) made with Unreal Engine, and you will find it has around three save files. Also, keep in mind, what if your game has multiple player profiles? Would you put all the players' data into one file, or each player's data in its own file? It is down to you how to organize it!

And due to the fact that the *.sav file is a binary data file, it is not directly readable by any app or text editor, and you either need Unreal Engine to access its data, or to make your way through some specific editors. So don't bother trying to open this file if you want to change some values, because it is not going to be straightforward.

Saving and loading game data in blueprints

When it comes to save and load values for your game, C++ is the king. While anything else within Unreal Engine is faster and easier to make with blueprints, actually saving and loading data takes too many nodes within a blueprint.

It could take exactly 15 nodes to store a value to the `*.sav` file, and the same amount of nodes in order to load a value and use it.

So, as we started in C++ by creating a class based on the `SaveGame` class, the same rule applies for the blueprint method. You will need to create a blueprint based on the `SaveGame` class, and in that case, I named it `BellzSaveGame` too, just as in the C++ example.

Feel free to add any variables within this blueprint, as those variables will represent exactly what we were adding within the `BellzSaveGame` header file.

But the most important part is creating a `SaveGame` variable within any blueprint that will be holding a logic to save or load data.

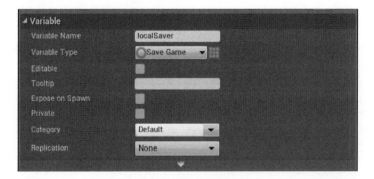

Finally, do the save or load itself. In either case, it is a matter of using one blueprint node call, which is **Load Game From Slot** in the case of loading, or **Save Game To Slot** in the case of saving. Regardless of which process you are using, there will be two main things in common. First, using the slot name you want to save to and load from. Second, you'll need to have a series of casting nodes to determine whether a slot or saving file already exists or not.

But the most important part is to always use the node called **Does Save Game Exist**, before proceeding to save or load, in order to make sure that a save slot has already been made before. If there isn't one, it's the correct time to call the node **Create Save Game Object**, in order to create one.

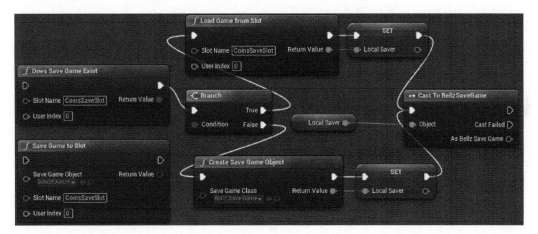

So basically, every time you need to load or save a value, you have to make sure that the value and its * .sav file already exists.

As you can guess now, if you would like to save a few bits of data, like the player name, gender, age, and score with some information about collectables and achievements, you will have at least something as complex as this!

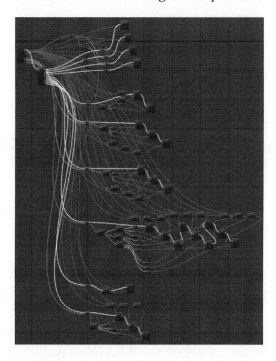

It is a screenshot from one of my early Unreal 4.1 games; it's the **Save Game** blueprint that has been used at that point. That was not easy to deal with.

So, in case you are working on a blueprint-based project, or Unreal C++ project and you would like to support saving data via blueprints, I would highly recommend picking a tool from the Unreal marketplace. The **Easy Save and Load** tool gives you the power of the blueprint and it is faster than C++.

Writing some C++ code to save or load data would take some time, and saving the data via blueprints would require lots of nodes and connections for each value you need to save or load. But with such a tool you can save or load values using only one node call, which saves time, effort, and keeps your graphs clean. It is the best solution when you have to save and load and organize tons of values easily, quickly, and cleanly. There is more about this at `https://www.unrealengine.com/marketplace/easy-save-load`.

Summary

Now you have gone through the process of saving and loading a player's data within an Unreal Engine game, using a type of logic, either C++ or blueprints.

All Unreal Engine based games follow the same concept of saving data, with the saved data stored in binary files. You have learned where to find and access those files.

Saving game data could be done in C++ or blueprints; both methods work fine, and it is up to you to decide which one to follow. You have learned about both methods, taking into account the pros and cons of each.

Now go ahead and keep saving different things in your game example. Try to save the entire map status and load it again. It will help you a lot, and once you are done let's move forward to the next chapter, where we will be discussing more complicated data loading, and will be looking at the data tables and spreadsheets.

11
Controlling Gameplay via Data Tables

Not all games are small, sometimes games are gigantic, and full of information, details, and most importantly, numbers. Let us imagine an RPG game, where you have to run, kill enemies, and collect stuff. Enemies could have different attributes, such as damage, powers, effect, health, and lots more. While the collected items might vary even more, where a collectable X could increase your health by 2%, another collectable Y could increase your health by 50%.

And that's the whole point behind data tables. It is a place where you can store data in a very organized way that is very friendly with the designer, and could be changed at any time, without the need to change the code. At the same time, the code can read it easily, regardless of any changes.

Data tables started for just a few specific types of games, such as *Tower Defense* or *RPG*, but very quickly it became an industry standard, and is used with all types of games, at least to store the localization data!

While data tables are essential, we will be diving into it, getting the guts of it, and learning how to use it in all circumstances.

By the end of this chapter, you'll be able to:

- Professionally create an Excel sheet for Unreal
- Understand the data table asset and all its different types
- Create the needed data structure for any data table
- Use the data table values within gameplay either in C++ or blueprint

Data table sheets

A data table sheet is something usually made by the game designers, and they pass it to the engineers inside the engine, so they can use it. It is basically just a table made in a third-party application.

You can use something like Excel to build the tables as Excel sheets, or you can just use something free and reachable like a Google spreadsheet, but in general it needs to be just a table.

Creating a table filled with information seems simple enough, but as it is going to be sent to Unreal, it requires a couple of specifications, in order for it to be processed:

- The first cell of the table, in all circumstances, needs to be called **Name**
- The table needs to be exported to a .csv (comma separated values), as it is currently the only acceptable data tables format
- The cell names have no spaces, because those names will be variable names in the future

When you are creating a table for your game, you have to make sure of those three things I mentioned.

By looking at Bellz, I decided to create only two table samples:

- The first one is a weapons table, which has the attributes for the player weapons:

	A	B	C	D	E
1	Name	Icon	DisplayName	Damage	CooldownTime
2		0 none_icon	Empty	0	0
3		1 sword_icon	The Hot Blade	5	1
4		2 axe_icon	The Sharpest	10	3
5		3 hammer_icon	The Mighty Hammer	15	6
6					

- The `missions` table holds the information for the game's different missions:

	A	B	C
1	Name	Kill	Collect
2	1	1	2
3	2	2	4
4	3	2	4
5	4	3	6
6	5	3	8
7	6	4	10
8	7	4	13
9	8	5	15
10	9	6	20
11	10	7	25
12			

Now create your own, and convert it to `.csv` and drag and drop it into Unreal Engine in order to import it for using!

Creating the data table asset

Creating a data table asset is actually very simple, you've already done the work by creating the Excel sheet itself and converting it into `*.csv`, but in fact this is not enough for it to work.

You see from the previous point, that after dropping the file into Unreal, it will ask you to "pick a structure" which means you can't proceed with the file without having a data structure, which we will be covering next.

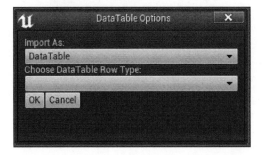

But what I want to cover now, is how to create a data table within Unreal. Let's say you don't want to create your work within Excel or a Google spreadsheet, and then convert it, and finally import it. You want to write your table directly within Unreal! And this is totally doable!

Dragging and dropping a *.csv file generating a data table asset, which you can create directly from within the content browser and the **Miscellaneous** section, will give you the same result. Despite that, you'll be asked for the data structure, but still you can create it directly within Unreal.

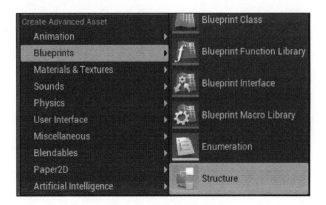

If it happens and you want to change anything within the table, you can always make a change within the data asset inside the Unreal Editor, regardless of whether the table was made inside or outside Unreal. But it is not recommended to always do updates and changes inside Unreal. If the table was made outside Unreal in the first place, then it is better to change it within the sheet, export to a .csv, and finally re-import it for the data asset. This way it is better to keep everything organized; changes should be made outside Unreal.

Now we know that if we don't have a data structure, we will be using the default values, which will do nothing. This means we need to create a data structure that fits the data tables we have.

Creating a data structure

So, now you've created the data table, and imported it into Unreal, but we still can't make sure of it, or in other words, the importing process is lacking a data structure, which made it only half import the process. Well, an unsuccessful one!

While there are always different paths to create things, Unreal follows the same rule. As I've mentioned earlier, we are going to learn how to do that process for C++ and blueprint. Well then, there are two ways to create data structures, and any fits any. Which means you can make:

- A blueprint data structure that is used within blueprint logic
- A blueprint data structure that is used within C++ code
- A C++ data structure that is used within C++ code
- A C++ data structure that is used within blueprint logic

What a variation we have!

But usually, I like to keep things familiar, so I use the blueprint-based data structures in case my game logic is blueprint based. And of course, the C++ based data structures used with the game logic based on C++. This makes much sense!

Blueprint data structure

Now all you need to do is, from the content browser, choose **Structure** from the **Blueprint** option of the **Add New** menu. This will create a data structure for you.

Now you have a data structure asset, but it is empty. Just double-click in order to open it inside the data editor. And all that you need to do, is to match the signature. Which means you create assets, with the names of the cell names in your Excel sheet and the same data type.

For example, for my weapons table, I can create (keep in mind that Bellz data structures are made in C++ and not in blueprint):

- **String**: **Icon**
- **String**: **DisplayName**
- **Integer**: **Damage**
- **Integer**: **CooldownTime**

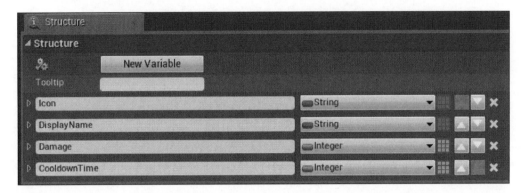

Now, I have a data structure that fits the same signature of my imported data asset. Now try to import the weapons table again and set its import data structure to that data structure which fits the signature.

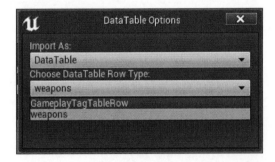

The resulting data asset will be fully imported now and can work just perfectly, and if you double-click on this asset file, you will find it looks just the same as the Excel sheet.

	Icon	DisplayName	Damage	CooldownTime
1	none_icon	Empty	0	0
2	sword_icon	The Hot Blade	5	1
3	axe_icon	The Sharpest	10	3
4	hammer_icon	The Mighty Hammer	15	6

C++ data structure

Now creating a data structure will require us to create a new class, a new C++ class, and we can base it on anything. I like to use **Actor** as my base.

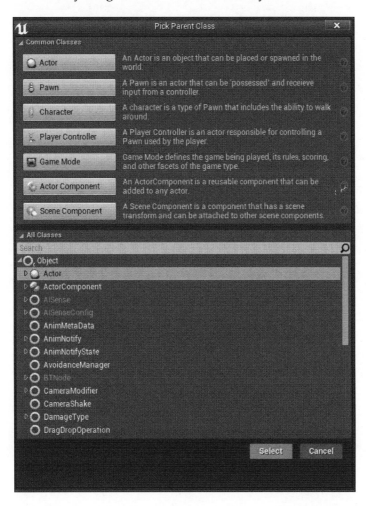

And as always, ladies first! Oh, I mean header files first. My header file setup is going to be simple, but it is very important, as much counts on that.

GameDataTables.h

Starting with the `include` statements as always, and as you can see, nothing fancy, but I have included a new header file that will allow me to manage the data table, which is `DataTable.h`:

```
#include "Engine/DataTable.h"
#include "GameFramework/Actor.h"
#include "GameDataTables.generated.h"
```

Then I started to directly build my structs. Remember the ones we created in blueprint? Now it is the time to create ones in C++. I built two structures using the word `struct` and the macro `USTRUCT`.

The first one is called `FWeaponStruct`, which is the type of `FTableRowBase` which is the equal of data table asset in a blueprint case. Within this struct, I've defined the same four variables I used within the blueprint sample, which are:

- `FString Icon`
- `FString DisplayName`
- `int32 Damage`
- `int32 CooldownTime`

Then, the most important part of creating the struct, is the constructor, which basically holds the struct name `FWeaponStruct()`, and some default values:

```
USTRUCT(Blueprintable)
struct FWeaponStruct : publicFTableRowBase
{
  GENERATED_USTRUCT_BODY()

public:

  UPROPERTY(VisibleAnywhere, BlueprintReadOnly)
    FString Icon;

  UPROPERTY(VisibleAnywhere, BlueprintReadOnly)
    FString DisplayName;

  UPROPERTY(VisibleAnywhere, BlueprintReadOnly)
```

```
      int32 Damage;

   UPROPERTY(VisibleAnywhere, BlueprintReadOnly)
      int32 CooldownTime;

   //default constructor
   FWeaponStruct()
   {
      Icon ="None";
      DisplayName ="None";
      Damage = 0;
      CooldownTime = 0;
   }
};
```

The second part of the code was to create the second table, which is for the missions, and is called FMissionStruct. Nothing fancy about it, I used the same concept as in creating the previous one, and setting a constructor for it. The only difference here, is the variable types and name, as it basically needed to match the signature of the Excel sheet (or the .csv file in other words):

- int32 Kill
- int32 Collect

The code is as follows:

```
USTRUCT(Blueprintable)
Struct FMissionStruct : publicFTableRowBase
{
   GENERATED_USTRUCT_BODY()

public:

   UPROPERTY(VisibleAnywhere, BlueprintReadOnly)
      int32 Kill;

   UPROPERTY(VisibleAnywhere, BlueprintReadOnly)
      int32 Collect;

   //default constructor
   FMissionStruct()
   {
      Kill = 0;
      Collect = 0;
   }
};
```

The last part of this class code is generating the actor class body. The point here is that you can't write the structs before the class, which is a C++ standard; as long as you are going to use those structs within the class itself, they need to be defined earlier.

At the beginning, the class has to be created, and extended from the `Actor` class, which is a default step, and usually it is autogenerated for you, as is the constructor and the couple of default methods (`begin play` and `tick`):

```
UCLASS()
class BELLZ_APIAGameDataTables : public AActor
{
  GENERATED_BODY()

public:
  // Sets default values for this actor's properties
  AGameDataTables();

  // Called when the game starts or when spawned
  virtual void BeginPlay() override;

  // Called every frame
  virtual void Tick( floatDeltaSeconds ) override;
```

Now, when the game starts, we somehow have to access the tables we have imported into the content browser. Which means we have assets which need to access it, but there must be a way to do that.

In fact, here comes the importance of the data structures, so while we have set the structures, and been able to import the assets, we can now create a `UDataTable` property for each table and mark its metadata to allow us to assign it in the **Details** panel:

```
//I used editanywhere, so I'll be able to assign it in the details
panel
  UPROPERTY(EditAnywhere, BlueprintReadWrite, Category = "Game
DataTables")
  UDataTable* WeaponsTable;

  UPROPERTY(EditAnywhere, BlueprintReadWrite, Category = "Game
DataTables")
  UDataTable* MissionsTable;
```

Then we create an array, `TArray`, of each data structure type (two for now, as there are two tables to be loaded) in order to store all the data from the table within its own data structure array:

```
//UPROPERTY(VisibleAnywhere, BlueprintReadWrite, Category = "Game
DataTables")
    TArray<FWeaponStruct*>AllWeaponsData;

    //UPROPERTY(VisibleAnywhere, BlueprintReadWrite, Category = "Game
DataTables")
    TArray<FMissionStruct*>AllMissionsData;
```

And finally, creating a method, that will be called, whenever we want to open the tables and execute them, which I called `OnFetchAllTables()`:

```
UFUNCTION(BlueprintCallable, Category = "Game DataTables")
    void OnFetchAllTables();
```

That's all that we want for the header file, two structures, and the class. Within the class, we need to define a table property for each table we want to use, and an array of the structure type of each table, and finally a method to access the tables and read them.

GameDataTables.cpp

As always, the `include` statements come first, but because my logic does not involve anything unexpected and all are normal and typical functions, the `include` statements are still the default ones for this class:

```
#include "Bellz.h"
#include "GameDataTables.h"
```

You will find that the code is split into two main pieces, the default methods and the `OnFetchAllTables()` method area. The default methods are left as they are here too. By this, I mean the `begin play`, `tick`, and the constructor, are left as the defaults. I did nothing with them. So you've got the chance to leave them or delete them. But I have left them only because I might need them in the future, especially the `begin play` method.

Also, I was initially going to assign the table assets to this class instance in code, within the constructor, but I found it is easier and involves less typing when we just set them in **public**, and assign them directly in the editor, within the **Details** panel. So feel free to do what makes you happy with this part:

```
// Sets default values
AGameDataTables::AGameDataTables()
```

```
{
  // Set this actor to call Tick() every frame.  You can turn this off
to improve performance if you don't need it.
  PrimaryActorTick.bCanEverTick = true;

}

// Called when the game starts or when spawned
void AGameDataTables::BeginPlay()
{
  Super::BeginPlay();

  //In case I want to call it at the beginning, but the most safe way
is to call it from the outside, probably from the player class
  //OnFetchAllTables();
}

// Called every frame
void AGameDataTables::Tick( floatDeltaTime )
{
  Super::Tick(DeltaTime );

}
```

And now for the huge piece, and where the magic happens, this is the `OnFetchAllTables()` method. It is basically running through a tidy and ordered process, which makes sense, and it is as follows:

1. First, I have created an `FString` and named it `ContextString`, and set its default value to `Name`. This will be used for the search.

2. Starting from this point, we will be coding for the `weapons` table, and then repeating the same thing for any other tables we have.

3. Then I created an array for the name `TArray<FName>` and named it `weaponsTableRowsNames`. This is for the first column of the table of weapons, this is used to return the cells names, which means the name of each cell at the beginning of each row. These cells have been named as numbers. Later we will convert these names to numbers, to be used for looping.

4. Then we run a `for` loop with the amount of rows (the total number of `weaponsTableRowsNames` array members).

5. Within each iteration of the loop, convert the number of the row into a string name, `IndexString`.

6. Then convert this string called `IndexString` into an `FName` variable type, called `IndexString`.

7. The previous two conversions have been made for only one reason, to be able to use the method `FindRow`, which requires an `FName` variable to be passed through it. Neither `int` nor `string`.

8. Then create a new struct of the weapons struct type, `FWeaponStruct` (as we are processing the weapons table now), and call it `aStructRow`.

9. Assign the current row data, to this newly created struct using `WeaponsTable->FindRow<FWeaponStruct>`.

10. Finally, assign `aStructRow` to the array we have created at the header file, the one called `AllWeaponsData`.

11. Now by the end of this loop, the `AllWeaponsData` will have all the data of the table stored within it.

After that, do a quick for loop to look within the `AllWeaponsData` array, and print all its data to the screen.

Then redo the whole process for any other tables which need to be read and stored, which in my case, is one more table for `missions`. And the end result of code will be this:

```
void AGameDataTables::OnFetchAllTables()
{
  //Any will be okay, not necessarily to be this cell name
  static const FString ContextString(TEXT("Name"));

  //Get all the row names and store them temporary here, the point is
to define the amount of rows, the best way yet!
  TArray<FName>weaponsTableRowsNames = WeaponsTable->GetRowNames();

  //usually we used 0 as the start index, but a table have it' first
row indexed as 1, other wise it will crash
  for (int32i = 1; i<weaponsTableRowsNames.Num() + 1; i++)
  {
    FString IndexString = FString::FromInt((int32)i);
    FNameIndexName = FName(*IndexString);

    FWeaponStruct* aStructRow = WeaponsTable-
>FindRow<FWeaponStruct>(IndexName, ContextString, true);
    AllWeaponsData.Add(aStructRow);
  }
```

```
    //GEngine->AddOnScreenDebugMessage(-1, 2.f, FColor::Red,
FString::FromInt(AllWeaponsData.Num()));

    //Just a print to screen to check if I got all the values correctly!
    for (int32 c = 0; c <AllWeaponsData.Num(); c++)
    {
        FString message = TEXT(" Number: ") +FString::FromInt(c)
+TEXT(" Name: ") +AllWeaponsData[c]->DisplayName+TEXT(" Icon: ")
+AllWeaponsData[c]->Icon +TEXT(" Damage: ") +FString::FromInt(AllWeapo
nsData[c]->Damage) +TEXT(" Cooldown: ") +FString::FromInt(AllWeaponsDa
ta[c]->CooldownTime);
        GEngine->AddOnScreenDebugMessage(-1, 10.f, FColor::Red, message);
    }



    //Get all the row names and store them temporary here, the point is
to define the amount of rows, the best way yet!
    TArray<FName>missionsTableRowsNames = MissionsTable->GetRowNames();

    //usually we used 0 as the start index, but a table have it' first
row indexed as 1, other wise it will crash
    for (int32 e = 1; e <missionsTableRowsNames.Num() + 1; e++)
    {
        FString IndexString = FString::FromInt((int32)e);
        FNameIndexName = FName(*IndexString);

        FMissionStruct* aStructRow = MissionsTable->FindRow<FMissionStruct
>(IndexName, ContextString, true);
        AllMissionsData.Add(aStructRow);
    }
    //GEngine->AddOnScreenDebugMessage(-1, 2.f, FColor::Red, FString::Fr
omInt(AllMissionsData.Num()));

    //Just a print to screen to check if I got all the values correctly!
    for (int32 x = 0; x <AllMissionsData.Num(); x++)
    {
        FString message = TEXT(" Number: ") +FString::FromInt(x) +TEXT("
Kills: ") +FString::FromInt(AllMissionsData[x]->Kill) +TEXT("
Collects: ") +FString::FromInt(AllMissionsData[x]->Collect);
        GEngine->AddOnScreenDebugMessage(-1, 10.f, FColor::Green,
message);
    }
}
```

Reading from data tables

Now we come to the last part of creating and using a data table within Unreal Engine, and it is the most fun part of this process.

While the book mainly uses C++ in order to build Bellz, I would not only like to mention how to make use of the data from C++ code, but also I would like to show you how to use it from within a blueprint. Which means data tables are now fully supported within both systems. In the early stages of Unreal, using data tables was something for C++ users only, but things have changed now.

As you have seen in the previous section, we were only building the data structures, which here represents a form that matches the Excel sheet form, but in a form of code. In order to be able to read the data from the files, we first need to choose which file to read, and secondly, get the data from it within a loop, usually.

Reading data through C++

Now for the easiest part of code. Remember *Chapter 2, Setting Up Your Warrior*, when we built the player controller? There was a variable type of AGameDataTables which we named TablesInstance within the Gladiator.h header file. This will mainly be holding all the information we need, or in other words, an instance of what the data manager has. This will make it easier every time we need to read or get some data:

```
#include "GameDataTables.h"
```

Calling the OnFetchAllTables() method now is even more easy. I like to do it at the beginning of the level, so in each level start, I just go through the data holder in the level, and then read all the data at once, and temporarily store it.

While there are several ways to do it, I usually like to use TActorIterator in order to search for all data holders in the map, and then call whatever function I want:

```
void AGladiator::BeginPlay()
{
  //Ask the datamanager to get all the tables data at once and store
them
  //AGameDataTablesdataHolder;
  for (TActorIterator<AGameDataTables>ActorItr(GetWorld()); ActorItr;
++ActorItr)
  {
    if (ActorItr)
    {
      //print the instance name to screen
```

```
        //GEngine->AddOnScreenDebugMessage(-1, 10.f, FColor::Green,
ActorItr->GetName());

        //Call the fetch to the tables, now we get all the datat stored.
Why? simply because keep readineverytime from the table itself is
going to cost over your memory
        //but the most safe method, is just to read all the data at
once, and then keep getting whatever needed values from the storage
we've.
        TablesInstance = *ActorItr;
        TablesInstance->OnFetchAllTables();


    }
  }
}
```

Now while we have all the code working perfectly fine, let's just do one more little thing to read it.

As you used to create blueprints based on the C++ code we make, go ahead and create a blueprint based on the GameDataTables class, and then drag an instance of this blueprint into the scene. That means you have an instance of a data holder. I gave mine a fancy gizmo, though!

Now from the **Details** panel of the blueprint instance, you can select which data asset files are to be used as **WeaponsTable** and **MissionsTable**. Just set the correct ones there:

Now once you hit **Run**, the expected behavior is:

- As long as there is a player in the map, the `begin play` method of the `Gladiator` (the player) class, will be executed
- That will allow it to search for any class instance in the map that is a type of `AGameDataTables`
- When one is found (the one you just put there), it will call the method `OnFetchAllTables()` on it
- This method will go through all the tables, and temporarily save what has been found in the tables inside the `AllWeaponsData` array and `AllMissionsData` array
- Finally, all the data will be printed to the screen:

And now anytime you need any data from the table, you just need to access the data holder (the instance inside the map) and do your shopping between data!

Reading through blueprints

Reading data through blueprints is even easier, as you can do it using only one node call. Unreal Engine has a small section within the nodes list that is composed of two nodes only (so far!). It is called **Data Table**; you can use either of them to read data from a certain table:

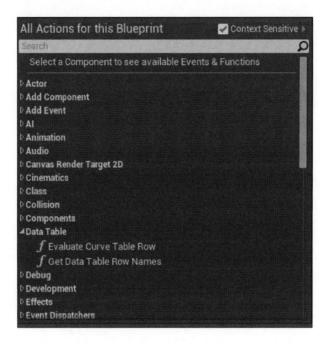

As there are different types of tables, you can use a different node that fits the situation, but in general, you can use the **Evaluate Curve Table Row** option with curve assets

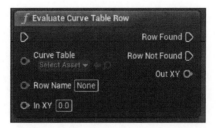

And you can use the **Get Data Table Row Names** node with the tables based on data structures. Just like the two tables of Bellz.

You might find it easier to read the data through blueprints. It is up to you. Just remember that as long as you are creating a C++ project, you are still able to execute any amount of the logic through blueprints, as C++ alone will never work, and you will need at least 10% blueprints within your project.

Summary

After this tasty chapter, you now have a better understanding of data tables management within the Unreal Engine environment, and you are able to use any type and any size of data table without any problems.

You've learned what the data table is and what it is used for, and most importantly how to prepare one for Unreal Engine. Unreal has its own policies and you learned what is going to respect those policies.

The data table files you made, regardless of the app, should be converted to .csv, in order to convert it to a data table asset. You also learned what the data table asset is and what is the different data type assets that you can use.

A data table is useless without a form, guidelines, and a data structure to follow, it's the link between the Excel sheet form and the code. Without a data structure, there is a missing pipe within the flow, and you've learned how to build it within C++.

The reason for creating data tables, is to derive some values during gameplay, in order to keep it balanced. And while Unreal Engine provides the game developers with two different methods of building the game logic, you have learned how you can make a use of the data tables you've made and how you can read data either within C++ or blueprints.

Now go ahead, build the tables you want. They don't have to be weapons or missions. Based on them create some, build their structures, and most importantly, be able to read them during the game. And once you are done, you will find me waiting for you by the door of the next chapter, where we are going to make some NOISE.

12
Ear Candy

While all games have audio and sound effects mixed with a nice background music, a lot of players either mute the game or do not even put their headphones on at all! But you can change all of this, if your game idea and its design and concept somehow depends on the sound effects, the narrations, and so one.

What I want to say here is that the audio element is an essential part of any game, and you can not only make it sort of candy that beautifies your game, but you can enforce it to be a core element within the game, so that if the player ignored it, the experience would not exist.

Audio types within the game can vary between music or sound effects. Sound effects themselves can vary between UI effects, gameplay effects, or voiceovers, but whatever the goal that an audio file is being used for within the game, the process of importing the file and using it within the game is the same, regardless of the audio file format.

And that's our topic here: audio files, how to get them into Unreal, and how to make the best use of them within the Unreal ecosystem.

By the end of this chapter, you will be able to:

- Import audio files and specify their settings
- Understand the difference between sound assets
- Use the sound cue editor to build some audio cues
- Understand how to use audio volumes, in order to control audio through the environment
- Play sound effects at any moment of your game via C++ code, blueprints, notifications, or something else

While we have a good set of targets, I would suggest you to go first and download some free sound effects, music, or even purchase online the ones you want, and make a good library of the sound files that match your game needs. But if you are creating Bellz, just like me, then you'll find all the sound files within the book project, just migrate them as we discussed in *Chapter 1, Preparing for a Big Project*.

Importing audio files

When it comes to importing an audio file, it is done in the same way as any other type of file you want to get into Unreal. You could either do it by dragging it into the content browser directly or through the right-click menu of the content browser, or even by hitting the big **Import** button in the content browser, just like any other asset. But the point here is, the type of audio files that you can import.

While all other engines support various types of audio files, such as *.wav, *.mp3, *.ogg, and so on, not all platforms support the same file formats. Unreal Engine accepts only the *.wav* file, nothing else. That means if you are trying to import an audio file of type *.mp3 for example, Unreal will not reject it but at the same time it will not be considered as an audio file, and probably will be imported as a movie, that you can't neither play nor watch.

Sometimes you can think of this as a bad thing. But in fact it is a very neat and powerful thing, as you have to export all your audio files, regardless of their usage, as *.wav files, and all of them with the same set of parameters. Regardless of the targeted platform, Unreal Engine will work on making those *.wav files work on the platform's beloved format. And this came from the fact that WAV data is saved in bulk as PCM.

And because of that, Epic and the community came up with a specific export setting for audio files that makes the best use out of the engine, and it is easy to apply in any audio application you are using to produce the files. In general, when you are about to export a sound effect or music file, you have to make sure you apply the following settings in your third-party app:

- **Specifications**: PCM, ADPCM, DVI ADPCM
- **Format**: .wav
- **Bit rate**: 16
- **Speaker channels**: Mono, stereo, 2.1, 4.1, 5.1 6.1, 7.1

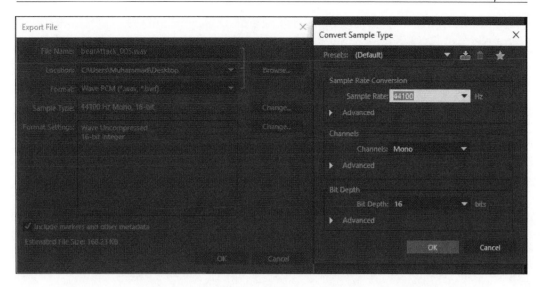

And keep in mind that Unreal Engine currently supports importing uncompressed little-endian 16-bit wave files at any sample rate (but a sample rate of 44,100 Hz or 22,050 Hz is recommended by the Epic team).

Once your audio file is inside Unreal Engine, it will no longer be called an audio file, but rather a sound wave asset and will be colored in purple. This sound wave asset has more settings that you can apply for it, just like importing a three-dimensional model, after getting the file into Unreal, you can apply some settings and compressions for it inside Unreal's model editor. The same applies here, double-clicking on this sound wave asset will open the sound wave asset editor, where you can apply some compressions, or standard settings for the wave file.

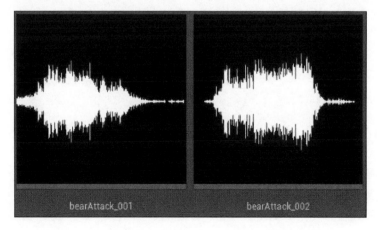

Once you open the sound wave editor for a certain file, you can find the following options adjust them in a way that fits your files. And yes, you have to do it for almost all sound files you import into Unreal!

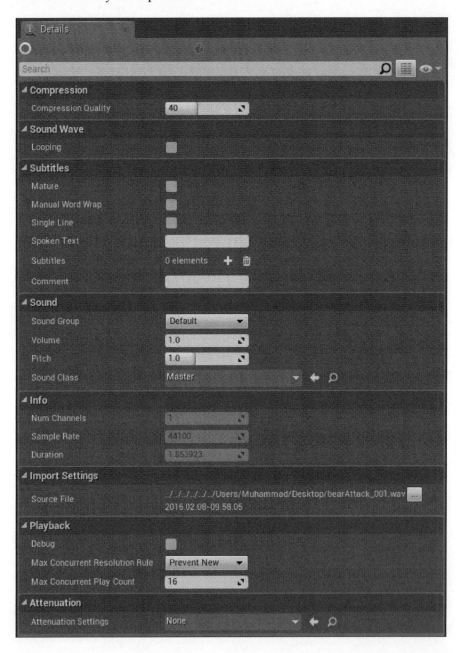

Let's look at the settings:

- **Compression**: This section has the following option:
  - ○ **Compression Quality**: This is a slider for compression versus quality; while **1** means the best compression, the maximum value (**100**) means the best quality

- **Sound Wave**: This section has the following option:
  - ○ **Looping**: Usually when you play a sound using a cue, you have to define if it is looped or not. But while there are several ways to play a sound, you can set a looping status by default that does not depend on a cue.

- **Subtitle**: This section has the following options:
  - ○ **Mature**: The only time you need to set this option to `true` is in the case of adult and/or mature content.
  - ○ **Manual Word Wrap**: When you are using subtitles for the audio, you have two ways to split line breaks, either manually or automatically generated. If you don't want the line breaks to be autogenerated, then turn on this option.
  - ○ **Single Line**: Setting this option to `true` will display the subtitles as a sequence of single lines.
  - ○ **Spoken Text**: What does the audio say?
  - ○ **Subtitles**: IThis represents the subtitle cues. If you leave it empty, then the previous value will be used.
  - ○ **Comment**: Just comments for yourself and the other team members; probably the localization people will be using this field. But nothing here will be displayed to the players.

- **Sound**: This section has the following options:
  - ○ **Sound Group**: Just give your sound file a group to list it
  - ○ **Volume**: The default playback volume for your sound
  - ○ **Pitch**: The pitch amount for the sound; it represents a simple linear multiplier to the sample rate
  - ○ **Sound Class**: Choose a sound class that this sound belongs to; you can leave it at **Master** if you don't have classes in the content browser

- **Info**: This section has the following options:
  - ° **Num Channels**: The total number of channels of the multichannel data
  - ° **Sample Rate**: The cached sample rate for displaying within the editor tools
  - ° **Duration**: The total duration of the sound on seconds

- **Import Settings**: This section has the following option:
  - ° **Source File**: Where are the source files in the disk?

- **Debug**: This section has the following option:
  - ° **Debug**: A useful option you need to set while debugging sound issues. It is basically going to display the sound file name/data as long as it is playing, on the screen. But only if you set **Stat Sounds -debug**, from the console variables.

- **Concurrency**: This section has the following options:
  - ° **Override Concurrency**: Whether to override the concurrency or not.
  - ° **Sound Concurrency Settings**: It works only if the previous option was set to `true`. And basically this option gives you the chance to choose a sound concurrency asset to be used. You can create a sound concurrency as an asset within the content browser.
  - ° **Concurrency Overrides**: If this sound is using concurrency, the settings for it will be here.
  - ° **Max Count**: Represents the maximum number of allowable concurrent active voices for voices playing in this concurrency group.
  - ° **Limit to Owner**: Set this if you want to limit the concurrency to the sound owner (the actor that is playing the sound).
  - ° **Resolution Rule**: What is the concurrency resolution that should be used in case the sound reaches the maximum voice count?
  - ° **Volume Scale**: Represents the amount of attenuation to apply to each voice instance in this concurrency group.
  - ° **Priority**: The sound priority over other sounds. The higher the value, the higher the priority.

- **Attenuation**: This section has the following options:

  ○ **Ignore Focus**: Tells us whether to ignore the focus or not.

  ○ **Attenuation Settings**: The attenuation settings asset to be used for the sound. You can browse for it in the content browser.

Now you go ahead, and set the settings you want for all your audio files. Sometimes the default values work well, but at other times you have to set certain options. But most importantly you probably will have to visit the settings area to set at least one value, which is the volume.

As you might have noticed in games, each layer of audio has its own volume value, and that is something particular to the game and its requirements. This is something mostly done by the audio engineers, and while there isn't a working value that fits all types of game, Epic games advise developers to use this formula in most cases:

- Dialog: 1.4
- Music: 0.75
- Weapons: 1.1
- Ambience: 0.5

Sound assets

As you might have seen, many of the settings for a sound file count on having specific types of assets. One time, you might need a sound class while at other times you might need a sound concurrency, and even more types of assets within other situations.

And that's because the Unreal Engine sound audio system has lots of those assets in order to give you the opportunity to get the best out of your audio file. Not every single change within a sound file needs to be made within a third party; you can still make a change in the way a sound file is heard using those different types of asset.

All the sound assets types could be made within the content browser, either from the right-click menu or from the big green button called **Add New**. With any of the methods you decide to use, you will find all the sound-related asset types listed under the **Sounds** submenu.

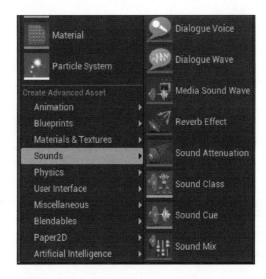

As you can see there are nine supported types of sound asset files, the majority of them are represent some kind of data structure, where you have to set a bunch of options and values, while a few of them represent a logical asset, where you have to connect some nodes within a graph. Let's get look at each in more depth, and the best usage of each asset type.

Dialogue Voice

Dialogue Voice is not actually very useful on its own, as it is a preparation asset to be used within a dialogue wave asset.

Within **Dialogue Voice**, you can set only two types of information: the gender of the spoken dialogue, and its plurality.

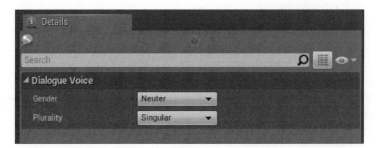

Dialogue Wave

The **Dialogue Wave** asset is one of the most important sound asset types. With the information you make within a **Dialogue Voice** asset, you can import it inside the **Dialogue Wave** asset in order to use it. This type of asset has its own editor responsible for the correlation between the dialogue audio and the subtitle text.

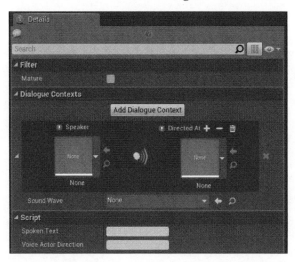

Media sound wave

This type of asset represents an implementation of a sound asset from a media player asset (a media player asset is the `UMediaPlayer` object, a video, for example). The rest of the options and settings you can set for it are then all like a normal sound wave asset you've imported.

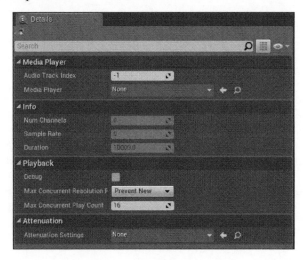

Reverb effect

Within Unreal Engine lots of things are performed inside maps during gameplay through volumes. One of those things is sound. While you can have audio volumes around your map, you will need to apply settings for those volumes in order to play the audio in a certain way or a different tone. And that's where the **Reverb** effect asset is important. With that asset you can define lots of properties that will be applied to any audio inside the volume.

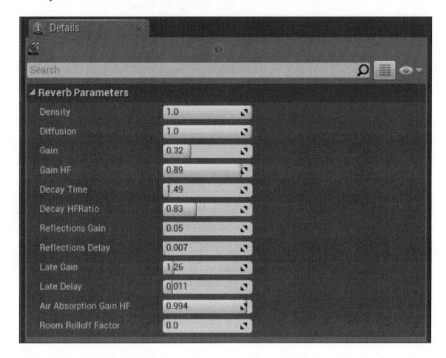

Sound attenuation

Remember that when we spoke about importing sound files, some settings related to sound attenuation? Well, what if you have set those settings for a 100 files, and, once you realize that you have been choosing some wrong options, you want to apply some changes to all of them?

Well, the good news is, you don't have to redo all of them. So you can create a sound attenuation asset that holds the options and properties you want and apply this asset to the sounds. And at any time you have to make changes, you just do it once inside the asset file!

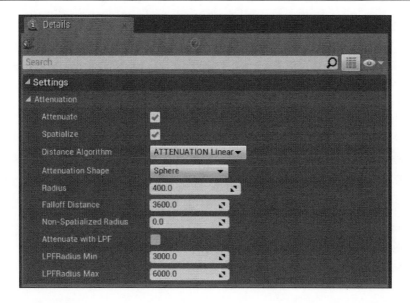

Sound Class

In the same way you can apply sound attenuation settings to lots of files at once, the **Sound Class** asset does just the same job, but for a different set of properties.

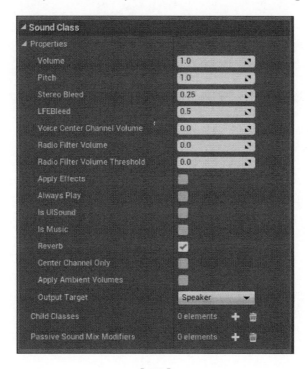

Sound cue

A sound cue is a place where you can combine audio effects or apply audio modifiers using sound nodes and create final output within an output node. So it is basically like a small audio editing app, and the asset is the outcome of that app. It uses nodes called sound nodes in order to achieve this result.

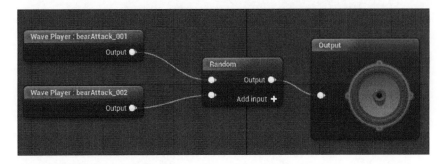

Sound mixes

Remember running Winamp in the old days, or even any recent media player that gives you equalizers?

Well a sound mix does exactly the same thing: it allows you to set equalizer settings and modify the properties of the **Sound Class** assets.

Sound cue editor

The sound cue editor's main job is to make sounds more appealing and creative, by applying pieces of logic. The sound cue editor is accessible directly by clicking over a sound cue asset. You can have tons and tons of those assets around the project, code, logic, and maps, and it is a replaces for directly using the sound wave asset.

Then what is the difference between using this asset type and the sound wave?

Well, you can apply some parameters, randomizations, and much more. But the most common reason to use the sound cue asset is to apply randomization to assets. So let's give an example from Bellz, and then you can just follow the recipe, improvise with different sound nodes, and you'll get great results!

When a bear is attacking, there are several audios being played. But, as you can see, I used several nodes, in order to make it sound unique each time.

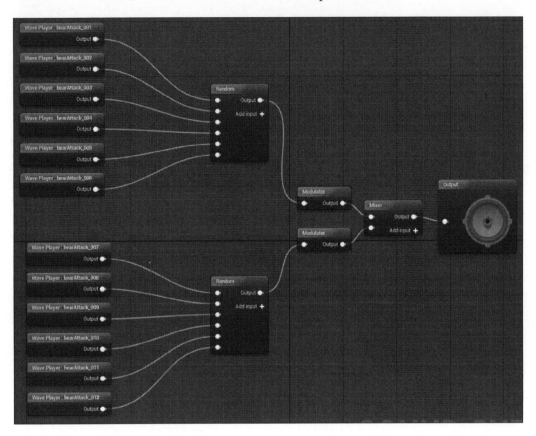

I used the following options:

- **Random**: In order to choose a different sound file randomly every time
- **Modulator**: In order to apply a different volume or pitch modification every time the sound plays
- **Mixer**: In order to play different sounds together

Connecting all these to the output will result in a different these every time. Try to keep playing and pausing from the top bar controls, and you'll hear it. And that's about it the sound cue editor; just make variations and try to make the sound play uniquely every time.

Audio volumes

Audio volume works like any other volume within Unreal Engine, which means it represents a type of effect that takes place inside the bounds of that invisible volume.

You can find the **Audio Volume** actor in the same place as all the other volumes, which means under the **Volumes** section of the **Modes** panel. Alternatively, you can just create a brush and convert it to an audio volume as we have done several times during *Chapter 3, Designing Your Playground*.

After inserting the audio volume, all that you can do is either position it, scale it to fit the area of effect, or set its parameters. While the audio volume contains some of the standard parameters that are found within any other volume, such as the **Transform** settings, **Brush** settings, and **Actor** setting, there are another three major sections of settings that give this volume its personality.

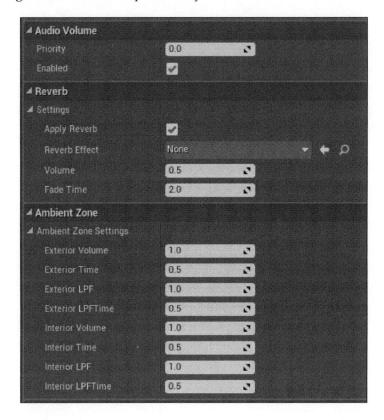

They are as follows:

- **Audio Volume**: This section has the following options:
  - **Priority**: If this volume overlaps another, this value will define its priority over the other
  - **Enabled**: Define if this volume works or not

- **Reverb**: This section has the following options
  - **Apply Reverb**: Define if the reverb effect works or not
  - **Reverb Effect**: You have to browse for the **Reverb** effect asset from the content browser, the one that has the parameters you want to use

○ **Volume**: The volume level of the Reverb effect

○ **Fade Time**: The amount of time used to fade the currently active Reverb settings into those held by this volume

- **Ambient Zone**: This section has the following options:

  ○ **Exterior Volume**: The required volume of sound outside this volume when the player is inside the volume

  ○ **Exterior Time**: The amount of interpolation to apply the previous volume value (**Exterior Volume**)

  ○ **Exterior LPF**: The required frequency cutoff (in Hertz) of sound outside this volume when the player is inside the volume

  ○ **Exterior LPF Time**: The amount of interpolation to apply the previous value (**Exterior LPF**)

  ○ **Interior Volume**: The required volume of sound inside this volume when the player is outside the volume

  ○ **Interior Time**: The amount of interpolation to apply the previous volume value (**Interior Volume**)

  ○ **Interior LPF**: The required frequency cutoff (in Hertz) of sound inside this volume when the player is outside the volume

  ○ **Interior LPF Time**: The amount of interpolation to apply the previous value (**Interior LPF**)

Now that you totally understand all the parameters that you can set, go ahead and throw some audio volumes within your environment and keep testing them, to see how it looks and feel when you hear the audio in different ways within a specific area. The best practice would be if you have a cave in your map; an audio volume will work just great there with the correct values for the parameters.

Playing sound effects

When it comes to playing any type of sound, Unreal gives you more than one method and you have to pick the one that fits you and the situation of that sound. The most common and popular methods I've found are:

- **Through C++ code**: You can play the sound of any `AudioComponent`, by simply using the member function `Play()` and, yes, just one line to run a sound.

```
AudioComp.Play(float StartTimer);
```

- **Through blueprint nodes**: Within a blueprint you can simply play sound using any of the **Play Sound** nodes. You can play a 2D sound, which means it will have the same volume always, or play it at a location in order to fade the sound in and out while getting closer or further away from it.

- **Through animation notifications**: Just as we used to set an animation notification to call some parts of the code, in the same way you can add a notification of the type **PlaySound** and it has its own options within the notifications menu.

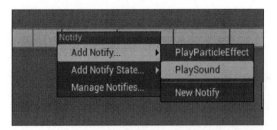

After adding it, selecting the notification itself, will give you a set of options at the **Details** panel for that specific notification, which will be mainly to choose a sound or sound cue to be played among other sound properties that you are already familiar with right now.

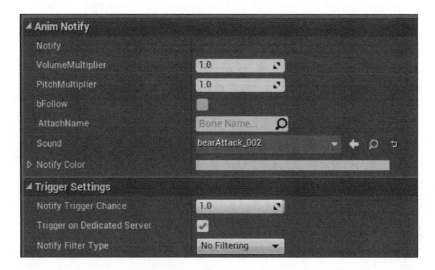

- **Drag and drop**: By dropping any sound wave asset or sound cue asset inside the map, it will run directly as soon as the game starts, and I guess this method only works well with ambience.

While there is no specific method to play sounds, you have all of them at hand. Depending on the situation, you can decide which one to go with. Sometimes you'll have to fire it from the logic itself, either C++ or blueprints. But other times it is better and more accurate for it to be tied with the animation frames, or even throwing it into the map might get the job done. It is up to you and the goal of that sound!

Summary

Congratulations, you have just learned the necessary tools and techniques to be a noisy games developer. Games without audio makes for a bad experience; the minimum amount of audio and effects is essential to deliver an experience.

Regardless of the usage of an audio file, you have learned all the properties that you can tweak for a sound wave file. Whether it is background music, dialog, or effects, it doesn't matter. All of them share the same properties at the end of the day.

Of course Unreal Engine has a wide range of sound assets, a really wide range. Each has its own job, but all of them are here to allow you to be productive and give you the chance to control the tiniest detail that might be heard.

Sound cues are an amazing solution. Lots of other engines make you write your own tools to modularize the same set of sound files you have, but with the sound cue asset and its editor, it becomes very easy to modularize a small amount of sounds and shuffle between them in order to make variations.

Sometimes the visual experience has more impact than sounds, and you learned how to use the audio volumes and what parameters to tweak, in order to give each area of the map its own personality.

Playing a sound can be tricky; there are different methods that you can follow to play a piece of sound, but it all depends on the situation, and you have learned about the four methods provided by Epic.

Now, go ahead, be noisy, and add some ear candy before moving on!

13
Profiling the Game Performance

Once you have completed the gameplay section, and you have a game ready to be built and shared with players, you have to spend some time making sure that the game is as free from issues as possible, and its performance is well balanced, with no frame rate drops, no glitches, and most importantly no crashes.

The debugging and profiling phase might take too long, it depends on how you have constructed your game, and how much care you gave earlier to the game code, blueprints, and graphical and rendering items. A major part of the debugging is for the code, but this is a typical debugging via Visual Studio which you are already familiar with, and debugging code here works the same as it does anything else. But the parts we are going to focus on during this chapter are the ones that could be made directly through the editor itself.

Of course, there are a lot of profiling tools and performance analyzers out there, but the majority of them are paid tools, and not that cheap. And here comes our super hero, Epic, with its amazing set of tools, that areas free as the engine itself. Epic is doing a great job with the Unreal ecosystem. There are a lot of tools and editors within Unreal that are used to serve different jobs and tasks while you are optimizing and freeing your game from bugs, and that's what we have to do right now.

By the end of this chapter, you will be able to:

- Understand how to debug blueprints in the editor using the blueprint debugger
- Use the collision analyzer and understand its job
- Use the editor and game console commands

- Create FPS charts and read them to analyze the game performance

- Switch between the different view modes and the visualizers to define the rendering performance issues

- Use the GPU visualizer

- Understand the device manager and the importance of the device profiles

While we have a huge table of targets, let's get started and launch the game editor. One thing to keep in mind while we are debugging is that the majority of the editors and tools are always listed under the **Window** menu at the **Developer Tools** section as defined in the following screenshot:

The blueprint debugger

Debugging code is a process which usually involves using breakpoints inside the IDE (which is Visual Studio here), but what if the game logic, or even parts of it have been made in a form of blueprints, then how could we debug those parts?

Well, Unreal Engine supports breakpoints for the blueprints logic as well, and that makes it easier to debug any graph-based logic. You can simply add a breakpoint to any node within a blueprint by simply right-clicking over the node, and choosing **Add Breakpoint**. It will be represented by a red circle at the top-right corner of the node:

Later, this choice will be replaced by a few other ones such as:

- **Remove Breakpoint**
- **Toggle Breakpoint**
- **Disable Breakpoint**

As expected, once you run the game, and the logic is about to execute the node that holds the breakpoint, then the game stops, and Unreal launches the blueprint for you, with the node highlighted:

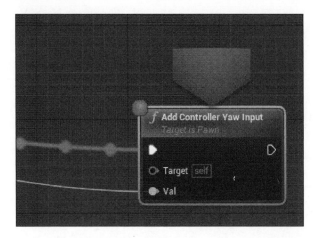

That's one way of using the breakpoints. And it is a great thing to do! However, when we debug the code via breakpoints, we can do a stack track as we would in a code breakpoint within Visual Studio. Which means we can follow its roots: The method, action, event, or node called before we call the node with a breakpoint. And the thing before that thing, and so on. We can keep tracking the whole sequence of logic.

That's exactly the usage of the blueprint debugger. Once you have the game paused because of a breakpoint, you can directly open the blueprint debugger, and there you'll find the **Execution Trace** point of that breakpoint:

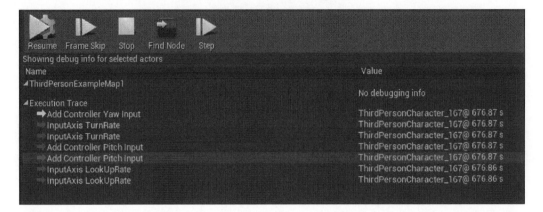

Reading this trace is exactly like how we do it in C++ and Visual Studio. You can keep tracking, reading values of the different variables until you spot the location of the problem. And, as with any other debugging tool, the blueprint debugger gives you the same set of buttons you find in something like Visual Studio or Xcode, which includes:

- **Resume**
- **Frame Skip**
- **Stop FPS Chart**
- **Step**

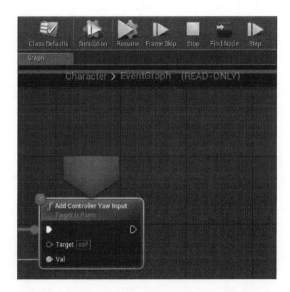

So if you have a logic error or bug that is related to a blueprint logic, then go ahead and throw some breakpoints at the suspicious locations and fire your blueprint debugger to do a typical tracking as you would do with Visual Studio. And remember, clicking on any part of the trace will take you directly to the responsible node in your blueprints, just like a typical code trace, but let's call it a node trace!

The Collision Analyzer

The only case where you might need to use this editor is when you have collision, overlapping or hitting events problems. As you can see from the tool name, it is all about and for physics collisions.

One of the most interesting things about this tool is it is very easy to use, and it is a tool that could be used at any time of the project development. Which means you can use it in the **Edit** mode while building your game, or while the game is running via the **Play In Editor** (**PIE**). Any time you hit the **Record** button, the tool will serve you directly:

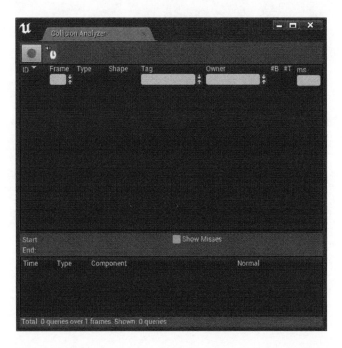

Once you hit **Record**, and let's say it's at runtime, the tool will start recording all the collisions that happen in the game, regardless of how weak or powerful they are, and regardless of whether they are at the camera view or not. Any single collision taking place will be recorded. Once you feel you're done, you can just hit the **Stop** button.

The result you have is very important, as you can understand what collisions have taken place, and what were the parties of each collision event, and which class or blueprint is responsible for that, and, most importantly you can learn about the time spent and the hit or collision times in a single frame.

Sometimes physics goes weird, and an event or hit registers twice; you have no way that you can catch it and understand the reason, except by using **Collision Analyzer**.

One of the coolest things that you can learn about your game collisions is that, when you choose any of the recorded collisions from the list, they will show you the exact position where this collision took place, and the exact position where the collision ended!

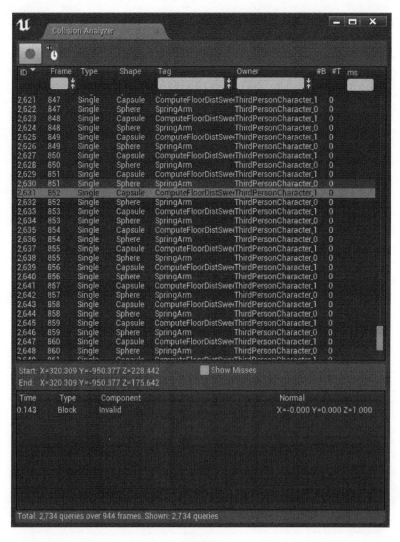

Also, the analyzer gives you a total of the collisions that took place at the time of recording, which means that you can understand out if you have more collisions than you should have or not, and again you can start working on that.

In a nutshell, the tool records everything for you, but what to do with the recorder results? It is something back to you and your needs. If you don't know yet why you need some results, then no problem, you can hit the **Save** button to save it in a form of a *UCA file, and you can open it later using the same tool!

The console

Any version of the Unreal Editor, or any game built with Unreal Engine, could have a console within it. This console has tons of variables that you can turn on or off, sometimes to display stuff, and other times to just hide something away.

If you don't know how to display the console, it is usually done using the input key ` for any game or any other game engine, and that's the default button for it within Unreal Engine, but you can change it in **Input Settings** of **Project Settings**.

Unreal Engine provides a number of console variables, which could be used at runtime in order to debug the game. However, some of those console variables are called **show flags**, which are implemented there in order to allow you to toggle a lot of rendering features at runtime. But that is only in the executable builds; in edit time (inside the editor) it is even easier, as the editor is a convenient place to have lots of menus and buttons, The Epic team puts them in one of those menus, which will be discussed later in this chapter in the *The view modes and visualizers* section:

In the game, you can use the **Show** command. Use the **Show** command to get a list of all show flags and their states. Use `showflagname` to toggle a feature.

All the show flags are exposed as console variables, for example the console show bloom, `showflag.Bloom 0` or in configuration `*.ini files: showflag.Bloom = 0`:

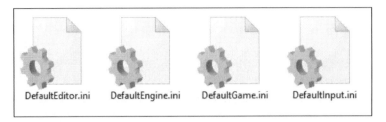

Keep in mind that some features will consume performance even if the feature is not enabled and not rendering anymore! Yeah, I know it sounds silly, but, for example, disabling the show flag `show particles` will hide the particles. The particles are hidden, but simulation time is still running in order to make the particles work properly when re-enabling them at a later time! So, it is not rendered, but it still calculates for the possibility of enabling it again. It is not the only example, but there are tons of other things that are disabled, but unfortunately are still running underground.

The FPS charts

The console is not only made for immediate toggles or displays or even an immediate value change. Using console commands such as `StartFPSChart` and `StopFPSChart` will allow you to generate a performance chart over a period of time:

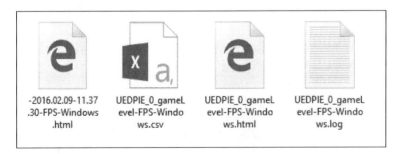

Using such a command will generate a `*.csv` file in the `Profiling` folder which is located at `ProjectFolder]\Saved\Profiling\SubwayPatrol\FPSChartStats)\` `[Date of today]\`.

Then you can easily load that `*.csv` file with Excel or any similar app. Then you can check the values you want which is very straightforward. Once you open the file in Excel, just mark the cells you want to visualize, and create a chart for it:

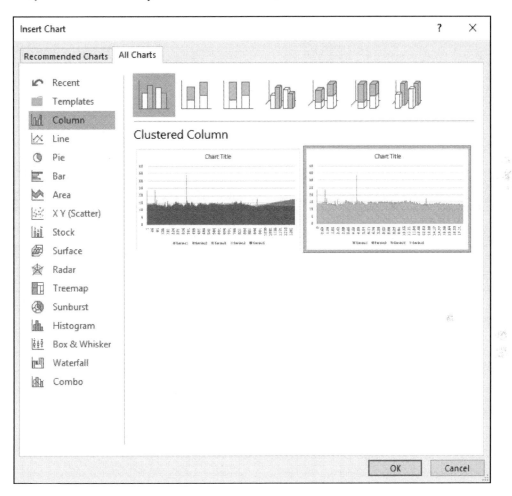

It might be a very useful step to get the stat unit times over a period of time where you suspect some performance issues:

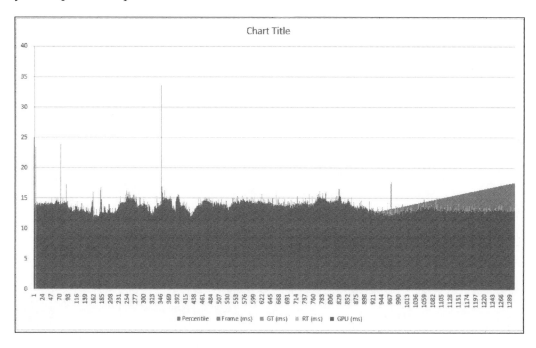

The *.csv file is not only what you get, but it is the most important one. You also get a *.log file which contain lots of useful information along with two tables of HTML files that hold some more info about the frames. And everything mostly named with the map/level name:

mapname	changelist	datestamp	OS	CPU	GPU	Res Qual	View Dist Qual	AA Qual	Shadow Qual	PP Qual	Tex Qual	FX Qual	avg FPS	% over 30 FPS
2016.02.09-11.37.30	2818968	2016.02.09-11.37.48	Windows 10	GenuineIntel Intel(R) Core (TM) i7-3770 CPU @ 3.40GHz	NVIDIA GeForce GTX 880MX	100	3	3	3	3	3	3	73.75	99.81

The view modes and visualizers

The view modes are one of the easiest ways in Unreal Engine that you can use to isolate some behaviors. They look like just a combination of show flags within the editor UI, but they hold much of Unreal's power. And they are almost the same as the show flags we discussed previously that can use the ViewMode console command to switch between them (check the previous paragraph, if you have already forgotten). But their job is limited to displaying some of the final picture aspects, or even the full final picture. As you know, the result you see on screen is basically a combination of different kinds of layers, and here you can separate them!

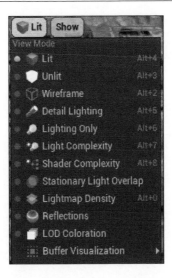

As you can see, their names imply what exactly you should expect on switching to one of them. For example, the **Reflections** view mode will help you to easily see and focus on the reflections only. Another benefit is that you can use the shortcuts as defines to make your workflow even faster; just hold the *Alt*, and keep swapping between numbers to have a look over all of them quickly. I do it that way! Some of the most important view modes are:

- **Unlit**: This view mode shows the diffuse color of the surfaces without any lighting or shadowing effects:

- **Wireframe**: This view mode shows the wireframe of all the meshes within the map (static, skeletal, or even brushes or decals), and it is quite helpful while optimizing:

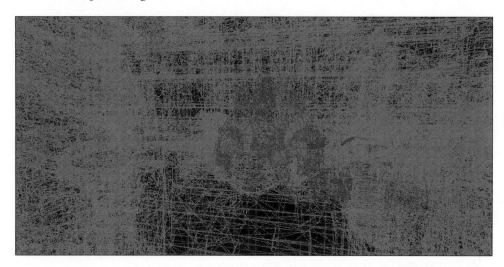

- **Light Only**: This view mode shows the light data only, just light and shadow. It is the total opposite of the **Unlit** view mode, where we see diffuse colors only without shadowing:

- **Lightmap Density**: This view mode displays a color code, where the green color means the meshes or parts have the normal light maps resolution (texel density). The blue color means this resolution is less and the red color means it is high:

- **Reflections**: This view mode will make everything you see within the map as reflective, and then you can study the reflectivity around the map, which makes it easy for you while placing the reflection capture actors:

And that's not all the list, even by the end of the list, you find an extendable list called **Buffer Visualization**, where you will find more options to visualize. But keep in mind that it is different, which means it contains more options. Feel free to keep investigating them all, but in general, that's what you are going to find in the menu:

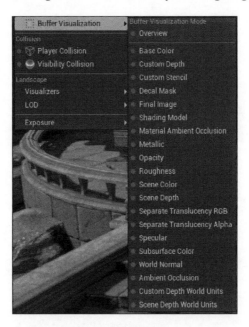

Generally, using the **Overview** choice has always been my favorite in order to get an overview of the most important buffers and compare the results in real time:

At the same time, there are visualizers, which are almost the same as the view modes, but serve different purposes and display different results. The visualizers are there in order to enable you to debug or view what Unreal is doing behind the scenes!

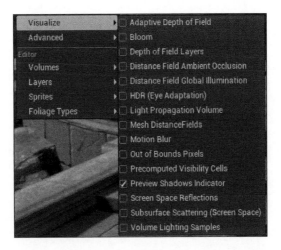

The visualized modes could be rendering steps or paths like the depth pass, or specialized views, like the motion blur vector visualizer. And, while the view modes allow you to display one at a time, the visualizers allow you to display different amounts of options at the same time. The view modes' UIs were built based on the toggle buttons while the visualizers' UIs were built using checkboxes. While some of the visualizers will display only a result for you, others will be displaying lots of useful statistics too. For example, the **Depth Of Field (DOF)** visualizer:

The GPU visualizer

The GPU visualizer is the place where you can see a visualization of each unit performance within the GPU. As you might know, the GPU has many different units working in parallel in order to do all the requested calculations. But sometimes some of these units hit their bounds, and can't process any more or any faster, and here comes the lag and performance issues based on the rendering pipeline. It is common, by the way, and it doesn't mean your content is that bad, but you can be bound by different units for different parts of the frame every day with the most complex and at the same time with the simplest projects!

But using the GPU visualizer will allow you to look at the parts where there is a bottleneck, and then you would know exactly what needs fixing. Because the visualizer is not embedded inside the editor UI by default, we have to launch it through the console (the same way you did before for the show flags), but this time you need to display the editor console not the game console. It is done in the same way, by using the console shortcut while being focused on any of the other editor panels, it will pop up the editor console for you. Just input the command name `r.ProfilerGPU.ShowUI` and it will appear:

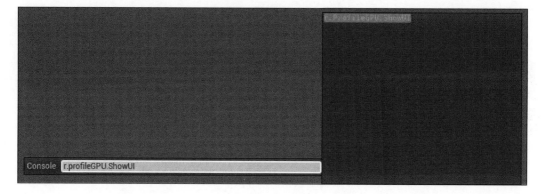

One thing to keep in mind, for some reason it might not appear on Mac editor builds. But it is okay with Windows editor builds. Also sometimes it might cause you some performance lag, but that is quite normal as it is based on slate (the UI solution used to build the editor UI) which is rendered in the GPU and needs to be updated every frame in order to display the correct results for you:

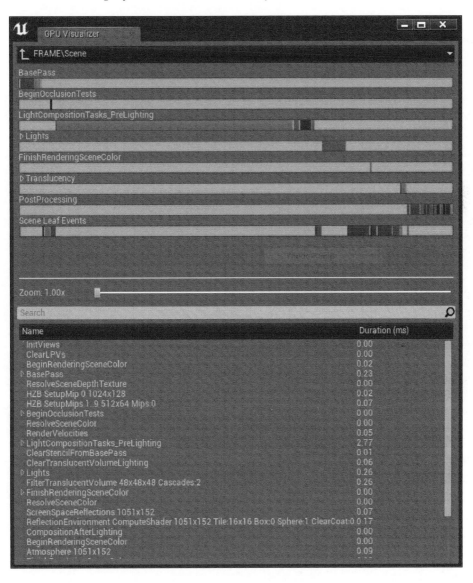

While everything is calculated in **milliseconds (ms)**, you will be able to easily define what causes much time to be rendered and therefore you can start checking the reason and optimize it. There is no key solution that the GPU visualizer will provide to you in order to fix your bottlenecks, but it will lead you in the right direction by letting you know what takes more than usual during the frame.

The Device Manager

The Unreal Device Manager, is nothing more than a device manager!

In fact, this tool has not that much to do with either development or profiling, but knowing it might be useful, especially when it comes to building the game in the next chapter, where you have the chance to deploy it directly to a device:

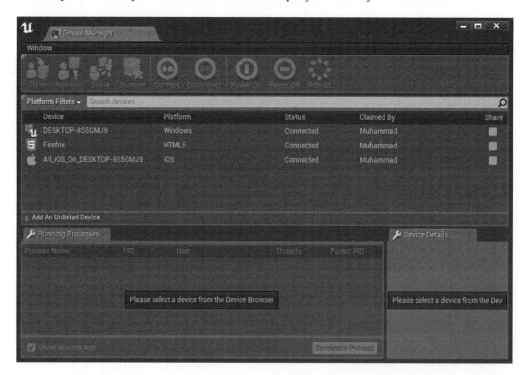

The Device Manager gives you the chance to add devices to the Unreal environment; any type of device that can be connected to your PC is acceptable. It also allows you to read some information about the selected device, check a list of the running processes, and even shut it down or restart it if you want.

The most important part here is when you have a device which doesn't know if it is supporting a certain feature of the engine, then you can simply connect the device, and add it to the list. You could check the **Device Details** section of the Device Manager to learn about the supported and unsupported features on that device:

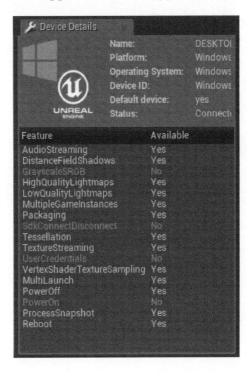

Device Profiles

When we talk about scalability and extensibility in game engines, Unreal is really the master! Not to mention the amount of settings and options you can do for the different platforms, but here at **Device Profiles**, you can do even more detailed tasks in no time:

Let's say your game is going to be shipped for all consoles that is supported by Unreal Engine, and that includes mobile devices, and let's even be more detailed and say it will be supporting all the available iOS devices. So what size of textures would you put in the final game *ipa?

Here comes the power of **Device Profiles**, Unreal gives you a huge list of platforms that you can mark as included or not via the pin next to the name of each one:

Try to unpin any of the profiles from the left side and you'll see them being removed from the table at the right.

Once a device is pinned, and included, you have the chance to set different settings for it through **Console Variables** and/or **Texture LOD Settings**. For each device, you can just hit the **Tool** icon, and then you can set the settings you want per device type:

The window of the settings looks the same for all platforms, but once you start doing changes per platform or per device, the window will look different each time you open it for a device. And remember, you can always rename the device profile with a name of your choice by changing the value of the base profile name from the profiles table:

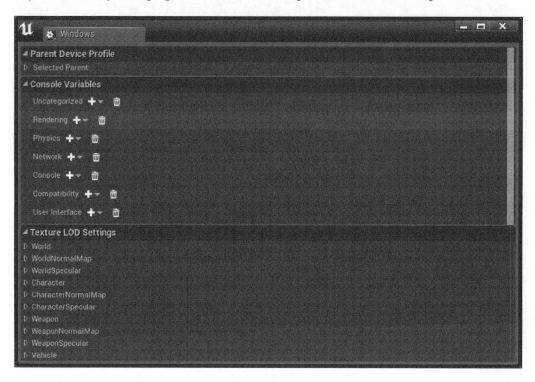

And while Unreal gives you all the possible profiles that you could think of, you still have the choice to add even more profiles by simply setting **Profile Name** and choosing **Profile Type** and hitting **Create Profile**:

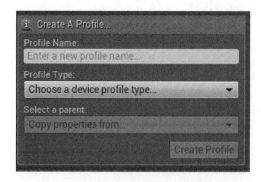

Summary

Now you have done a great job, and I'm sure you found a few things to tweak in your game, as I did with mine. As you know, there is no perfect content, and there is always something to change, update, or fix.

While debugging is usually done within the IDE, which is Visual Studio in our case, the code debugging is not everything when it comes to Unreal Engine, and you've learned about the different tools that are provided by Unreal in order to cover that aspect.

Now you understand the blueprint debugger, and while our game is a C++ game, we still have few blueprints to debug and check whether there are some errors in them. **Collision Analyzer** is a good place to spend some time, but only if you are facing some physics engine problems.

Some games have consoles, but any Unreal game by default has a very powerful console, and you learned where to get it and why, and what you can do with it.

If the game frame rate has a problem, then there is nothing better than using the console to generate some FPS charts and then loading them within something like Excel in order to convert the generated number tables to something visual and understandable.

Sometimes rendering behaves weird; turning on and off some features comes in handy in those situations, and you learned about the view modes and the visualizers.

Device Manager and **Device Profiles** are two extra tools embedded within Unreal. They are not very popular, but both are necessary to make sure the game is as good and smooth on the end user's device as it is on yours.

Now that you have learned a lot of things, I would suggest you to go ahead and run through all the tools once without looking at the book, just to make sure you can use them on your own without a reference, and once you are ready and satisfied enough, go ahead to the next chapter, where you will finally be porting the game!

14
Packaging the Game

Now we come to the most interesting part of this book, and the most interesting part in the journey of developing a game. It's time to put everything together into a game file that we can ship and share without the need to have the editor or the engine itself in the end user machine.

This seems to be the end of our journey, but hang in there! If the game you have built/are building is meant to be a real game, which needs to be released for players and distributed to vendors, then it's just the start of another journey!

A game is not just an art, code, and a game design packaged within an executable. You have to deal with stores, publishers, ratings, console providers, and making assets and videos for stores and marketing, among other minor things required to fully ship a game.

Apart from that, this chapter will take care of the last steps you need to do within the Unreal environment in order to get this packaged executable fine and running. Anything post-Unreal, you need to find a way to do it, but from my seat, I'm telling you have done the complex, hard, huge, and long part; what comes next is a lot simpler!

By the end of this chapter, you will be able to:

- Prepare your project to make a building
- Set different build settings to match the build requirements
- Add different videos and splash screens to your game
- Package the game into an executable
- Cook the game content
- Understand and use Unreal's Project Launcher, patching the project and creating DLCs (downloadable content)

With all these interesting plans in mind, let's run the editor for one last time, and start packaging our game.

Preparing the project for building

Remember in *Chapter 1, Preparing for a Big Project*, when we went to **Project Settings** to do some tweaks? That was something we did at the beginning of the project and it will save us some time now.

There at the **Project Settings** section are tons and tons of settings, some of which are needed during the development time, and while building and editing the game, and during the final build.

Feel free to tweak the game as you wish, the physics, the inputs, the navigation, the AI, and so on, These types of settings vary between the different types of game. But in general there are certain settings that need to be changed for builds, and they are almost always the same.

Packaging settings

The most important part is to define what type of build you are making. Many of the engine parts will be dependent on that, lots of optimizations will or will not be applied based on that. So you have to define if a regular test build or a final build needs to be released.

In order to quickly set this value, Unreal provides you with a quick access for it. From the **File** menu, you can choose either **Development** or **Shipping**, from the **Build Configuration**, under the **Package Project** submenu:

From the same menu, you can just hit **Packaging Settings**, and that will take you directly to **Packaging Settings** inside **Project Settings**. This one is a shortcut as well, but usually you can access these setting from the **Edit** menu, and then **Project Settings**, which will not only take you to **Packaging Settings**, but also to the entire project settings.

So feel free to use it the way you want to, but here at **Packaging Settings** are the most important options we can tweak for the build:

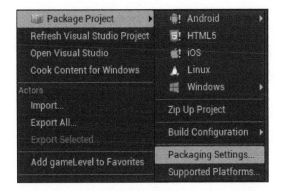

Packaging Settings contains lots of options affecting the game and its performance in different ways. While lots of project settings might remain untouchable from the moment you create a project to the moment you ship it, the options and settings within this section must be changed and/or tweaked at least once during the project lifetime. Because of their importance, I would like to break all of them down:

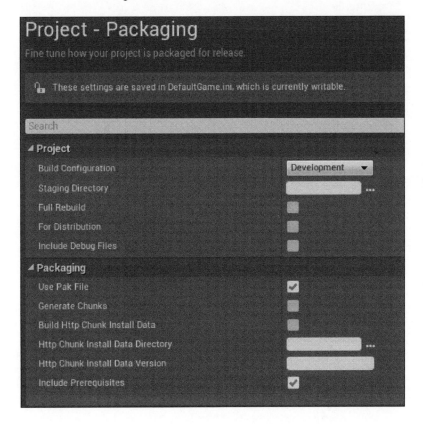

Here is what you can see in this section of the project settings:

- **Project**: This has the following options:
    - ° **Build Configuration**: It represents the type of build, and it is the same as the value you could change from the **File** menu (we discussed this in the previous section) and based on it, the engine will apply some optimizations and remove some unnecessary code and systems.
    - ° **Staging Directory**: It represents the directory where the final packaged project will remain; in other words, it's where you to put the final game!
    - ° **Full rebuild**: It's a Boolean value; setting it to `true` will force the project to make a full build, which will delete the old build, and replace it entirely with a new build. But setting this value to `false` means that every time you make a new build, some of the old files will not be replaced, and only the files and assets that have changed will be updated and replaced with new ones, which means less building time. So you have to decide which to go with. Personally, I like to keep it `false` as long as I'm making testing and development builds, but I do switch it to `true` when I'm making the final RC (release candidate) builds or the release build itself. Or perhaps switching it to `true`, when I find the game is acting weird, as conflicts might happen sometimes!
    - ° **For Distribution**: It is almost the same as the first option, where you have to define if the build is development or shipping, and I've no clue why Epic duplicated this choice, once in the form of a Boolean and another time in the form of a drop-down menu. But anyway, setting this option, will directly disable the **Build Configuration** option and gray it out.
    - ° **Include Debug Files**: It's a Boolean value that is related to development builds. Checking this option will allow including the debug files into the packaged game. Just check whether, if you really want it, it is going to increase the game size too much, but it will increase it, however, and you have to be serious about the game size, especially if you are targeting mobiles.
- **Experimental**: This has the following option:
    - ° **Native Blueprint Assets**: This one is still experimental, so you have to use it at your own risk. Enabling this choice will force the engine to convert all blueprints into C++ code. This process will take some time which means the build time will be a little more, but on the other hand the game performance will be better. If you kept it disabled, then all the logic made using blueprints will be packaged as `uasset` files into the final packaged game.

- **Packaging**: This has the following options:

  ○ **Use Pak File**: This is enabled by default and it is better to keep it enabled, as this option will make sure to package all the content inside one *.pak file, rather than keeping all the content scattered into tons of individual files. Those *.pak files are compressed formats (just like .zip), and they get decompressed when launching the game. So you will get a smaller build but start-up time will slightly increase (but not too much).

  ○ **Generate Chunks**: Enabling this option will work on generating .pak file chunks, and it is good for cases where the game is huge and needs to be installed from a server (**Streaming Installs**). The process of assigning the assets into specific chunks is usually done either through the editor or via delegates in C++ code.

  ○ **Chunk Hard References Only**: If the previous option was enabled, then enabling this one will make sure you pull in the hard dependencies of assets into the generated chunk, and all other dependencies remain in their original chunks.

  ○ **Build Http Chunk Install Data**: Enabling this option will generate data for the HTTP chunk installer; then it can be hosted in a web server for the user to installs it at runtime. But it also works only if you've enabled the **Generate Chucks** option.

  ○ **Http Chuck Install Data Directory**: The directory where the data will be built, only if the previous option was enabled.

  ○ **Http Chuck Install Data Version**: A version name or number for the HTTP chunk install data.

  ○ **Include Prerequisites**: Enable this option if you want to include prerequisites for packaged games, something like redistributable operating system components.

Now you understand what these options are for, and based on your game, its type, and its size, you will be choosing what is to be enabled and what is not needed for now. Most importantly, mark your game as **Shipping**, if it is going to be shipped. That will make it more secure with less development content.

Maps & Modes settings

The second and very important section of settings you will probably need to make sure of every time you are making a new game build of the game, is the **Maps & Modes** section, which is accessible directly through **Project Settings** under the **Edit** menu:

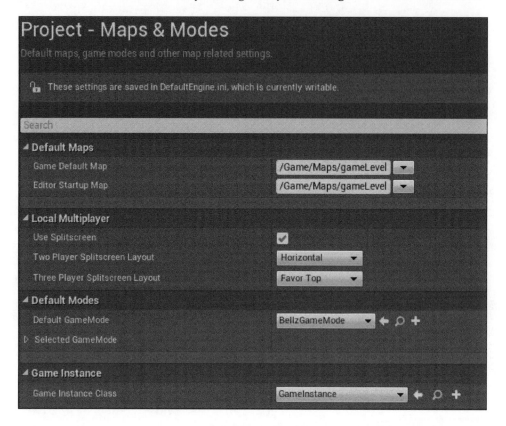

Usually any game made with Unreal Engine, or any similar technology, has lots of maps and levels but, when you build the game, how does the engine know which one should be launched first, or which one is the most important? Here within this section you have the chance to set these settings, and define what map needs to be launched first; then, using the game code, you can use this map to start launching all the other maps, but you need to pass only the first map to the engine during the packaging time. Here in the **Maps & Modes** settings there is a set of options that you might need to change or might not need to check at all however, in general, the **Game Default Map** is a necessary field you must check when you are making the build.

You can also do the following for your game from this section:

- **Default Maps**: This has the following options:
    - ○ **Game Default Map**: Which map is to be used as the default map that will be run directly after the splash screen
    - ○ **Editor Startup Map**: Define which map should be the default map that the editor has to load every time you run the editor

- **Local Multiplayer**: This has the following options:
    - ○ **Use Splitscreen**: If the game has more than one local player, does the screen have to be split, or will all the player will be playing on one screen?
    - ○ **Two Player Splitscreen Layout**: If the game is a multiplier with the previous option checked, then how would you like to divide the screen between two players? Vertically or horizontally:

- ° **Three Player Splitscreen Layout**: In a multiplayer that has the **Use Splitscreen** options selected, if there are three active players, then the screen will be split between them in a different way. As there must be one player who has the advantage of a full half of the screen. This option allows you to decide if that full half is on the top or the bottom of the screen:

- **Default Modes**: this has the following options:
    - ° **Default GameMode**: As we discussed in *Chapter 1, Preparing for a Big Project*, the importance of the game mode. We discussed in *Chapter 2, Setting Up Your Warrior*, how to define settings for it. You have to set the default game mode, from this section of **Project Settings**.
    - ° **Selected GameMode**: As the game mode is a set of settings, in this section you can set the different values for the game mode, such as the default pawn controller or the default HUD.

- **Game Instances**: This has the following options:
    - ° **Game Instance Class**: A drop-down list to select the class to use when instantiating the transient `GameInstance` class

Description settings

There are some game settings that you have to set, but no one will see them after you (I mean the players). The type of setting you need to change in this case is the game description. This set of settings you probably will change only once, at the first time you make the first build. The settings here remain almost the same with your game consistence, but you are free to change the settings here every time you make a build:

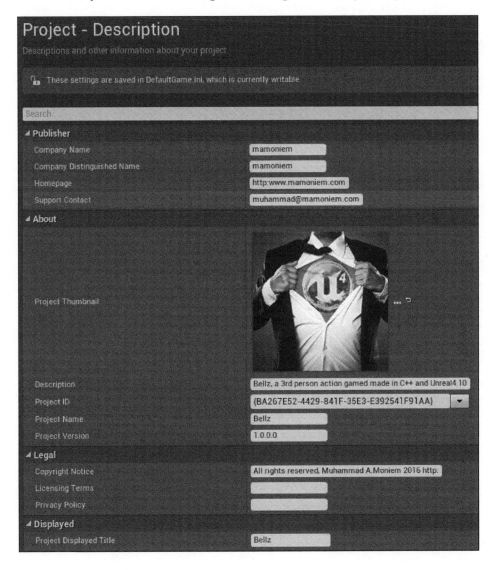

I'll not go through the settings you find in the section, as they are self-explanatory and will most probably not be seen by the user. You have to put in your company name, game name, website, build version, copyrights, and display title, and so on. But the most important option here is the **Project Thumbnail**, which will be used to display the game in the Unreal Launcher only. You have to make sure that you use a 192 by 192 pixel image for that. And remember, this is not representing the game icon that the players will see.

Platform settings

As you still inside **Project Settings**, you'll have a huge section of them called **Platforms**. This section might vary for your editor version. As for me, I'm using Windows. I have access to lots of platforms but, for example, if you are running Unreal Engine on Mac or Linux, you'll probably end up with a shorter list of platforms. This list contains only the platforms that you can target from your current OS:

While I'm using Windows and we are targeting Windows and the console, I'll be discussing in this section the Windows platform options that you can set. Feel free to explore all the other settings for the other platforms. But keep in mind that, while our game is targeting console quality, we still can't set the platform settings for XBox or PlayStation as this section of settings is locked until you get authorized by Microsoft or Sony and get the DevKit from them that will unlock the platform options for you inside Unreal Engine. Anyway, the options that we can set for the Windows platform are the following:

- **Targeted RHIs**: This has the following options:
  - **DirectX 11 (SM5)**: Check it to true if you want the game to support DirectX 11 features with Shader Model 5.
  - **DirectX 10 (SM4)**: Check it to true if you want the game to support DirectX 10 features with Shader Model 4.

- ◦ **OpenGL 3 (SM4)**: Check it to `true` if you want the game to support the OpenGL 3 features with Shader Model 4.

- ◦ **OpenGL 4 (SM5)**: Check it to `true` if you want the game to support the OpenGL 4 features with Shader Model 5. But this one is still experimental.

- **OS Info**: This has the following option:
  - ◦ **Minimum OS Version**: This option will probably be disabled if you have got the Unreal editor as a downloaded version. But if you got the Unreal editor source code, and you compile it in Visual Studio, then you can define which OS version is to be used. But anyway, Epic set it to Vista, which is good and a standard now. If you want to support lower versions, or unsupported Vista, then you have to compile the engine from the source code.

- **Splash**: This section has the following options:
  - ◦ **Editor Splash**: When you run the editor, there is small square splash screen with some information and text above it; it's called the project splash. Here you can define this image, make sure that it is in the `*.BMP` format and its size is almost 600 by 200 pixels.

  - ◦ **Game Splash**: The same as the editor splash screen, but this one is displayed after the player clicks the game icon and before the game launches, while the engine is starting. This must also be 600 by 200 pixels in the `*.BMP` format.

- **Icon**: This has the following options:
  - ◦ **Game Icon**: Here you can choose the game icon, the one that the player will be seeing when they want to run the game, and probably the same one that you will be using for the store. Make sure that this icon is in the file extension `*.ico` as that's the official icon extension for Windows. Also make sure that its size is 256 by 256 pixels.

Now while everything is almost in place, and we are ready to go, let's just change one more setting in **Project Settings**.

Adding different screens

A game may be not made by one company, and there should be a publisher and developer at least. Both of them may want to include their fancy logos as splash screens at the beginning of the game. Usually a game by default will include only the Unreal Engine logo at the beginning of it, and before launching any of the maps. But Unreal Engine gives you the choice to add any amount of splash screens in the form of videos, but all come after the Unreal Engine logo.

The splash screen or movie set of options that is provided by the Unreal Engine can be found under **Project Settings**, but this time within the **Movies** section. And these options include the following:

- **Movies**: This has the following options:
  - **Wait for Movies to Complete**: Setting this option to `true`, the game will wait for all the movies to be completed, and then run the game, even if the game loading has already completed.
  - **Movies Are Skippable**: Setting this option to `true` will allow the player to skip the start-up movies when they do inputs such as a mouse click for example. It is good to have this option, but usually the splash screen should not be skippable.

- **Startup Movies**: This is an array of elements, which means you have to define a number of movies you want to display, and the order in which you select the files inside the array will be the same order to display those movies. The most important part about this option is that you need to set these movies files within the `Content` folder in a folder named `Movies`:

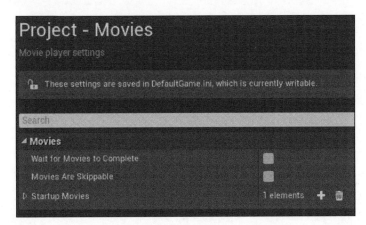

Set the ones you need to display, and mark the options you want to be true, and now you are really ready to export the game and run it. And that's what we are going to do next.

Packaging the game

Now when it comes to packaging the game process, I have to say it is the easiest and straightforward thing to do in this chapter. And while it is just a click of a button, sometimes it becomes a nightmare for people when packaging fails and errors start to show up. You can apply the packaging of the project to a certain platform, from the **File** menu, and then choose **Package Project** and then select your targeted platform, and that will start packaging right away:

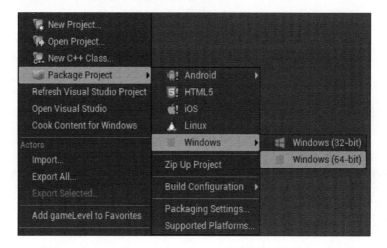

While the game is packaging, it is actually doing three different processes one after another, which are:

1. Build the project.
2. Cook the content.
3. Package the game.

During all that time all that you can do is just wait until it is done. As you can see, once the packaging starts, you'll see the progress bar at the top-right corner of the screen:

Personally, I like to hit the **Show Output Log** button, and watch it while packaging the project. It is not just informational; you can learn about the process of packaging your game and how Unreal Engine does it, the problems your game might have; most importantly, if the packaging process failed, this log screen will display as much information to you as possible, enough to lead you in the correct direction towards fixing it. And even if the failure does not show a clear error that you need to fix, you'll at least know at which phase the packaging process failed, and that's enough to fix it or ask for help from the Epic staff:

Once the packaging is done and successful message appears, you can find the game in the defined directory where you have defines, and from there you can launch the game using its executables. The executable extension and place might vary between the different platforms.

Cooking the content

Previously when we discussed the packaging process, I've mentioned that it happens in different phases, and one of those phases is called **cooking the content**. When it comes to packaging a game, Unreal is very smart and they thinks about how to make the best of your time as a developer.

Let's assume that you have made a huge game, about 10 GB in size. What if you have changed a single texture? Do you have to build the whole thing in order to test it? Or do you have to build the whole thing in order to publish it?

Unreal does a good separation between the game logic and its content, and as long as you want to rebuild the content itself, you can always do it by cooking. Content such as textures or sound files always have their own file formats, like PNG, JPG, WAV, or MP3, but when you package the game, you never find those files, as the engine works on converting those files to more encrypted and engine-friendly formats that match the targeted platforms. And that's called the cooking content process.

You can cook the project content at any time from the **File** menu, choosing **Cook Content for Windows**:

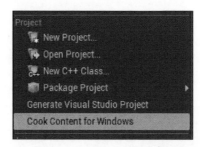

Project Launcher and DLCs

The first and the most important thing you have to keep in mind is that the project launcher is still in development and the process of creating DLCs is not final yet, and might get changed in the future with upcoming engine releases. While writing this book I've been using Unreal 4.10 and testing everything I do and write within the Unreal 4.11 preview version, and yet still the DLC process remains experimental. So be advised that you might find it a little different in the future as the engine evolves:

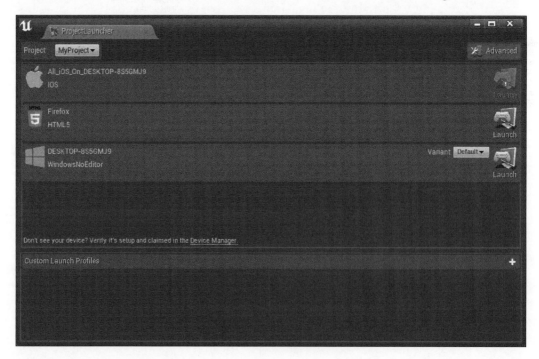

While we have packaged the game previously through the **File** menu using **Packaging Project**, there is another, more detailed, more professional way to do the same job. Using the **Project Launcher**, which comes in the form of a separate app with Unreal (Unreal Frontend), you have the choice to run it directly from the editor. You can access the **Project Launcher** from the **Windows** menu, and then choose **Project Launcher**, and that will launch it right away.

However, I have a question here.

Why would you go through these extra steps, then just do the packaging process in one click?

Well, extensibility is the answer. Using the Unreal **Project Launcher** allows you to create several profiles, each profile having a different build setting, and later you can fire each build whenever you need it; not only that, but the profiles could be made for different projects, which means you can have an already made setup for all your projects with all the different build configurations.

And yet even that's not everything; it comes in handier when you get the chance to cook the content of a game several times, so rather than keep doing it through the **File** menu, you can just cook the content for the game for all the different platforms at once. For example; if you have to change one texture within your game which is supported on five platforms, you can make a profile which will cook the content for all the platforms and arrange them for you at once, and you can spend that time doing something else. The **Project Launcher** does the whole thing for you.

What if you have to cook the game content for different languages? Let's say the game supports 10 languages? Do you have to do it one by one for each language?

The answer is simple; the **Project Launcher** will do it for you.

So you can simply think of the **Project Launcher** as a batch process, custom command-line tool, or even a form of build server. You set the configurations and requests, and leave it alone doing the whole thing for you, while you are saving your time doing something else. It is all about productivity!

And the most important part about the **Project Launcher** is that you can create DLCs very easily. By just setting a profile for it with a different set of options and settings, you can end up with getting the DLC or game mode done without any complications. In a word, it is all about profiles, and because of that let's discuss how to create profiles, that could serve different purposes.

Sometimes the **Project Launcher** proposes for you a standard profile that matching the platform you are using. That is good, but usually those profiles might not have all we need, and that's why it is recommended to always create new profiles to serve our goals.

The **Project Launcher** by default is divided into two sections vertically; the upper part contains the default profiles, while the lower part contains the custom profiles. And in order to create a new profile all you have to do is to hit the plus sign at the bottom part, where it is titled **Custom Launch Profiles**:

Pressing it will take you to a wizard, or it is better to describe this as a window, where you can set up the new profile options. Those options are drastic, and changing between them leads to a completely different result, so you have to be careful. But in general, you mostly will be building either a project for release, or building a DLC or patch for an already released project. Not to mention that you can even do more types of building that serve different goals, such as a language package for an already released game, which is treated as a patch or DLC but at the same time it has different a setup and options than a patch or DLC. Anyway, we will be taking care of the two main types of process that developers usually have to deal with in the **Project Launcher**: release and patch.

Packaging a release

After the new **Custom Launch Profile** wizard window opens, you have changes for its settings that are necessary to make our **Release** build of the project. This includes:

- **General**: This has the following fields:
    - Give a name to the profile, and this name will be displayed in the **Project Launcher** main window
    - Give a description to the profile in order to make its goals clear for you in the future, or for anyone else who is going to use it

- **Project**: This has the following sections:
    - ° Select a project, the one that needs to be built. Or you can leave this at **Any Project**, in order to build the current active project:

- **Build**: This has the following sections:
    - ° Indeed, you have to check the box of the build, so you make a build and activate this section of options.
    - ° From the **Build Configuration** dropdown, you have to choose a build type, which is **Shipping** in this case.
    - ° Finally, you can check the **Build UAT** (Unreal Automation Tool) option from **Advanced Settings** in this section. The UAT could be considered as a bunch of scripts creating a set of automated processes, but in order to decide whether to run it or not, you have to really understand what the UAT is:
        - ° Written in C# (may convert to C++ in the future)
        - ° Automates repetitive tasks through automation scripts
        - ° Builds, cooks, packages, deploys and launches projects
        - ° Invokes UBT for compilation
        - ° Analyzes and fixes game content files
        - ° Codes surgery when updating to new engine versions
        - ° Distributes compilation (XGE) and build system integration
        - ° Generates code documentation
        - ° Automates testing of code and content
        - ° And many others—you can add your own scripts!

    Now you will know if you want to enable it or not:

- **Cook**: This has the following settings:
    - ○ In the **Cook** section, you need to set it to by the book. This means you need to define what exactly is needed to be cooked and for which platforms it is enough for now to set it to **WindowsNoEditor**, and check the cultures you want from the list. I have chosen all of them (this is faster than picking one at a time) and then exclude the ones that I don't want:

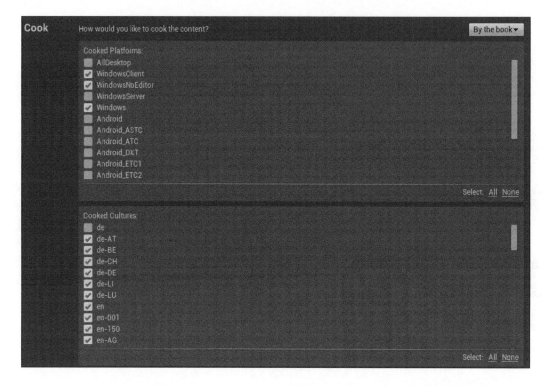

- ○ Then you need to check which maps should be cooked; if you can't see maps, it is probably the first build. Later you'll find the maps listed. But anyway, you must keep all the maps listed in the Maps folder under the Content directory:

- Now from the **Release / DLC / Patching Settings** section, you have to check the option **Create a release version of the game for distribution**, as this version going to be the distribution one.

- And from the same section give the build a version. This is going to create some extra files that will be used in the future if we are going to create patches or DLCs:

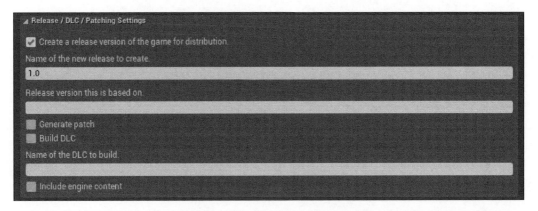

- You can expand the **Advanced Settings** section to set your own options. By default, **Compress Content** and **Save Packages without versions** are both checked, and both are good for the type of build we are making. But also you can set **Store all content in a single file (UnrealPak)** to keep things tidy; one .pak file is better than lots of separated files.

- Finally, you can set **Cooker Build Configuration** to **Shipping**, as long as we set **Build Configuration** itself to **Shipping**:

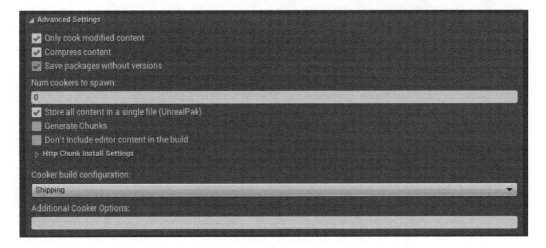

- **Package**: This has the following options:
  - ○ From this section's drop-down menu, choose **Package & store locally**, and that will save the packages on the drive. You can't set anything else here, unless you want to store the game packaged project into a repository:

- **Deploy**: The **Deploy** section is meant to build the game into the device of your choice, and I don't think it is the case here, or anyone will want to do it. If you want to put the game into a device, you could directly do **Launch from within the editor itself**. So, let's set this section to **Do Not Deploy**:

- **Launch**: In case you have chosen to deploy the game into a device, then you'll be able to find this section; otherwise, the options here will be disabled. The set of options here is meant to choose the configurations of the deployed build, as once it is deployed to the device it will run. Here you can set something like the language culture, the default startup map, command-line arguments, and so on. And as we are not deploying now, this section will be disabled:

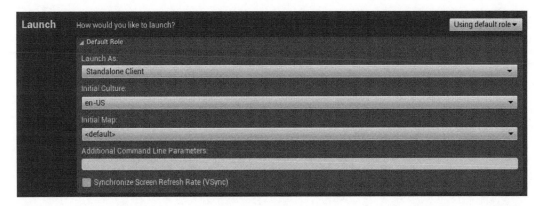

Now we have finished editing our profile, you can find a back arrow at the top of this wizard. Pressing it will take you back to the **Project Launcher** main window:

Now you can find our profile in the bottom section. Any other profiles you'll be making in the future will be listed there. Now there is one step to finish the build. In the right corner of the profile there is a button that says **Launch This Profile**. Hitting it will start the process of building, cooking, and packaging this profile for the selected project. Hit it right away if you want the process to start. And keep in mind, anytime you need to change any of the previously set settings, there is always an **Edit** button for each profile:

The **Project Launcher** will start processing this profile; it will take some time, but the amount of time depends on your choices. And you'll be able to see all the steps while it is happening. Not only this, but you can also watch a detailed log; you can save this log, or you can even cancel the process at any time:

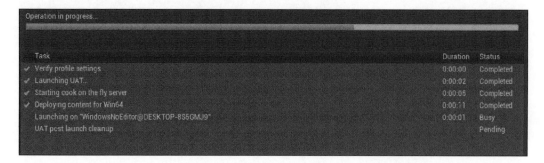

Once everything is done, a new button will appear at the bottom: **Done**. Hitting it will take you back again to the **Project Launcher** main window. And you can easily find the build in the `Saved\StagedBuilds\WindowsNoEditor` directory of your project, which is in my case: `C:\Users\Muhammad\Desktop\Bellz\Saved\StagedBuilds\WindowsNoEditor`.

The most important thing now is that, if you are planning to create patches or DLCs for this project, remember when you set a version number in the **Cook** section. This produced some files that you can find in: `ProjectName\Release\ReleaseVersion\Platform`. Which in my case is: `C:\Users\Muhammad\Desktop\Bellz\Releases\1.0\WindowsNoEditor`.

There are two files; you have to make sure that you have a backup of them on your drive for future use.

Now you can ship the game and upload it to the distribution channel!

Packaging a patch or DLC

The good news is, there isn't much to do here. Or in other words, you have to do lots of things, but it is a repetitive process. You'll be creating a new profile in the **Project Launcher**, and you'll be setting 90% of the options so they're the same as the previous release profile; the only difference will be in the **Cook** options. Which means the settings that will remain the same are:

- **Project**
- **Build**

- **Package**
- **Deploy**
- **Launch**

The only difference is that in the **Release/DLC/Patching Settings** section of the **Cook** section you have to:

1. Disable **Create a release version of the game for distribution**.

2. Set the number of the base build (the release) as the release version this is based on, as this choice will make sure to compare the previous content with the current one.

3. Check **Generate patch**, if the current build is a patch, not a DLC.

4. Check **Build DLC**, if the current build is a DLC, not a patch:

Now you can launch this profile, and wait until it is done. The patching process creates a *.pak file in the directory: `ProjectName\Saved\StagedBuilds\PlatformName\ProjectName\Content\Paks`.

This .pak file is the patch that you'll be uploading to the distribution channel! And the most common way to handle these type of patch is by creating installers; in this case, you'll create an installer to copy the *.pak file into the player's directory: `ProjectName\Releases\VersionNumber\PlatformName\`.

Which means, it is where the original content *.pak file of the release version is.

In my case I copy the *.pak file from: `C:\Users\Muhammad\Desktop\Bellz\Releases\1.0\WindowsNoEditor` to: `C:\Users\Muhammad\Desktop\Bellz\Saved\StagedBuilds\WindowsNoEditor\Bellz\Content\Paks`.

Now you've found the way to patch and download content, and you have to know, regardless of the time you have spent creating it, it will be faster in the future, because you'll be getting more used to it, and Epic is working on making the process better and better.

Summary

For the first time, you can run the project as a game, not from within the Unreal editor or the Unreal Launcher, but as a game from its own executable file.

Now you have got you hands-on the process of finalizing a game as a product, what is needed before making the build, and what settings should or could be fine-tuned for that purpose?

All games have different splash screens, based on the number of developers and publishers. You will need different types and numbers of splash screens, and you've learned during this chapter how to add splash screens to your game in different ways.

Packaging a game and cooking its content are two different processes, but both do similar things. You've learned when to use each process, and what the difference is between them.

The **Project Launcher** is a very powerful tool shipped with the Unreal ecosystem. Using it is not mandatory, but sometimes it is needed to save time, and you learned how and when to use this powerful tool.

Many games nowadays have downloadable content; it helps to keep the game community growing, and the game earn more revenue. Having DLCs is not essential, but it is good, having them must be planned earlier as we discussed, and you've learned how to manage them within Unreal Engine. And you learned how to make patches and DLCs using the Unreal **Project Launcher**.

Now all I can say is thank you for following along. Now, it's your time go ahead and play your game, share it with you friends, receive their feedback, fix it, and make another build. And most importantly, if you are happy with your project, don't forget to recommend this book to your friends.☺

Index

Symbols